Patterns Plus

A Short Prose Reader
with Argumentation

Eighth Edition

Mary Lou Conlin
Cuyahoga Community College

Houghton Mifflin Company Boston New York

Publisher: Pat Coryell
Development Editor: Kellie Cardone
Editorial Associate: Peter Mooney
Associate Project Editor: Lisa C. Sullivan
Senior Manufacturing Coordinator: Priscilla Bailey
Marketing Manager: Annamarie Rice
Marketing Assistant: Laura Hemrika

Ellen Gilchrist: Ellen Gilchrist, "Message in a Bottle" is reprinted by permission of Don Congdon Associates, Inc. First published in the February 2003 issue of REAL SIMPLE. Copyright © 2003 by Ellen Gilchrist. **S. I. Hayakawa:** "How Dictionaries are Made" adapted from LANGUAGE IN THOUGHT AND ACTION, Fourth Edition by S. I. Hayakawa and Alan R. Hayakawa, copyright © 1978 by Harcourt, Inc., reprinted by permission of the publisher. **E. J. Kahn, Jr.:** "The Discovery of Coca-Cola" from THE BIG DRINK: THE STORY OF COCA-COLA by E. J. Kahn, Jr. Copyright © 1950, 1959, 1960 by E. J. Kahn, Jr. Used by permission of Random House, Inc. **Mary Mebane:** From MARY by Mary Mebane, copyright © 1981 by Mary Elizabeth Mebane. Used by permission of Viking Penguin, a division of Penguin Group (USA) Inc. **Rick Reilly:** Rick Reilly, "Earning Their Pinstripes," SPORTS ILLUSTRATED, Sept. 23, 2002, p. 92. Reprinted by permission of Sports Illustrated. **Eliot Wigginton:** From THE FOX-FIRE BOOK by Eliot Wigginton. Copyright © 1968, 1969, 1970, 1971, 1972 by The Foxfire Fund, Inc. Used by permissin of Doubleday, a division of Random House, Inc.

Acknowledgments continue on page 327.

Cover image: © Sergio Spada/Graphistock

Printed in the U.S.A.

Library of Congress Control Number: 2003110178

ISBN: 0-618-42119-X

123456789-QWF-08-07-06-05-04

Contents

6 Comparison and Contrast   *145*

PARAGRAPHS

ESSAYS

Thematic Table
of Contents

3   The Natural Environment

The following selections consider our impact on the environment and its
  impact on us.

4   Animals and Humans

The following readings discuss animal and human behavior, from sports
  fans to human mistreatment of a frog and the sea.

5   Progress

The memorable but sometimes questionable effects of discoveries,
  inventions, and decisions made in the name of "progress," as well as our
  lack of progress in solving some of society's problems, are considered in
  the following readings.

6 Expectations and Reality

In the following readings, the writers show us that expectations, whether positive or negative, may not be realized or may turn out differently than anticipated.

7 Education and Learning

What we've learned and what we have yet to learn are considered in the
    following selections.

8 Food for Thought

The following readings consider things we like to eat and drink, things we
    shouldn't drink, and the celebration of the harvest that signals plentiful
    food for the year ahead.

9 The Working World

The nature of work, the definition of work, and the effect of not working are
    considered in the following readings.

10 Values

11   The Family

The following readings consider the positive and not-so-positive aspects of family life.

12   Childhood

In the following readings, the writers share their memories, lessons learned, risks taken in childhood and youth, and the significance of early parental involvement with their children.

13   Communication

In the following readings, the writers consider the many ways we communicate and fail to communicate effectively.

Writing Across the Curriculum
Table of Contents

19 Women's Studies

Preface

Patterns Plus: A Short Prose Reader with Argumentation provides students with an understanding of the thinking process, organizational principles, and rhetorical strategies involved in producing clear and effective writing. In this eighth edition, students are introduced to the uses of freewriting and brainstorming in defining ideas for their writing and to the process of collaborative writing. The study apparatus provides complete and clear explanations of the various rhetorical modes, and the paragraph and essay-length readings provide students with examples of how the modes can be used in organizing and developing their ideas.

New to the Eighth Edition

Patterns Plus, eighth edition, provides students with a variety of models for their own writing and with readings that stimulate lively and thoughtful classroom discussions. Features of the new edition include:

- Fifty percent new readings, including selections by such well-known writers as Henry David Thoreau, Ann Patchett, Rachel Carson, Pete Hamill, James Baldwin, and Konrad Lorenz.
- New women and minority writers, including Lesley Stern, Ellen Gilchrist, Sara Askew Jones, Diana Crane, John L. Jackson, and William Raspberry.
- New student writers, including Kirsten Bauman, University of Cincinnati Raymond Walters College; Julie Gifford, Pennsylvania State University; and Andy Lin, Dos Pueblos High School.
- New collaborative writing assignments.
- New Internet-based writing assignments (look for the globe icon).
- A revised introductory chapter to include new example paragraphs and essays.
- A revised Thematic Table of Contents.
- A revised Writing Across the Curriculum Table of Contents.

An Overview of Patterns Plus

Chapter 1, an introductory chapter, describes the basics of the writing process and the construction of paragraphs and essays. In chapters 2 through 10, the various techniques used in developing the main idea of a paragraph and the thesis of an essay are explained: *narration, description,* and the expository modes of *examples, classification and division, comparison and contrast, process, cause and effect, definition,* and *argumentation and persuasion.* These are the traditional *rhetorical modes*—the strategies for development that have proved effective in providing starting points for student writers. Chapter 11, "Combining the Strategies," contains student and professional essays that illustrate the ways writers combine various modes of development within a single essay.

Professional and student selections in *Patterns Plus* were chosen specifically to build students' confidence by showing them that the writing of short, effective compositions is within their reach. Selections range from simple, accessible paragraphs to longer, more challenging essays. The student writings that are included throughout the text will make students aware of the level of skill they can realistically expect to achieve.

The breadth of reading selections also allows the instructor a wide choice of topics—from serious and timely discussions related to discrimination, cultural differences, and social concerns to lighthearted pieces that reveal human foibles. As a stimulus to discussion, two sides of a controversial subject are sometimes provided. Students will probably respond quite differently to the argumentation and persuasional essays on the death penalty, television cameras in the jury room, and the smoking issue.

Apparatus

Patterns Plus offers a full range of study apparatus:

- *Headnotes* provide author information and a context for each reading selection to help students understand and enjoy the selection.
- *Words to Know* define unfamiliar words and clarify allusions that might be unfamiliar or regional.
- *Getting Started* questions prepare students to think critically about the topic presented in the reading selection or about topics for their own writing.
- Exercises promote comprehension and critical skills.
  Questions About the Reading are designed to stimulate thinking about the selection's meaning—expressed and implied—and

to help students gain fuller understanding of the writer's message.

Questions About the Writer's Strategies ask students to discuss the writer's *thesis statement, mode of development, point of view, figurative language*—or whatever strategy is particularly appropriate to a given selection—and thereby promote critical and analytical thinking.

Writing Assignments are related to the topic and development mode of the reading selection and are designed to encourage the student to generate ideas that can be developed into paragraphs and essays.

- The *Thematic Table of Contents* groups the readings in the text by such themes as "The Individual in Society," "Values," and "The Working World."

- The *Writing Across the Curriculum Table of Contents* arranges the readings by academic discipline, such as biology, education, and history.

- The *Glossary* provides definitions of all writing-process, rhetorical, and literary terms that are boldfaced throughout the chapter introductions and end-of-selection questions.

Support for Instructors

The Instructor's Resource Manual for *Patterns Plus* offers instructors a wide variety of supplemental materials:

- Part One supplies teaching suggestions that will allow flexibility in determining course content and structure.

- Part Two contains questions and their answers about the content of each chapter. The questions can be used as quizzes or to generate class discussion.

- Part Three provides suggested answers to the reading comprehension and Writer's Strategies questions that appear at the end of each reading selection in chapters 2 through 10.

- Part Four offers suggested questions and answers for the extra readings in chapter 11.

- Part Five includes a list of the reading levels according to the Fry and Dale-Chall readability formulas. Reading levels are arranged by chapter and by grade.

Acknowledgments

I would like to thank my good friends Ruth Silon, Cuyahoga Community College, for sharing her student's essay, "Students," and

Kim Flachmann, California State University, Bakersfield, for providing "An Intruder in the House," by her student Carol Adams. My thanks also to Lynn Schubert, Los Angeles Harbor College, for "My Suit," a paragraph by her student Ricardo Galvez; George D. Gess, George Fox College, for "Overindulgence," a paragraph by his student Heidi Hall; and Kathryn Kemmerer, Pennsylvania State University, Hazelton, for "The Art of Making Fimo Beads," by her student Julie Gifford.

I am further indebted to the following persons for their helpful suggestions for revisions and new reading selections for this eighth edition of this text:

Juanita Bass of LeMoyne-Owen College
Juliana F. Cárdenas of Grossmont College
David Elias of Eastern Kentucky University
Julia A. Galbus of the University of Southern Indiana, Evansville
Dr. Louis Gallo of Radford University
Julie Nichols of Okaloosa-Walton Community College
Randall Rehberg of the University of Wisconsin—Parkside

Finally, I again thank the people at Houghton Mifflin who worked with me on this, my twenty-second textbook with them: Patricia Coryell, Anamarie Rice, Peter Mooney, and Lisa C. Sullivan.

My twenty-some years of working with the staff at Houghton Mifflin have always been a joy.

Mary Lou Conlin

The Basics of Writing: Process and Strategies

"If you wish to be a good reader, read; if you wish to be a good writer, write."

Epicetus, *Discourses*. Bk. Ii, Ch. 18, sec. 2 (c. A.D. 100)

THIS BOOK TELLS you about the process and strategies that you can use to produce effective writing. It includes many paragraphs and essays—by both student and professional writers—that you can read and study as models for your own writing. By understanding and following the process involved in writing, by learning the strategies writers use to communicate their ideas, and by practicing in paragraphs and essays of your own, you can develop the skill and confidence needed to write effectively on many different subjects.

Purpose and Audience

It is important that you understand the writing process and learn a variety of writing strategies because you will need to write, in school and afterward, for different **purposes,** to different types of **audiences,** and for varied **occasions.** Your purpose might be to persuade (perhaps in a memo recommending a new procedure at work), to instruct (in a description of how to do a lab assignment), or to inform (in a note to your teacher explaining your absence from class). Your audience, or reader, may be fellow students or friends, and the occasion may be an informal activity; your audience may be your employer, and the occasion a formal report. In any case, you will need to make choices—as you work through the process of prewriting, drafting, rewriting, revising, and editing your work—about the writing strategies that will most effectively explain your ideas.

As a student, you will often have tests and assignments that require you to write either a **paragraph** or an **essay.** Although such compositions may differ in their length and content, a paragraph and an essay are alike in two important ways. First, each one should have a **main idea.** Second, the main idea should be fully explained or developed. In this book, you will learn the ways in which many writers go about finding a main idea and the strategies they use in explaining or developing it.

Finding a Main Idea

If you are like most writers, you may find it difficult to come up with a main idea of your own. You may stare out the window, get something to eat, play a game on your computer, or in some other way put off starting to write. When you find yourself stalling, you may find it helpful to do some prewriting exercises to generate ideas. One method is to sit down and write without stopping for five or ten minutes. This is called **freewriting,** and its primary purpose is to get you started writing.

As the term implies, freewriting is often disorganized and lacks a clear focus. Your freewriting might look like this:

> Need to wash my car. May rain though. What to write about? Maybe last night's ball game. What's that guy doing in his yard? He just mowed it yesterday. Ball game was great—all those homers and extra innings— exciting. Glad I went. Need to go to the store. Out of bread. What'll I get for dinner?

When you look over your freewriting, you can see that you wrote about the baseball game you saw last night. You could write about the exciting game.

Sometimes your instructor will suggest a topic to focus your freewriting. For example, suppose your instructor asks you to write a paragraph describing the room you are in. Your freewriting might then look like this:

> Looks like rain. Wonder if I closed my bedroom windows. What can I say about this classroom except that it's pretty much like all college classrooms. Seats with writing arms, blackboard, teacher's desk, tan walls with lots of dents in them. Have to pick Chad up from the day-care center at 4. Hope he won't be crabby like he was yesterday. What should I say about this classroom?

When you read over your freewriting, underline anything that strikes you as interesting or important. Your freewriting may trigger an idea that will focus your description. For example, you may notice that your classroom is like all classrooms, except that the walls have lots of dents. Choosing this as a main idea, you might then write a paragraph like this:

Main idea

The classroom is like all college classrooms except for the many dents in its walls. Like all classrooms, it has thirty chairs with writing arms, lined up in five rows with six chairs in each row; a blackboard that still has the assignment on it from the previous class and needs a good washing; the professor's desk, with a podium on it to hold his oft-used lecture notes; and tan, finger-marked walls. But for some unknown reason, chairs have been shoved hard and often against the walls, which have more and deeper dents than

Main idea restated

those in other classrooms. Only its dented walls make this classroom different from all college classrooms.

Suppose, however, that the assignment is to **collaborate** with one or more of your classmates in writing an essay about the environment. Collaboration means working with others on a project—in this case, writing an essay about the environment. Once the members of your collaborative group are determined, you will need to meet to discuss the assignment, determine each person's responsibilities, and schedule the project. One member of your group may emerge as the leader, or your group may elect a leader. The leader is responsible for coordinating the project and for seeing that each member of the group meets the schedule that is set for drafting, revising, and editing the assignment.

Next, each of you might want to do some freewriting in order to get started, but then you will want to do some **brainstorming** together. Brainstorming, like freewriting, is simply a way of putting your thoughts on paper to help you choose a main idea and develop supporting evidence for a paragraph or an essay. You will need to focus your thinking on words and ideas that relate to the environment, with one of you writing down what each person contributes. Your group's list might look like this:

trees	water
pollution	diapers
landfills	food
harmful	resources
paper	waste disposal
flowers	cars, airplanes—noise
smog	cars, exhaust
plastics	wasting resources—oil, coal, water, land

After your group finishes the brainstorming list, you will need to look for relationships among the words and ideas. For instance, your group could decide that the items can be clustered into two groups or categories: (1) things that the environment provides and (2) things that can harm or damage the environment.

Environment provides:	Environment damaged by:
trees	waste disposal—diapers, plastics
flowers	cars—exhaust fumes, noise
food	airplanes—noise
resources—water, oil, coal	wasting resources—water, oil, coal, trees

Based on these categories, your group may decide that the main idea for the group's essay could be "We depend on our environment for food, water, and other resources, but we are damaging our environment in several ways." Your group could then decide to **classify** the *ways* we are damaging our food, water, and other resources. After reviewing your brainstorming list and talking it over, your group might decide that the classifications could be *polluting, poisoning,* and *wasting*. You could say, "We are *polluting* the land and our water supply with waste disposal, *poisoning* the air with the exhaust from cars and airplanes, and *wasting* our resources by the overuse of paper and oil."

You might then decide to assign responsibility for providing supporting details for each of the classifications to different members of the group. Thus someone could be responsible for providing **examples** to support "polluting the land and our water supply with waste disposal"; someone else for "poisoning the air with the exhaust from cars and airplanes"; and someone else for "wasting our resources by the overuse of paper and oil."

Stating the Main Idea

The main idea of a paragraph is called the **topic.** This topic is usually stated in a sentence, called a **topic sentence.** The topic sentence usually expresses a general rather than a specific idea, and it may be placed anywhere within the paragraph. However, you will find that it generally helps to keep your writing clear and focused if you state your main idea at the *beginning* of the paragraph. In the sample paragraph that follows, the main idea (or topic) of the paragraph is stated in the first sentence, followed by the supporting examples. This is called general-to-specific, or **deductive,** order.

Topic sentence   History does seem to repeat itself, even in the way college students behave. In the 1840s students protested and acted in violent ways. Students at Yale, for example, objected to their mathematics course and burned their books in the streets. Some captured their tutor and kept him tied up all night, and others shot a cannon through the tutor's bedroom window. In the 1940s and 1950s students were a fun-loving, game-happy lot. They swallowed live goldfish, took part in dance marathons, and held contests to see how many people could crowd into a phone booth. The more daring males broke into women's rooms in "panty-raids," then festooned their own rooms with the ill-gotten silks. Then, in the 1960s, students repeated the activities of the 1840s. They objected to their courses, littered the campuses with their books and papers, and locked teachers inside college buildings. They protested against all forms of social injustice, from war to the food in the cafeteria. The more violent threw rocks at the police, and a few planted bombs in college buildings. In the 1970s students repeated the fun and games of the forties and fifties. They held contests to see how many people could squeeze into a phone booth. They had dance marathons. The more daring ran naked across campuses, in a craze called "streaking." The slightly less daring did their streaking with brown paper bags over their

Topic restated   heads. Yes, history does seem to repeat itself, even in the sometimes violent and sometimes fun-and-games behavior of the students on college campuses.

In the following paragraph, the writer has stated the topic in the first and second sentences.

Topic sentence   In the nineties and the early 1900s, gold teeth were as much a part of the fashion scene as peg-top trousers, choker collars, and chatelaine watches. There were, of course, certain practical reasons for this popularity. From the viewpoint of the average dentist, gold-shell crowns provided a simple method of securely anchoring artificial teeth; at the same time they covered ugly, broken-down, and discolored natural teeth, as well as much inferior dental work. And to the patient, gold seemed to represent the most in value received.

Charles I. Stoloff, *Natural History* (February 1972)

As you become more experienced, you may sometimes find it effective to place the topic sentence at the *end* of the paragraph. In the following paragraph the writer has stated the topic in the last sentence. This is called specific-to-general, or **inductive,** order.

We think of an ideal society as being a community—whatever its size—in which the people, the environment, and the institutions are in harmony. No nation, ours included, has ever achieved such a society. In fact, most Americans would say it is not really possible to establish an ideal society. But strangely enough, we keep trying. Time after time, a group of people will drop out of the mainstream of American society to try another "life style" based on the group's concept of an ideal society. Most of these groups have believed in holding their property in common—that is, they believed in a communistic or communal concept of property. Most of the groups have also used the word "family" to refer to all members of the group, rather than to a mother, father, and

Topic sentence — their children as the family unit. But the groups have differed widely in their attitudes toward sex, marriage, and other values and seldom lasted for very long as a consequence.

As you study the student and professional writings that follow, you will find that writers do not always state the main idea of their paragraphs and essays outright. Instead, they may prefer to suggest or to **imply** the idea. Notice that the writer must provide enough clues to allow the careful reader to **infer** (determine) the main idea. In the following paragraph, for example, the writer implies the idea that the man saw the berries reflected rather than actually floating in the water. The writer provides the clues the reader needs to infer the main idea by saying that the man struck the bottom of the river when he dived in and that he then looked up and saw the berries hanging over him.

> While walking along the river, he saw some berries in the water. He dived down for them, but was stunned when he unexpectedly struck the bottom. There he lay for quite a while, and when he recovered consciousness and looked up, he saw the berries hanging on a tree just above him.
>
> Paul Radin,
> "Manbozho and the Berries"

If you experiment with implying your main idea, be sure to give the reader enough clues to determine your meaning.

In a longer piece of writing, such as an essay, the main idea is called the **thesis** (rather than the topic). The thesis is usually stated in one or more sentences called the **thesis statement.** Like the topic sentence of a paragraph, the thesis statement is often placed near the beginning of an essay. In the essay that follows, the thesis is stated in the opening sentence.

Thesis — A safe city street must have three main qualities.

Topic sentence — First, there must be a clear demarcation between what is public space and what is private space. Public and private spaces cannot ooze into each other as they do typically in suburban settings or in projects.

Topic sentence

     Second, there must be eyes upon the street, eyes belonging to those we might call the natural proprietors of the street. The buildings on a street equipped to handle strangers and to insure the safety of both residents and strangers, must be oriented to the street. They cannot turn their backs or blank sides on it and leave it blind.

Topic sentence

     And third, the sidewalk must have users on it fairly continuously, both to add to the number of effective eyes on the street and to induce the people in buildings along the street to watch the sidewalks in sufficient numbers. Nobody enjoys sitting on a stoop or looking out a window at an empty street. Almost nobody does such a thing. Large numbers of people entertain themselves, off and on, by watching street activity. . . .

Jane Jacobs, *Death and Life of Great American Cities*
(New York: Random House, 1961)

In addition to noting the thesis statement, notice that each paragraph has its own topic sentence. The topic sentences support and clarify the thesis. The topic sentences are supported, in turn, by the specifics in each paragraph.

Experienced writers may place the thesis statement in later paragraphs or at the end of the essay. They may, indeed, only imply the thesis. For your own writing, the important point to remember is that an effective essay has a clear thesis statement, just as a well-made paragraph has a topic sentence. When you are reading, your task is to discover the writer's thesis. When you are writing, your task is to make your own thesis as clear as possible to your reader. And your best strategy, initially, is to *state your thesis at or near the beginning of your essay.*

Developing the Main Idea

The second important way in which paragraphs and essays are alike is that their main ideas must be explained or **developed** by the writer. The strategies used by writers to develop their ideas include:

narration	process
description	cause and effect
examples	definition
classification and division	argumentation and persuasion
comparison and contrast	

These strategies for developing the main idea are called **modes of development.** Although they have different characteristics, the modes of development have a common purpose: to provide the reader with the specific information needed to **support** or clarify the main idea. As stated earlier, the main idea is a general statement; the development provides the details to support or explain the main idea.

In developing a paragraph, the writer usually (1) begins with a topic sentence, (2) develops the main idea (topic) by a series of related sentences that explain the idea fully, and (3) concludes with a sentence that restates or summarizes the main idea. Look at the following paragraph diagram and compare it with the example paragraph about the classroom on page 3. Notice that the example paragraph begins with a topic sentence; develops the main idea (topic) with the sentences about the chairs, blackboard, desk, and walls; and then concludes by restating the topic sentence.

Paragraph

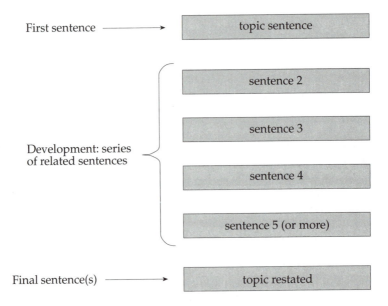

First sentence ⟶ topic sentence

sentence 2

sentence 3

Development: series of related sentences

sentence 4

sentence 5 (or more)

Final sentence(s) ⟶ topic restated

Next, compare the paragraph diagram with the essay diagram that follows. Notice that in developing the essay, the writer starts with a thesis statement, which is generally part of the introduction and may make up the whole first paragraph. Then the writer develops the thesis in a series of related paragraphs, called the **body** of the essay. Usually, each paragraph has its own topic sentence. The conclusion, which may restate the thesis or summarize the essay's important points, is usually found in the final paragraph.

Essay

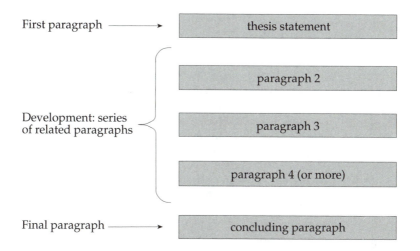

First paragraph ⟶ thesis statement

Development: series of related paragraphs ⟶ paragraph 2

paragraph 3

paragraph 4 (or more)

Final paragraph ⟶ concluding paragraph

Now look at the following essay developed by a group of students for the environment assignment. Notice that the thesis is stated in the first paragraph, which is called the **introduction** of the essay. The thesis is developed, or supported, by the next three paragraphs that make up the body of the essay. In these paragraphs, each classification of the ways the environment is being damaged has been used as the topic for a body paragraph and items from the brainstorming lists (see page 3) have been used as examples to develop the topics. The final paragraph, called the **conclusion** or concluding paragraph, restates the thesis and sums up the main points of the essay.

Thesis statement (introduction)

Modern conveniences have made our lives easier, but often at the expense of our environment. Science and society, which have been so quick to create and adopt new consumer goods, have been slow in creating and adopting practices to protect the environment from the same consumer goods. As a result, just through everyday living, we are damaging the environment we depend on and wasting our resources.

Development (body paragraph)

For one thing, we pollute the land and our water supply with the by-products of modern life. We fill our garbage dumps and landfills with throwaway plastic products and "disposable" diapers that will not disintegrate for hundreds of years, if ever. Industries accidentally or willfully spill oil and chemicals into the ground or streams and pollute our water supply.

Development (body paragraph)

For another thing, we poison the air with exhaust from the cars and airplanes that have become such an important part of our lives. In some areas, the exhaust from cars creates smog that poisons our lungs and causes respiratory ailments. Air pollution also causes acid rain that, in turn, destroys rivers, lakes, woods, and farm crops.

Development (body paragraph)

Finally, we are wasting our resources shamefully. For example, we use far more water than we need to in brushing our teeth and taking showers. Even something as "harmless" as letting dripping faucets go unrepaired wastes a lot of valuable water. We water our lawns through automatic sprinkler systems that run even in rainstorms. We also waste oil by driving millions of cars hundreds of millions of needless miles each year and by keeping our houses warmer than we need to. We are even dangerously close to depleting our "renewable" resources. We cut down our forests with abandonment in order to eat from paper plates, drink from paper cups, and carry products home from the store.

Thesis and important points restated (concluding paragraph)

Yes, we have come to depend on technology to fulfill our needs, but we still need our natural environment. Unless we start developing technology to protect our natural world, it may soon pollute and poison us.

The essay has also been developed by using **classification, examples, cause and effect,** and **persuasion** as modes of development. The *classifications* are the *ways* we are damaging the environment: polluting, poisoning, wasting. *Examples* are plastics, diapers, and oil and chemical spills; exhaust fumes from cars and airplanes; using too much water to brush our teeth and water our lawns; driving needlessly; overheating our houses; and using paper products. In turn, the examples are *causes* of three *effects:* pollution, poisoning, and wasting. The smog created by car exhaust is also a *cause* of lung and respiratory ailments (*effects*). The essay also seeks to persuade readers to stop damaging the environment.

Notice, too, the use of the words *for one thing, for another thing,* and *finally* at the beginning of paragraphs 2, 3, and 4. These are called **transitional** words, and their purpose is to help the reader identify the connection among the ideas in a composition and to move the reader along from one idea to another.

Although the modes of development are often combined as they are in the students' collaborative essay, a single mode of development will often be dominant in a composition. For instance, if you are writing a **descriptive** essay, that does not mean you cannot use **examples** to illustrate your description, but it does mean that most of the paragraphs will be descriptive. Or you might write a **cause-and-effect** essay in which you **narrate** a series of events that constitute a cause and another event that is the effect. In general, however, you will learn to be comfortable with the modes of development if you first study them individually; and this text is organized so you can do that. You will see that chapters 2 through 10 deal with a single mode of development and bring together paragraphs and essays in which that mode dominates. Chapter 11 contains essays that combine the modes, even though one mode may still dominate.

Before each paragraph or essay, you will find a note that tells you something about the reading, definitions of words that might be unfamiliar to you, and a question that either will help you think about the reading or will provide a writing idea. Following each reading selection are questions about the reading, questions about the writer's strategies, and suggestions for your own writing assignments.

The Glossary at the back of the book defines and explains the technical terms you will learn to use. These terms are boldfaced throughout the text. If you encounter a boldfaced term and cannot recall what it means, turn to the Glossary to refresh your memory.

The ability to state an idea and to develop it so that it is clear to your reader is essential to all forms of composition. The writing strategies covered in this text will help you develop those abilities. However, to produce an effective piece of writing you will generally need to follow this process:

- **Prewriting** (freewriting, brain storming), to get started and to define your idea
- **Drafting,** to learn what your idea is about
- **Rewriting,** to clarify your idea and to improve or add to the strategies used to develop it
- **Revising,** to improve the organization and content
- **Revising,** to polish the organization and content
- **Editing,** to improve word choices and sentences and to correct punctuation and spelling

Your instructor may also want you to keep a journal as a way to record your thoughts and experiences, to keep you writing, and perhaps to give you ideas for writing. Your instructor may also want you to compile a portfolio—a collection of all your drafts and revisions—as part of your course and to demonstrate your writing progress. Some instructors may want you to collaborate with your classmates on various writing assignments. Still other instructors may give you the option of submitting your drafts by computer and receiving their corrections and suggestions the same way. In any event, you should expect to draft, rewrite, revise, and edit all of your writing assignments until they are clear and convincing to your reader. You can then apply your skills to the many kinds of writing that will be required now, at school, and later, in your career.

Narration

HAVE YOU EVER seen a bad car accident, a fire, or a robbery? Have you had an especially sad or happy experience that made a lasting impression on you or made a difference in your life? If you later mention one of these **events** to friends, they will probably want to know more about it. What individual **incidents** made up the event? How did it happen? At what time? Where did it take place? On the spot, you become a narrator or storyteller and try to give a clear and lively account of the event. Thus you are already familiar with **narration,** one of the modes of development that writers frequently use to illustrate and explain their ideas. The purpose of narration is to interest the reader in a story that illustrates a particular idea clearly.

Narration is frequently used to tell about personal experiences. You have a variety of personal experiences every day. Your car won't start, you miss the bus, and then you are late for your class. Such experiences, although important to you, will not necessarily make for an effective narrative. For a narrative to be effective, the writer needs to describe an experience that has some unusual meaning or significance for both the writer and the reader. Usually, an experience is significant because it taught you—and may teach your reader—something new, something you never before realized about life. For example, in the following paragraph, the writer tells about a personal experience that taught him about being responsible, not only for making decisions but also for accepting the consequences of those decisions.

As I was growing up, my father and I often disagreed about how I should spend my time. He began telling me, "If you get yourself into it, you'll have to get yourself out." But

Topic sentence I learned what it meant to be responsible for the consequences of my decisions only after I went to a weekend party

Incident 1 when I should have studied for a math exam. I needed a good grade on the exam to stay eligible to play basketball.

Incident 2 The consequences of my decision to go to the party were clear when I got my exam back with a notice that I was on academic probation. I spent two semesters of almost steady

Incident 3 studying before I was back in good standing. Now, whenever I have a difficult decision to make, I remind myself, "If

Topic restated: significance of narrative you get yourself into it, you'll have to get yourself out." It was a tough lesson, but I learned that making a decision means taking the responsibility for its consequences.

Effective narrative writing, like all good writing, is carefully organized. Since a narrative describes events, its organization must be governed by some form of time **order.** The writer often tells about events in the order in which they took place. This method of organization, called **chronological order,** ensures that the sequence of the incidents will be logical.

In the following sample paragraph, the writer uses narration to give a factual account of an event: the discovery of Wheaties. Notice that this writer has chosen to explain the different incidents in a simple chronological order.

Topic sentence Like gravity and penicillin, Wheaties was discovered by accident. In 1921, a health clinician named Minnenrode, in

Incident 1 Minneapolis, was mixing up a batch of bran gruel for his patients when he spilled some on a hot stove. He heard it

Incident 2 crackle and sizzle, and had a taste. Delicious, he thought. He

Incident 3 took his cooled gruel to the Washburn Crosby Company, which in 1928 would merge with three mills to become

Incident 4 General Mills. Favorably impressed, Washburn Crosby gave Minnenrode use of a laboratory. Alas, his flakes crumbled

Incident 5 too easily and turned to dust in a box. Exit Minnenrode, enter George Cormack, Washburn Crosby's head miller. Cormack tested 36 varieties of wheat. He cracked them, he

Conclusion steamed them, he mixed them with syrup, he cooked them, he dried them, he rolled them. Finally he found the perfect flakes.

Steve Wulf,
"The Breakfast of Champions"

Notice the **details** in this paragraph. In addition to re-creating the incidents that are significant to his topic, the writer uses descriptive words to tell what happened. Minnenrode "spilled" the gruel, heard it "crackle" and "sizzle," and found that the flakes "turned to dust in a box." By using words that provide descriptive detail, the writer adds variety and interest to his narrative. (**Description,** a mode of development in its own right, is the subject of the next chapter.)

Notice, too, that this paragraph contains only the incidents or details that contribute directly to the story. Avoiding irrelevant incidents and details is essential to effective narrative writing. Perhaps you have heard some long-winded person tell a story and found yourself wishing that the person would skip some of the trivial details. You should keep this in mind when you are writing and limit yourself to the details that are *essential* to the main idea of your narrative. In the following essay, for example, the writer does not include any incidents that happened before the robbery. He concentrates on those incidents and details that explain his actions and reactions only during key moments. As you read the essay, think about the details the writer provides and try to form an image of the scene in your mind.

Thesis statement	1 Recently I was unfortunate enough to be in a store when a robbery took place. I learned from that experience that a pointed gun makes people obey.
Incidents arranged as they occurred in time	2 I had stopped at the store on my way home from work to get a loaf of bread. I was at the check-out counter when a man standing nearby pulled out a gun and yelled, "Everyone on the floor and away from the cash register!"
Frozen in place	3 My first reaction was fear. Around me, people dropped to the floor. But I felt frozen where I stood.
Gun pointed	4 As I hesitated, the robber pointed his gun at me and yelled again, "On the floor!" Then I felt angry. I was bigger and stronger than he was. I was sure I could put *him* on the floor in a fair fight.
Sank to floor	5 But the gun, small enough to be cradled in the palm of my hand, was bigger and stronger than I was. I sank obediently to the floor.
Robbery took place	6 All of us watched silently as the robber scooped money out of the cash register into a paper bag. Then he ran out the door, jumped into a car that was waiting, and the car raced away.
After robbery	7 Everyone stood up and started talking. A clerk called the police, who asked if anyone could describe the robber or the car. No one could.
Dialogue Significance of narrative restated	8 Then one man, blustering defensively, told the clerk just what I was thinking. "Listen. Tell them when a gun is pointed at me, it's all I'm looking at. One look and I'm going to do whatever I'm told."

Look at each paragraph in this essay. The first paragraph is an introduction in which the main idea or thesis of the essay is stated. Each successive paragraph deals with an incident or a set of incidents in the narrative. Each incident contributes key information to the essay and moves the story forward in time. The final paragraph concludes the narrative by restating the main idea of the essay.

As you can see, the narrative mode is used for more than just retelling what happened. In addition to reporting the action, narrative writing often explains the *reactions*—emotions and thoughts—of the narrator and others involved. At other times, the writer may leave it to the reader to determine the narrator's feelings and reactions.

In this and other ways, the writer establishes a particular **point of view** for the essay. Point of view involves three elements: **person, time,** and **tone.** The essay may be written in the **first person** (*I/we*), **second person** (*you*), or **third person** (*he/she/it/they*). The time in which the essay is set may be the past, present, or future. The tone is the attitude (serious, humorous, angry, sad) that the writer adopts.

In a narrative essay, the point of view creates the context for the incidents described: that is, who saw or experienced the events, when the events occurred, and how the writer felt about the events. Narration is generally written from the first- or third- person point of view—that is, from the point of view of the person who observed or was a party to the event. Usually, too, the person—the narrator—is kept consistent throughout the narrative, although writers may sometimes use different narrators to express another view or opinion of an event.

Because narration deals with an event or personal experience that already has happened, it is usually written in the past tense. Experienced writers may change the verb tense from the present to the past in what is called a "flashback"—but in general the tense should be kept consistent.

In narration and the other modes of development, an important factor in point of view is whether the writer is being objective or subjective. An **objective** essay presents the **facts**—the basics of what occurred or what is being described—without including the writer's own interpretations or personal opinions of those facts. The writer tries to portray the subject of the essay as truly as possible and does not try to influence how the reader will react. A **subjective** essay, by contrast, expresses how the writer feels and may try to get the reader to feel a certain way. It may state an opinion or reveal the writer's emotions, or it may present facts in such a way that the reader will draw a conclusion favored by the writer. The Wheaties story is an example of objective writing; it presents the facts without interpreting them. The other two examples are written more subjectively, expressing the writers' own feelings about and interpretations of the events described.

Often, writers give clues that indicate that they are being subjective. Phrases like "in my opinion" or "I felt" or "I learned" signal a subjective interpretation. (Just because an essay is written in the first person does not mean it is entirely subjective, however.) As you will see in some of the selections in this text, writers may not always tell you when they are being subjective. Some writers may even take an objective tone when they are being quite subjective—perhaps, for instance, by presenting certain facts about a subject but not others. No matter what mode of development is used in an essay, you should try to make sure just how subjective or objective the writer is being.

Narrative writing is called **nonfiction** if the story or event is true and actually happened. All of the preceding examples are nonfictional accounts. This kind of factual narrative is found in biography, history, and newspaper writing. Narrative is also the predominant mode used in short stories and novels. If a story is not true or did not actually occur, it is called **fiction.**

In fiction and nonfiction narrative writing, writers use **dialogue** as a "technique" to re-create what characters or people in the narrative said. In the essay on the store robbery, notice that the writer often tells you exactly what was said and encloses the statement using quotation marks to let you know he is quoting word-for-word conversation. Quoted dialogue can help the writer accurately express the incidents in a narrative and can add variety and color. To practice working with dialogue, listen to your friends talking with one another and see if you can reproduce something like their conversation in dialogue in your own narratives.

Writers use narration to tell about personal experiences, about other people's lives and experiences, and about factual or historical events, such as the discovery of Wheaties. Narration adds interest, suspense, and clarity to writing, as you will find in the reading selections that follow. Consequently, it is a writing skill well worth mastering.

The questions and assignments at the ends of the readings in this chapter will help you to recognize and apply the principles of narration. They will give you practice with the concepts of chronological order, narrative detail, subjective and objective writing, and dialogue.

The Hunt

Lesley Stern

In this paragraph, the writer conveys the tension and suspense felt by the narrator as he observes a prowler who enters his bedroom and ransacks the closet. Lesley Stern is the author of The Scorsese Connection, The Smoking Book, *and coeditor of* Falling for You: Essays on Cinema and Performance.

Words to Know

accretions   accumulations, collections
dissipate   ease, lessen
voluminous   large, huge

Getting Started

How would you feel and what would you do if an intruder entered your bedroom at night?

———————————

The door edges open and in the crack light flickers. A figure moves into the room, a dark silhouette. The figure turns into the light and he sees: it is her. Only her, a figure as familiar as his own body. The tension begins to dissipate, but slowly, uneasily. It is as though knots have formed through his being from tip to toe. He holds his breath and watches as she moves across the room, easing the wardrobe door open, carefully trying to avoid the habitual squeak. I must oil the hinges, he thinks. With her back to the bed, shielding the flashlight beam, she scrambles among old clothes piled at the back of the wardrobe; she burrows into the bottom of voluminous coat pockets, turns shirts inside out, baggy jeans upside down. He knows that she will already have gone through the house searching in jars, behind books in the bookcase, at the back of untidy drawers filled with junk. It happens once a year or so: the evil spirit comes upon her in the night, and she invades her own house, excavating the accretions of daily living, wanting desperately to find a remnant of the past, a sign of life. "Not much to ask," she'd say if pushed, "a little thing." That thing which is so simply and satisfyingly itself: a cigarette.

———————————

Questions About the Reading

1. Where is the narrator when the event takes place?
2. Who is the "intruder" who enters the room?
3. What does the "intruder" do?
4. Is this the first time the "intruder" has acted as she does?
5. Why does the intruder act this way?

Questions About the Writer's Strategies

1. What is the main idea of the paragraph?
2. Is the main idea stated or implied?
3. Is the paragraph objective, subjective, or both?
4. What order does the writer use?
5. What is the point of view of the paragraph? Does it change? If so, where and why?

Writing Assignments

1. Write a narrative paragraph about an experience you had that was scary.
2. Write a narrative paragraph about a happy event you are anticipating.

3. Use the Internet to find out more about the writer and make an entry in your journal about Lesley Stern's birthplace, education, occupation, and honors.

Why Harlem Is Not Manhattan

John L. Jackson

A young black man insists that Harlem is not part of Manhattan.

Words to Know

distinction   difference
Dominican   a country (Dominican Republic in the West Indies)
queue   line or file of waiting people
scissored   cut

Getting Started

Has anyone ever made you feel "different" or "left out" because of where you live?

Standing at the end of a too-long line of customers inside a too-crowded fast food restaurant in northern Manhattan, I listened attentively as Dexter, a twenty-three-year-old black man, argued across the shiny McDonald's countertop with the Dominican cashier who was trying patiently to take his order. Dressed in white, gray, and black fatigues, with neatly coifed dreadlocks down to his shoulders and two-summers-old Air Jordans on his feet, Dexter held up that queue by waving a colorful coupon in the palm of his right hand. Scissored out from an insert in that Sunday's local newspaper, the coupon redeemed a ninety-nine-cent Big Mac in every part of New York City (so read the fine print) "except the borough of Manhattan," where Big Macs, with this very same square of paper, were discounted to $1.39 instead. Well, hearing the cashier, Pam, make that borough-specific distinction several times, Dexter became increasingly annoyed. He crossed and uncrossed his arms with emphatic gestures. He sighed audibly and repeatedly. Squeezing a dollar bill and a dime in his outstretched left hand (the ten cents was "for tax," he declared numerous times), Dexter made his case: "This is Harlem," he stated with electrified finality, "not Manhattan! If they meant Harlem, if they meant Harlem, they should have written Harlem! Harlem is not Manhattan! So, I'm paying $1.10 for my Big Mac."

Questions About the Reading

1. Where does the event take place?
2. Who is the person the event is about?
3. What does he look like?
4. What does he want?
5. Do you think his demand is justified? Why or why not?

Questions About the Writer's Strategies

1. What is the point of view of the narrative?
2. Is the narrative objective or subjective?
3. What order does the writer use in the narrative?
4. What "technique" does the writer use to clarify Dexter's demand and emphasize his frustration?

Writing Assignments

1. Write a narrative paragraph about an experience you or an acquaintance has had redeeming a coupon at the grocery store.
2. Write a narrative paragraph about an unusual or exciting event that happened in your city or neighborhood.

The Discovery of Coca-Cola

E. J. Kahn, Jr.

E. J. Kahn, Jr. has written about the American scene for The New Yorker *for more than forty years. He has written about America at war, about Frank Sinatra, about Harvard, and about burlesque. He has also discussed that most American of drinks, Coca-Cola, in a book titled* The Big Drink. *In a paragraph from that book, he tells us of the invention of Coca-Cola as a medicine and the discovery that led to its becoming a soft drink.*

Words to Know

audit analyze, figure out, verify
composition contents, ingredients
concoction a mixture of ingredients
dollop a large portion or serving
factotum an employee
testimonially in honor of

Getting Started

Coca-Cola was first sold as a medicine. How do you imagine it became a popular soft drink?

The man who invented Coca-Cola was not a native Atlantan, but on the day of his funeral every drugstore in town testimonially shut up shop. He was John Styth Pemberton, born in 1833 in Knoxville, Georgia, eighty miles away. Sometimes known as Doctor, Pemberton was a pharmacist who, during the Civil War, led a cavalry troop under General Joe Wheeler. He settled in Atlanta in 1869, and soon began brewing such patent medicines as Triplex Liver Pills and Globe of Flower Cough Syrup. In 1885, he registered a trademark for something called French Wine Coca—Ideal Nerve and Tonic Stimulant; a few months later he formed the Pemberton Chemical Company, and recruited the services of a bookkeeper named Frank M. Robinson, who not only had a good head for figures but, attached to it, so exceptional a nose that he could audit the composition of a batch of syrup merely by sniffing it. In 1886—a year in which, as contemporary Coca-Cola officials like to point out, Conan Doyle unveiled Sherlock Holmes and France unveiled the Statue of Liberty—Pemberton unveiled a syrup that he called Coca-Cola. It was a modification of his French Wine Coca. He had taken out the wine and added a pinch of caffeine, and, when the end product tasted awful, had thrown in some extract of cola (or kola) nut and a few other oils, blending the mixture in a three-legged iron pot in his back yard and swishing it around with an oar. He distributed it to soda fountains in used beer bottles, and Robinson, with his flowing bookkeeper's script, presently devised a label, on which "Coca-Cola" was written in the fashion that is still employed. Pemberton looked upon his concoction less as a refreshment than as a headache cure, especially for people whose throbbing temples could be traced to overindulgence. On a morning late in 1886, one such victim of the night before dragged himself into an Atlanta drugstore and asked for a dollop of Coca-Cola. Druggists customarily stirred a teaspoonful of syrup into a glass of water, but in this instance the factotum on duty was too lazy to walk to the fresh-water tap, a couple of feet off. Instead, he mixed the syrup with some charged water, which was closer at hand. The suffering customer perked up almost at once, and word quickly spread that the best Coca-Cola was a fizzy one.

Questions About the Reading

1. Why did the drugstores in Atlanta honor John Pemberton by closing on the day of his funeral?
2. How is Frank M. Robinson significant to the story of Coca-Cola's origins?
3. Sherlock Holmes, the fictional detective in a series of short stories and books written by Arthur Conan Doyle, and the Statue of Liberty appeared in the same year as Coca-Cola. Why would Coca-Cola officials like to point out these facts?
4. The writer describes the way Pemberton mixed Coca-Cola and distributed it. What does the writer's explanation tell you about the standards that existed in 1886 for the production and sale of patent medicines? Which words and phrases help describe the standards?

Questions About the Writer's Strategies

1. Is the main idea of the paragraph directly stated? If so, in which sentence(s)? If not, state the idea in a sentence of your own.
2. What is the point of view in "The Discovery of Coca-Cola"? Could the writer have used another point of view, such as first person? Why or why not?
3. Does the writer include any details that are not essential to the idea of the narrative? If so, why did he include them?

4. What tone does the writer achieve by his description of how Robinson checked a batch of syrup? What is the effect of using the word *nose*? Why is the word *audit* appropriate?
5. The writer uses the words *dollop* and *factotum* in telling about the customer being served Coca-Cola in the drugstore in 1886. Why are these words more effective than *large serving* and *employee* would be?

Writing Assignments

1. Write a narrative paragraph in which you tell about an accidental discovery of your own.
2. *Working Together* Join with a classmate to write a narrative paragraph in which you describe the incidents that you imagine led to the discovery of fire or the wheel.
3. Write a narrative paragraph in the first person telling about something you did to help a friend, relative, or organization. Try to show how your action was significant to *you*.

Freedom

Iu-choi Chan (student)

*Sometimes a single event can tell us a great deal about a person, culture,
or way of life. In the following paragraph, a young Chinese man tells
about his daring attempt to escape from a country where he felt oppressed
to a place where he could feel free. Although this attempt failed, Iu-choi
Chan has since managed to come to the United States. He wrote this
paragraph while he was a student at California State University in
Bakersfield.*

Words to Know

Hong Kong a former British colony on the coast of China
sentries persons or soldiers posted to guard an area or position

Getting Started

What obstacles have you had to overcome to achieve a goal?

Two years ago, I attempted to escape from mainland China to Hong
Kong. I planned and prepared well. I dressed up like a farmer and
walked for two days from my village to the border between China and
Hong Kong. That night, I was very excited and nervous, but I tried to
keep calm. At the border there were a lot of sentries who tried to catch
people like me, so I put some mud on myself to avoid being noticed. It
was not easy for me to pass through the sentries, but I bit my tongue and
climbed across the swampy area. Finally, I reached the river that runs
across the border. I plunged into it. It was icy cold, and I used all my
strength to swim as fast as I could. In about twenty minutes, I touched
land. I had made it! My happiness was beyond description. But when I
stood up, a Hong Kong policeman was immediately beside me. My
dream was shattered. I was taken to a police station to wait for a truck
that takes unsuccessful refugees back to China. The police put me in the
truck with a great many other people, and we were driven like a herd of
buffalo back to China. I had lost my freedom again.

Questions About the Reading

1. Which statement indicates the distance the young man lived from the Hong Kong border?
2. Describe the border area between China and Hong Kong.
3. Do many people try to leave mainland China and go to Hong Kong? Which details support your answer?
4. Why do you think the young man dressed like a farmer when he tried to escape?
5. The writer says, "I had lost my freedom again." What does the word *again* tell you about what happened to him before? Do you think the sentence reflects his opinion of life in mainland China?

Questions About the Writer's Strategies

1. Is the main idea of the paragraph directly stated? If so, in which sentence(s)? If not, state the main idea in a sentence of your own.
2. In what order are the major incidents of the story arranged? Could the order be changed? If so, in what way?
3. The writer compares the return of the refugees to China to being "driven like a herd of buffalo." Does this comparison help you see his situation?
4. What is the point of view in the narrative? Could another point of view be used? Using the first three sentences of the paragraph as an example, explain how you could change the point of view.

Writing Assignments

1. Think of a goal you have set for yourself but that you have not yet reached. Write a narrative paragraph in which you (a) state the goal; (b) explain what has happened to prevent you from reaching the goal; and (c) tell what you will do in the future to achieve the goal.
2. Write a narrative paragraph in which you tell what you or another person did to succeed in reaching a particular goal.
3. What career have you chosen for yourself? Write a narrative paragraph in which you tell what experiences made you choose the career.

When We Were Colored

Clifton L. Taulbert

In his story of growing up in segregated Glen Allan, Mississippi, Clifton Taulbert remembers his "colored" childhood for the love and strength given him by his extended family of relatives and friends.

Words to Know

agrarian agricultural or rural

antiquated old, out-of-date, obsolete

delta the area at the mouth of a river or inlet created by sediment

gentry people of an upper class or group

pilgrimage a journey to a special or sacred place

solace comfort, consolation

verified proved to be true

Getting Started

How do you feel when you return to a familiar, childhood place?

It was a beautiful October day in the 1970s. It was not quite like those other October days when I was a child growing up in this southern cotton community, but it was beautiful nonetheless. I had come home for my yearly pilgrimage to see Glen Allan, Mississippi, to remember the life I once knew and visit my older relatives. Somehow I always felt better after visiting those tired people who had given me strength when I was a child. So many changes had taken place in Glen Allan. "Colored" people were now "black," soap operas had replaced quilting bees in their homes, and the schools their children attended were now integrated. But the land was the same; the rich delta land had not changed. And the cotton smelled as it did in the early '50s when I picked it as a way of life. Now, however, the quarter of a mile long cotton rows seemed shorter and instead of the bent backs and scratched hands of hundreds of coloreds picking cotton, there were scores of big red machines harvesting the white fields. As always, the land was giving life, being faithful, fruitful and productive, providing stability and a sense of worth.

I made it a point to visit my old aunt, Mozella Alexander. She insisted I sit and listen as she vividly recalled the times when her grandparents owned a plantation five miles from Glen Allan—a plantation they called

Freemount. As we sat in her shotgun house that was falling on one end
and propped up on the other, she rocked, swatted flies and told me all
about old man Sidney Williams, Miss Phoebe, Rosa Morgan, Tom
Williams and the rest that were known at the turn of the century as "the
big colored landowners."

As she talked, her smooth black face shone with a pride that I don't   3
know if I'll ever possess. "Son, my pa and your great-great grandpa
were somebody. Oh chile, they had plenty land, mules, hogs and chickens and jest 'bout eberthang."

She talked with increasing excitement. Even though she was renting   4
a run-down house, she knew that she was descended from the colored
landed gentry. I guess that's why she was labelled "uppity." Even at her
age she walked straight as an arrow.

"All out dar in de colony was colored when I wuz a chile. Yez sir my   5
ole grandpa worked dat land like it was no t'morrow."

I knew the land she spoke of, although Freemount no longer existed.   6
It was near the colored colony, a large parcel of land which I'd also heard
was once in my family. I remember some of the older people saying,
"Chile y'all folks shore had some land out dar in de colony." But for
some reason those sayings never reached my belly. Land ownership and
the sense of worth it brings seemed to have died out during my parents'
time. I responded to this story as if it might be colored folklore. All my
life most of the land owners had been white. When I'd go to the colony,
it was their stately homes I'd see first. It never dawned on me that these
houses, so seemingly permanent on their sites, were not the beginning.
Little did I know they were built upon the sweat and blood of a different set of land owners, black men and women who tamed the land and
gave it such an appropriate name, "Freemount."

Aunt Mozella talked for hours and I listened politely. At last I   7
attempted to take my leave, but she stopped me.

"Set down, son. Lemme give ya something. And you hold onto it. It's   8
valuable. No matter what happened to me, I'se always held onto these."

She got up and walked over to a trunk that was probably twice her   9
age. She was old, colored and proud, with not a wrinkle in her cinnamon
face. As she bent over her trunk and undid the double locks, I looked
around at her tattered home, wall papered with pages from the Sears
catalog. I wondered what of value she could possibly give me, her educated grand nephew.

Turning from the trunk she stood in front of me holding in her black 10
hands a bundle of papers tied securely with old rags. Her cinnamon face
shone as she pressed the papers to my hands.

"Here son, take 'em. Hold 'em. Yessir, here's de proof. It's all here. All 11
dat my grandaddy worked for is right here."

I would later learn that in that moment, she had released to my gen- 12
eration the legal proof of our family's land ownership. All I had heard as
a child was true.

I stood there at the foot of her iron bed holding the ancient papers. I'd 13
been led to believe that coloreds never kept their papers. Nervously I
untied the bundle and unfolded the fragile deeds. I was holding not the
copies but the actual documents signed in ink by my great-great-grand-
fathers Sidney Williams and Ben Morgan, and the land commissioner for
the State of Mississippi. Almost a century later these deeds spoke to me
from their faded pages and verified for all time to come that Freemount
had once really existed.

My discovery of these deeds affected me oddly. All my life, growing 14
up in the colored section of the little Mississippi town of Glen Allan, I
had been taught to respect the owners of the large plantations. In the
agrarian South, land ownership more than any other factor decided who
had status; the more land a person owned, the more he was worth. The
realization that I was the descendant of black plantation owners gave me
a sudden sense of pride. At the same time I felt cheated. The land which
should have been my birthright had been lost, taken from my family
during the Depression, sold without my great grandparents' knowledge
at a tax auction for money they'd never known they owed. I'd grown up
in the '50s, under a system of segregation which enforced on all people
of my race an inferior status—a sense of worthlessness which was
wholly illegitimate, but which I had striven all my life to overcome.

On further reflection, I realized that many of the values of the 15
Southern culture had been illegitimate, even, perhaps, the value placed
on land ownership. For the truth is, man cannot really own the land; we
are only trustees for a time. Eventually the land will claim us and we'll
return to our mother earth. Knowing this gives me some solace as I look
at antiquated deeds dated in the late 1800s and signed over to my great-
great-grandparents by the vice-president of the Yazoo and Mississippi
Valley Railroad Company and its land commissioners. This land, once
called Freemount, has probably had more trustees and names than we'll
ever know.

If land ownership is not a legitimate measure of a people's worth, I 16
wondered, what is? I began to think about my childhood and other values I'd learned as I grew up in an environment much like that experienced by thousands of other colored Americans. Even though segregation was a painful reality for us, there were some very good things that
happened. Today I enjoy the broader society in which I live and I would
never want to return to forced segregation, but I also have a deeply-felt
sense that important values were conveyed to me in my colored childhood, values we're in danger of losing in our integrated world. As a

child, I was not only protected, but also nourished, encouraged, taught, and loved by people who, with no land, little money and few other resources, displayed the strength of a love which knew no measure. I have come to believe that this love is the true value, the legitimate measure of a people's worth.

I was barely seventeen when I left my childhood home in Glen Allan 17 and boarded the Illinois Central north to Saint Louis and into the 1960s, which would forever change the fabric of our society. Today my children are growing up in a world where "color" is something that comes in a box of crayons—a world of Bill Cosby and Yves St. Laurent. I have written *Once Upon A Time When We Were Colored* because I want my children to know of the life-style that gave them their father and their mother. It is very difficult to master the present and make a meaningful contribution to the future unless you understand and appreciate the past. In our desire as black Americans to put segregation behind us, we have put ourselves in danger of forgetting our past—the good with the bad. I believe that to forget our colored past is to forget ourselves, who we are and what we've come from.

This book is not the story of Freemount and the years when blacks 18 owned the land. It is the story of a mostly landless people, the coloreds, who lived in Glen Allan and other small Southern towns during the last years of segregation. I have written it to recall a treasure more valuable and enduring than land ownership. It is the treasure that stood out in my colored childhood when there was so little else, and it has been a source of strength to me in all the years since then. That treasure is the nourishing love that came to me from my extended family of aunts, uncles, parents, grandparents, great-grandparents, cousins, neighbors and friends. Rich in love, this congregation of black maids, field hands and tenant farmers worked the cotton fields, fished Lake Washington, gathered at St. Mark's Missionary Baptist Church to sing and pray, and gathered at the Greenville train station to bid farewell to loved ones moving north. In ordinary daily living through very difficult times, they showed themselves to be a great people. They are the reason I want today's world to remember an era that in our haste we might mistakenly forget—that era when we were called colored.

Questions About the Reading

1. Why does Taulbert make his yearly pilgrimage to Glen Allan?
2. What changes have taken place in Glen Allan since Taulbert's childhood? What things have remained the same?

3. Whom did the writer visit in Glen Allan and what did the person value highly?
4. Does the writer share the person's opinion of what is highly valuable?
5. Why does the writer think it is important to his children for him to go back to Glen Allan?
6. What does the writer feel is the most valuable "treasure" he gained from his childhood in Glen Allan?

Questions About the Writer's Strategies

1. What is the thesis of the essay? Is the thesis stated? If so, in which sentences? If not, state the thesis in a sentence of your own.
2. What is the point of view of the essay in person, time, and tone?
3. What is the main idea of paragraph 15? Is the main idea directly stated or is it implied? If directly stated, in which sentence(s)?
4. What order does the writer use in paragraphs 2 through 13?
5. Identify the descriptive details in paragraphs 2, 9, and 10.

Writing Assignments

1. Write a narrative essay in which you explain the influence of relatives or friends on your thinking about or attitude toward life.
2. Write a narrative essay in which you imagine you are visiting a place that you lived in as a child. Explain the significance the place had in shaping your personal values or your attitude toward life.

Message in a Bottle

Ellen Gilchrist

Ellen Gilchrist is the author of many novels, short stories, poetry collections, and nonfiction works. In this essay, she tells the story of her battle with and recovery from alcoholism.

Words to know

barged into   intruded where not invited
behaviorist   a psychologist whose treatment is based on a
  person's behavior
psychoanalyst   a specialist in the treatment of mental disorders
psychotherapy   treatment by applying various forms of mental
  therapy
recurring   repeated action or event

Getting Started

Do you have a habit you think you should break?

As I approached the age of 40, four things happened that changed my 1
life: I went into psychotherapy, I ran a marathon, I stopped drinking, and
I started writing again for the first time in seven years.

Of these four things, the most important was that I stopped drinking. 2
Without that, the other three might never have been possible.

To understand how I quit drinking you first have to understand how 3
I became a drunk. I never meant to drink too much. I meant to be a beautiful woman raising a glass of wine to my lover, then dancing the night
away in a Balenciaga gown. I meant to be like Dorothy Parker and Edna
St. Vincent Millay. I didn't know they were alcoholics any more than I
knew I was one.

I lived in a world where alcohol was served at every meeting and 4
every function and anyone over 16 was allowed, even expected, to drink.
It was served at weddings, baptisms, christenings, parties. Women
drank sherry after church; while playing bridge; while getting their hair
done at the beauty parlor; before, during, and after sports events; and
even at bedtime—the latter called a nightcap, supposedly because it kept
your head warm while you slept. From the first whiskey I was given
(one New Year's Eve by the junior high school basketball coach) to the

last terrible night (when I fell down a flight of stairs and suffered a concussion), if I drank alcohol, I ended up drunk.

Once, during the days when I was drinking, I went down to New 6 Orleans's Oschner's Clinic and had a six-hour operation to undo a tubal ligation because I had told my husband that I wanted to have a child for him. After I said it, I had to prove it. The surgery was terrible. And unsuccessful.

Once when I was drinking, I went down to the French Quarter in New 7 Orleans and tried to get the whores in a whorehouse to come home and live in our house and stop being whores.

I should make a list of things I did when I was drinking that no one 8 would believe anyone would do, much less a nice girl from a nice family who had been educated in good schools and raised by sober parents.

During those years, I tried to quit, but I didn't know how, because I 9 didn't understand what was wrong with me. I remember seeing an article in a women's magazine called "How to Tell You're an Alcoholic." I bought the magazine and ran home to read the article. It was a test. There were 10 questions, and if you answered yes to more than six, you were an alcoholic. I answered yes to most of them. I hid the magazine, but I couldn't stop thinking about the questions.

I was two people when I was a drunk. On the outside, I was energetic, 10 bright, optimistic, attractive. On the inside, I didn't know what was wrong with me. I couldn't understand why everything I did turned to dust, why my marriages didn't last, why I couldn't achieve my goals, why years were going by and my talents were being wasted. My grandfather used to say he would rather a child of his be dead than be a drunk. Many times I wanted to be dead during the years when I drank. I could not understand why it kept happening—why time after time I would set out to have two drinks and end up sleeping God knows where, having lost my car keys, my shoes, my sanity, my health.

When I was in my late 30s, I was saved from my addiction. I was 11 saved with knowledge and information and with the help of two great psychiatrists: a behaviorist and a psychotherapist.

On the morning that the good, sober, happy part of my life began, I 12 was out running on the Tulane University track with my best friend. I was living in New Orleans at the time. It was a lovely spring morning, cool for New Orleans, and perfect for running, but I was in a bad mood and feeling guilty. The night before, I had barged into my friend's house while she was on a date with a gorgeous French rugby player. I had been drunk when I arrived, and after I got there, I got drunker.

I don't know why she even came out to the track to meet me the next 13 morning, but she did. After we had run about three laps, she brought it up.

"I don't want you to come over anymore when you're drinking," she 14
said.

"I know," I answered. "I'm so sorry. I don't know why I did it."   15

"Maybe you need to see a psychiatrist," she suggested. "Diana is see- 16
ing one who got her to stop." Diana was a beautiful friend who had been
queen of a Mardi Gras ball. A very big deal in New Orleans.

"Maybe I will," I answered. "What's his name?"   17

"His name is Chet Scrignar," she answered. "He's a behaviorist. 18
Diana's crazy about him. She says he's really helped her."

I made an appointment for the following afternoon.   19

Dr. Scrignar had once been a psychotherapist but quit because he 20
couldn't stand the slowness of "the talking cure." Psychotherapy was not a
good fit for his personality, so he switched to behaviorism, which attempts
to deal with problems by using quicker and more practical methods.

He attacked my problem with every tool in his kit. He put me on 21
Antabuse, a drug that makes you nauseated when you drink alcohol. He
hypnotized me. He begged me. He charmed me. He took me for long walks.
He marched me down to the Tulane School of Medicine and made me look
at slides of decaying livers. He taught me that alcoholism is a disease.

It was spring when I began to work with Dr. Scrignar. I had to learn many 22
things and unlearn many others. At first I kept going to the endless round
of parties that is the life of uptown New Orleans society. Finally I
stopped. I was finding other things to do. I began running six miles every
morning in Audubon Park. I played tennis. I sat in meditation. I practiced
yoga. I read and read and read. I began to write seriously for the first time
in seven years. I was waking up. I was freeing myself from the guilt that
people who drink too much carry with them all the time.

After a year, I stopped seeing Dr. Scrignar and began seeing a psy- 23
choanalyst who helped me understand the underlying cause of my
addiction. I called my analyst "the crying doctor" because sometimes I
would go into his office and cry over things that I didn't know bothered
me. I didn't know it bothered me to abandon my dreams of becoming a
writer after I started having children. Once I figured that out, I began to
write seriously.

Many times I have tried to turn these experiences into fiction. I was 24
successful when I saw the humor in the situation, less so when I got too
serious with the material. Nonetheless, once of the recurring characters
in my stories managed to quit drinking also. There is great fun, even joy,
in watching a real or imagined person survive a crisis. Helping my characters, in the end, helped me heal myself.

Questions About the Reading

1. What did the writer think she would become in life?
2. How old was she when she had her first drink? Who gave it to her?
3. What are some of the things she did when she was drunk?
4. What happened that made her decide to get help to stop drinking?
5. What are the four things that changed in her life? What was the most important change?
6. What did the writer discover bothered her?

Questions About the Writer's Strategies

1. What is the thesis of the essay? Is it stated or implied? If stated, where?
2. What is the "message" of the essay?
3. Is the essay objective or subjective or both? Justify your answer with examples from the essay.
4. What technique does the writer use in telling about the incident that made her decide to seek treatment for her alcoholism?
5. What point of view does the writer use? Is it consistent throughout the essay? Could another point of view be used? Why or why not?

Writing Assignments

1. Write a narrative essay in which you explain how you have broken— or would break—some habit such as overeating or smoking.
2. Write a narrative essay explaining how friends or family members stopped smoking or lost weight.

3. Use the Internet to research Dorothy Parker and Edna St. Vincent Millay and, in your journal, explain what they had in common with Ellen Gilchrist.

The Jeaning of America— and the World

Carin C. Quinn

In "The Jeaning of America—and the World," Carin Quinn tells about Levi Strauss's development of blue jeans, the sturdy and reliable American pants that are now famous worldwide. Quinn also explains some of the reasons for the popularity and success of blue jeans.

Words to Know

Alexis de Tocqueville (1805–1859)   French aristocrat, traveler, and author; noted for his four-volume work *Democracy in America*, which was based on his travels in the United States in 1831 to study the American penitentiary system and democracy.

appropriated   took over

bureaucrats   government officials, particularly those who rigidly follow rules and regulations

ensuing   following, subsequent

idiosyncratic   individual, unique

mother lode   rich, original vein of ore

proletarian   of the working class

rigors   hardships

ubiquitous   seeming to be everywhere at the same time

Getting Started

Do you believe that success in life comes from hard work, good luck, or a combination of the two?

This is the story of a sturdy American symbol which has now spread   1
throughout most of the world. The symbol is not the dollar. It is not even Coca-Cola. It is a simple pair of pants called blue jeans, and what the pants symbolize is what Alexis de Tocqueville called "a manly and legitimate passion for equality." Blue jeans are favored equally by bureaucrats and cowboys; bankers and deadbeats; fashion designers and beer drinkers. They draw no distinctions and recognize no classes; they are merely American. Yet they are sought after almost everywhere in the world—including Russia, where authorities recently broke up a teenaged gang that was selling them on the black market for two hun-

dred dollars a pair. They have been around for a long time, and it seems likely that they will outlive even the necktie.

This ubiquitous American symbol was the invention of a Bavarian- 2 born Jew. His name was Levi Strauss.

He was born in Bad Ocheim, Germany, in 1829, and during the 3 European political turmoil of 1848 decided to take his chances in New York, to which his two brothers already had emigrated. Upon arrival, Levi soon found that his two brothers had exaggerated their tales of an easy life in the land of the main chance. They were landowners, they had told him; instead, he found them pushing needles, thread, pots, pans, ribbons, yarn, scissors, and buttons to housewives. For two years he was a lowly peddler, hauling some 180 pounds of sundries door-to-door to eke out a marginal living. When a married sister in San Francisco offered to pay his way West in 1850, he jumped at the opportunity, taking with him bolts of canvas he hoped to sell for tenting.

It was the wrong kind of canvas for that purpose, but while talking 4 with a miner down from the mother lode, he learned that pants—sturdy pants that would stand up to the rigors of the diggings—were almost impossible to find. Opportunity beckoned. On the spot, Strauss meas-ured the man's girth and inseam with a piece of string and, for six dol-lars in gold dust, had [the canvas] tailored into a pair of stiff but rugged pants. The miner was delighted with the result, word got around about "those pants of Levi's," and Strauss was in business. The company has been in business ever since.

When Strauss ran out of canvas, he wrote his two brothers to send 5 more. He received instead a rough, brown cotton cloth made in Nîmes, France—called *serge de Nîmes* and swiftly shortened to "denim" (the word "jeans" derives from *Gênes*, the French word for Genoa, where a similar cloth was produced). Almost from the first, Strauss had his cloth dyed the distinctive indigo that gave blue jeans their name, but it was not until the 1870s that he added the copper rivets which have long since become a company trademark. The rivets were the idea of a Virginia City, Nevada, tailor, Jacob W. Davis, who added them to pacify a mean-tempered miner called Alkali Ike. Alkali, the story goes, complained that the pockets of his jeans always tore when he stuffed them with ore sam-ples and demanded that Davis do something about it. As a kind of joke, Davis took the pants to a blacksmith and had the pockets riveted; once again, the idea worked so well that word got around; in 1873 Strauss appropriated and patented the gimmick—and hired Davis as a regional manager.

By this time, Strauss had taken both his brothers and two brothers-in- 6 law into the company and was ready for his third San Francisco store. Over the ensuing years the company prospered locally and by the time of his death in 1902, Strauss had become a man of prominence in California. For three decades thereafter the business remained profitable though small, with sales largely confined to the working people of the West—cowboys, lumberjacks, railroad workers, and the like. Levi's jeans were first introduced to the East, apparently, during the dude-ranch craze of the 1930s, when vacationing Easterners returned and spread the word about the wonderful pants with rivets. Another boost came in World War II, when blue jeans were declared an essential commodity and were sold only to people engaged in defense work. From a company with fifteen salespeople, two plants, and almost no business east of the Mississippi in 1946, the organization grew in thirty years to include a sales force of more than twenty-two thousand, with fifty plants and offices in thirty-five countries. Each year, more than 250,000,000 items of Levi's clothing are sold—including more than 83,000,000 pairs of riveted blue jeans. They have become, through marketing, word of mouth, and demonstrable reliability, the common pants of America. They can be purchased pre-washed, pre-faded, and pre-shrunk for the suitably proletarian look. They adapt themselves to any sort of idiosyncratic use; women slit them at the inseams and convert them into long skirts, men chop them off above the knees and turn them into something to be worn while challenging the surf. Decorations and ornamentations abound.

The pants have become a tradition, and along the way have acquired   7 a history of their own—so much so that the company has opened a museum in San Francisco. There was, for example, the turn-of-the-century trainman who replaced a faulty coupling with a pair of jeans; the Wyoming man who used his jeans as a tow-rope to haul his car out of a ditch; the Californian who found several pairs in an abandoned mine, wore them, then discovered they were sixty-three years old and still as good as new and turned them over to the Smithsonian as a tribute to their toughness. And then there is the particularly terrifying story of the careless construction worker who dangled fifty-two stories above the street until rescued, his sole support the Levi's belt loop through which his rope was hooked.

Questions About the Reading

1. What reasons does Quinn give for the success of blue jeans? Identify the sentences that support your answer.
2. What are the main incidents in the development of blue jeans?
3. Speculate about why Levi's brothers lied to him about their status in America. Why do you think the writer included this detail?

4. What conclusions can you draw about Strauss's character?
5. How do you think Quinn feels about Levi's jeans and their popularity?

Questions About the Writer's Strategies

1. What order does the writer use for paragraphs 3 through 6? What is the purpose of the first paragraph of the essay? What is the purpose of the last paragraph?
2. Is the thesis of the essay stated? If so, in which sentence(s)? If not, state the thesis in a sentence of your own.
3. What are the main ideas in paragraphs 3, 4, 5, and 6? Are the main ideas directly stated?
4. What is the point of view in person, time, and tone in the essay?
5. Could the first sentence in paragraph 5 be made into more than one sentence? Why or why not? Could the third sentence in paragraph 5 be made into more than one sentence? If so, how? If not, why not?

Writing Assignments

1. *Working Together* Join with some classmates to write a narrative essay explaining how your classmates achieved success by working hard, being lucky, taking a risk, or being innovative. Describe the series of events that led to the successes.
2. Write a narrative essay about an important opportunity that you once had. Explain how the opportunity arose, how you took or did not take advantage of it, and what the results of your action were.

Daughter's Doll Teaches
Mom Lesson on Race

Connie Schultz

*Mothers may usually know best, but Connie Schultz, a reporter for the
Cleveland (Ohio)* Plain Dealer, *learned that when it came to choosing a
doll, her daughter had a perfectly logical reason for the one she wanted.
(Connie Schultz, "Daughter's Doll Teaches Mom Lesson on Race"* ©
2000 The Plain Dealer. *All rights reserved. Reprinted with
permission.)*

Words to Know

balked   refused

furrowed   wrinkled, rutted

nuzzling   caressing with the nose

venue   location, site

Getting Started

What was your favorite plaything as a child, and why did you like
it?

Sometimes our kids teach us lessons we thought we were teaching   1
them.

That's how Addy made her way into our family's life five years ago.   2

Addy is an American Girl doll. She is based on the main character in   3
a series of books about a slave girl whose family escaped to freedom in
the 1800s.

Addy is black. My daughter is white. But from the moment Cait read   4
her first sentence about Addy, she was convinced she and that slave girl
were practically twins. And since her father and I had recently separated, it didn't take much lobbying on Cait's part to get exactly what she
wanted from this mother steeped up to her furrowed brow in guilt: An
Addy doll. An almost-$100 Addy doll, to be precise.

That Christmas morning, my then 8-year-old daughter greeted her   5
new friend with squeals of delight. Not only did she get Addy, she and
Addy got matching nightgowns, which Cait quickly snatched up before
running off to her bedroom.

A few minutes later, there they were: Addy and Cait, cheek to cheek   6
and dressed in matching white, ruffly nightgowns. "Don't we look alike,

Mommy?" Cait said, her face beaming as she wrapped her arms around her doll.

I looked at my blue-eyed daughter, as pale as a calla lily, squeezing   7 her doll with the creamy brown skin and big dark eyes, and wondered what she could be thinking. Tread gently here, I told myself.

"How do you and Addy look alike?" I asked.   8

Cait just smiled as she brushed back Addy's hair. "Oh, you know," she   9 said, nuzzling the doll's cheek. But I didn't know, and I felt left out, blinded to the bigger picture only my daughter seemed to see.

For the next two months, Cait took Addy everywhere she went. You 10 can learn a lot about strangers by their reaction to a pretty black doll in a white girl's arms. One woman, who was white, glared at me as we stood in line at a McDonald's. "You *made* her buy that, didn't you?" she hissed, shaking her head as she looked at Cait clutching Addy to her chest. "There is no way she would have asked for a doll like that."

A young black woman working at a local drugstore stared at Cait and 11 Addy and then politely leaned in to whisper to me. "Did she want that doll?" When I nodded my head, she winced. "Why?"

"We're a lot alike," piped up Cait. I looked at the bewildered woman, 12 shrugged my shoulders and smiled.

I thought of Addy recently after talking to a mother with two adopted 13 sons from Korea. For years, Linda has sent her boys to a camp for Korean children adopted by Americans. "I thought it was a good idea," she said. "All year long they are with kids who don't look like them, who didn't come from Korea, and everything I had heard and read said this is a good thing to do."

One of her sons, however, balked last year, announcing he did not 14 want to go to that camp again. Her 10-year-old did this in what is all children's venue of choice for serious conversations: In the car, while his mother was driving.

Linda was surprised, but undeterred. "Don't you like to be some 15 place where everyone is like you?" Her son's response so startled her she nearly ended up on a tree lawn: "Isn't the important thing supposed to be liking who you are and not being like everyone else?"

Linda smacked her forehead in recounting this conversation. "You 16 know, you raise them to believe certain things, to get beyond the issues of race and gender and all that, but then you're blown away when you realize they're there, all your lessons took, and *you're* the one who isn't getting it."

At that point I was required to welcome Linda into the Clueless 17 Mothers Club, of which I am president. Then I told her about Addy, and how I finally found out why Cait wanted the doll in the first place.

"Addy and I are so alike," Cait said yet again as I tucked them into 18
bed one night. "How so?" I asked. Cait reached up and touched my face.
"Addy had to leave with her mom, just like you and me."

I froze. For eight years I had been teaching my daughter that it's 19
what's on the inside that counts. Obviously, only one of us had been
listening.

And you know what? Cait was right. She and Addy, they're so alike. 20
They're practically twins.

Questions About the Reading

1. When did Cait get Addy, the black doll?
2. Why did Cait want Addy?
3. How did people react to Cait having Addy?
4. What did Linda's Korean son tell her when she asked why he didn't want to go back to camp?
5. What is the lesson the writer learned?

Questions About the Writer's Strategies

1. Where is the main idea (thesis) of the essay? Is it stated more than once? If so, where?
2. What is the order the writer uses in the essay?
3. What technique does the writer use to re-create what Addy, Linda, and the writer said?
4. Is the essay objective or subjective?

Writing Assignments

1. Write a narrative essay telling about your favorite plaything as a child and explaining why it was your favorite.
2. Write a narrative essay telling about why you wanted to learn to drive a car and the first time you drove someplace by yourself.

The Deli

Carmen Machin (student)

Carmen Machin was a student at East Los Angeles College when she wrote this account of running a small food store in New York. She is especially effective at letting us see what happened exactly as she saw it at the time. Her account gives us a good idea of her own refreshing character: a bit wide-eyed and innocent but ready to discover things, to learn, and to take the world as it comes.

Words to Know

albeit although, even though
brogue accent
fortitude strength
naiveté innocence
purloined stolen
sorties entries, invasions
syndrome symptoms, feelings

Getting Started

In what ways are people and situations not always as they first appear?

My husband and I were about a year into wedded bliss, when we 1
were made an offer we couldn't refuse. There was a delicatessen whose
owner was anxious to sell. He was moving to another state. We could
have the store at payments we could afford. We accepted. There was an
apartment behind and connected to it which was included in the deal.
We had no idea what the neighborhood was like, but with youthful
energy and optimism, we moved in.

The first week was tragic. As the days passed and the end of the 2
month approached, we realized that if things continued as they were, we
would not only be unable to make the payments, but would probably
have to close the doors. In the midst of this anxiety was the surly attitude
of the customers. One lady in particular seemed to relish my discomfort
and attempts at self-control while she, on each of her sorties into the
establishment, accused us, now of underweighing the cold cuts and salads, or then, of miscounting her change. For weeks I remained courteous

and patient before her onslaught. I did not want to alienate the very few customers that we had.

Then suddenly, we began to see new faces. Our business started a def- 3 inite upward swing. Even our first customers seemed more pleasant. All, that is, except HER. The day came when I felt I could no longer tolerate her attacks, and still smiling, I suggested that since we did not seem to be able to satisfy her, that it might be a good idea if she went elsewhere. She burst out laughing and in her thick Irish brogue, proclaimed to the other customers who were there at the time, that at last she had made me show some "backbone." Then she turned to me and said: "I wondered how long you'd be taking it." She went on to marvel at the intestinal fortitude or innocence of two "spics" moving into an Irish neighborhood. I stood there in complete awe, as the other customers assured me that they had, at first, abandoned the store when they heard that "spics was buying," but that, thanks to Madeline Hannon, for that was our tormentor's name, they had, one by one, come back.

New York is a great big city; most folks call it unfriendly, and yet, I 4 never found it so. This area, from 96th Street to 100th Street, between Amsterdam and Columbus avenues, was absolutely small townish. Everyone knew everybody else and most were related in some way. Outsiders who moved in had to prove themselves worthy of acceptance or remain forever strangers. We were fortunate. Even the local gang, called "The Dukes," on whose turf our place was located, accepted us wholeheartedly.

The "Dukes," unknown to us, had terrorized all the shopkeepers in 5 the area. In order to be able to stay in business without being harassed by vandalism, shoplifting, out and out robberies, and, in certain cases, beatings, the Dukes were paid whatever they felt the traffic could bear. In their opinion, we were to be no exception.

One day three of the young men swaggered into the store. At the time, 6 my husband was in the cellar arranging a shipment of merchandise that had just arrived, and I, expecting him momentarily, was preparing a sandwich which was to be my lunch. As I glanced up, I saw one of them quickly grab some Hostess Cupcakes and put them in his pocket; another leaned against the fruit bin which was immediately minus an apple. Such was my naiveté that I firmly believed the only reason anyone stole food was hunger. My heart broke and at the same time opened and embraced them in the mother syndrome. They asked to speak to my husband. "He's not here at the moment, but if you don't mind waiting, he should be back in a jiffy." They nodded.

As they started to turn to walk around the customer area, I pro- 7 ceeded to introduce myself and, at the same time, commenced making three more sandwiches. While I made small talk (actually, it was a mono-logue), they stood silent, looking fiercely, albeit hungrily at the master-pieces I was concocting: Italian rolls, piled high with juicy roast pork and, on top, my husband's wonderful homemade cole slaw. I placed them on paper plates along with pickles and plenty of potato chips, then I said, "Come on, you'll have to eat in the kitchen, because we're not licensed to serve in the store. Do you want milk or soda?" "Don't you know who we are?" "I've seen you around, but I don't know your names," I replied. They looked at me in disbelief, then shrugging their shoulders, marched as one into the kitchen which was the first room behind the store. They ate to their hearts' content and, before they left, emptied their pockets, depositing each purloined article in its appointed place. No apologies were given, none were expected. But from that day on, we were protected, and the only payment we ever made was that which we also received: friendship, trust, and acceptance.

Questions About the Reading

1. Explain how the writer proved she was "worthy of acceptance." Did she use the same method in each of the two incidents she tells about in the narrative?
2. What final conclusion can you draw about Madeline Hannon's character? Was she prejudiced? Were her friends prejudiced?
3. Why do you think Madeline and her neighbors behaved as they did?

Questions About the Writer's Strategies

1. In paragraph 4, the writer says, "Outsiders who moved in had to prove themselves worthy of acceptance." What purpose does this statement serve in the essay?
2. What order does the writer use in explaining the incidents that took place? Are there any paragraphs in which the writer seems to change that order?
3. What is the point of view of the narrative? If the writer had known at the time of the incidents what she knew when she was writing, do you think the events would have proceeded in the same way and with the same outcomes?
4. The writer does not use very much dialogue in her narrative. Rewrite paragraphs 6 and 7, changing some of the descriptive statements into quoted dialogue.

Writing Assignments

1. Write a narrative essay about an experience in which you did not fully understand what was happening until after the event—perhaps, for instance, when you were the target of a practical joke, or when you misinterpreted a friendly gesture as a romantic overture.
2. Write a narrative essay in which you tell about a person who achieves a goal only after standing up to another person.
3. Write a narrative essay about a situation in which you were at a serious disadvantage. Tell how you were able to work around that disadvantage.

3

Description

DESCRIPTION PROVIDES THE reader with a "word picture" of a specific person, the flavor of a special place, or the look of a particular object. To help the reader visualize the object, the writer chooses key details to develop the description: a certain liveliness in a person's eyes, the movement of ocean waves, the design of a favorite chair.

We saw in chapter 2 that writers use descriptive words to add color and vividness to the details they describe. The specific descriptive words the writer chooses depend on the particular **impression,** or image, the writer wants to create. For example, the writer can create the impression of a person who is likable by describing the person's face as "friendly" and "good natured." The writer can create the opposite impression by using such descriptive words as "shifty" or "scowling." In the following paragraph, the writer develops an effective impression of a chair by the buildup of details and descriptive words that re-create the object for the reader.

Detail:
location

Detail:
appearance

Detail:
appearance

The chair was the one piece of furniture I wanted to take with me when I closed up my parents' house for the final time. To look at it, sitting in the same kitchen corner where it had been for fifty years, you'd wonder how it could be my favorite chair. It was nothing but a straight-backed wooden chair, its seat scratched here and there from the soles of a small boy's shoes. The only thing unusual about it was the intricate design carved into its back. But the carving was what made the chair meaningful to me. I had sat in that chair many times as punishment for errors in my ways. I suppose my mother thought it was defiance that led me to sit cross-legged on the seat with my back to her in the

Details:
decoration of
chair

kitchen. But it was not defiance. Rather, in that position my eyes and then my fingers could trace the intertwining leaves and flowers of the design carved in the back of the chair. Each time I sat there I seemed to see lines and shapes I hadn't seen before: a heart-shaped leaf, a budding rose, a blade of grass. Perhaps that chair had something to do with my lasting interest in well-made antique furniture. Who knows? I do know that when I drove away on that last day, the chair, carefully wrapped in several old quilts, lay tenderly cradled on the back seat of my car.

Notice that the chair is described only as being a straight-backed wooden chair with a scratched seat and a design carved into its back. However, the writer creates the dominant impression that the chair—in spite of being associated with childhood punishment—remained beautiful to him and probably influenced his lifelong interest in fine woods and antiques. The words *intricate, trace, intertwining, heart-shaped,* and *budding* describe and help the reader picture the design in the back of the chair. And in the last sentence, the phrases *carefully wrapped* and *tenderly cradled* convey indirectly the writer's feelings about the chair. The reader must be given enough detail not only to picture an object but also to understand what touched or moved the writer to single it out.

In descriptive writing you will often find stylistic devices that help convey both the essential qualities of the subject and its significance to the writer. Consider the following paragraph.

A baseball weighted your hand just so, and fit it. Its red stitches, its good leather and hardness like skin over bone, seemed to call forth a skill both easy and precise. On the catch—the grounder, the fly, the line drive—you could snag a baseball in your mitt, where it stayed, snap, like a mouse locked in its trap, not like some pumpkin of a softball you merely halted, with a terrible sound like a splat. You could curl your fingers around the baseball, and throw it in a straight line. When you hit it with a bat it cracked—and your heart cracked, too, at the sound. It took a grass stain nicely, stayed round, smelled good, and lived lashed in your mitt all winter, hibernating.

In this paragraph, the writer uses a **figure of speech** called a **simile** to help enhance the description of the baseball. A simile takes items that are considered unlike and then compares them in a way that shows an unexpected similarity. Usually, a simile uses *like* or *as* to establish the connection between the items. For example, three similes in this paragraph are "like skin over bone," "like a mouse locked in its trap," and "not like some pumpkin of a softball."

A figure of speech related to the simile is the **metaphor,** which also compares unlike items, but does so without directly stating the connection with *like* or *as*. Metaphors may be used to express an idea that is rather abstract, as in "the *scales* of justice." But they can be used for other effects, too, and they may only be **implied** by the use of a certain verb— "The swimmer *waddled* across the sand."

Read the paragraph that follows. What is the metaphor for the matron and for the electric car? Is there another metaphor?

> In 1900, electric cars were a common sight on city streets. They were high, boxy, and heavy—those early electric cars—and they couldn't get up much speed. Nor could they be driven very far before the battery had to be recharged. So by the 1930s, the electric car was a curiosity piece that now and then sailed out of a carriage house, usually with a stern-faced matron at the steering tiller. Car and driver were somehow suited to each other: heavily built, elegantly appointed, and quietly majestic. They were quality products. They didn't guzzle fuel, raise their voices above a murmur, or create a public problem as they floated across the streets. But they both disappeared in favor of slim-lined, stripped-down models that drink high-powered fuels, make noise in the streets, and create a public nuisance. Now maybe only a few people would like to see that old-style matron come back. But these days, most of us would like to have a car that didn't use gas, was really quiet, and didn't pollute the environment. That's why our engineers have worked to solve the battery problem: so we can have electric cars again.

Personification, another figure of speech, attributes human qualities or abilities to animals or objects. For example, after Red Riding Hood observes that the wolf has big teeth, the wolf answers, "The better to eat you with, my dear!"

Exaggeration, which is called **hyperbole,** is also used. "I could have danced all night" might be possible for a few people, but for most of us, it would be hyperbole.

The organization of a description also contributes to its effectiveness. The writer may arrange the details in **order of importance,** usually moving from the less important to the more important details. The details in the paragraph on pages 47–48 are arranged so that they build to the most significant point—the deeper meaning of the chair to the writer. The writer may choose to arrange the details according to space, called **spatial order.** When a description is organized according to space, the writer takes a physical position in a room or at a scene and then describes what can be seen from that position, using some consistent order such as moving from left to right, from foreground to background, or from top to bottom.

In creating a description, the writer must identify the important characteristics of the object or scene being described and then find the words—nouns and verbs, as well as adjectives and adverbs—that best express these characteristics. In the essay that follows, the student describes the house in which she is living. Notice that she describes the house in **spatial order**—first from the outside and then as she walks through its rooms. Notice, too, that the descriptive details provide the reader with an image of both the house and its owner.

View of the outside of the house	It's really not a striking house, nor is it an old charming house. It is, in fact, very plain—just like the houses on each side of it. As I climb up the hilly driveway, its <u>whiteness</u> stares blankly back at me, reminding me that I am not the
Details: preciseness of the landscaping	owner but just a temporary, unwanted trespasser. There are flowers lining the driveway, which push their faces toward the sun as they lie in their bed <u>perfectly spaced</u>, not too close and not too far apart, <u>perfectly coordinated</u> to reflect all the colors of the spectrum. Through the windows of the house
Thesis statement	nothing but my reflection can be seen. They are like the house, clean and tinted, allowing no one a look in, keeping life in the house shut off from the rest of the world, uninviting of intrusion, only interested in cleanliness, only leading the people inside to a feeling of loneliness.
Entering the house	Upon <u>entering the house</u> the smell of Pinesol and disinfectant engulfs my nostrils and shoots directly to my brain,
Details: cleanliness and coldness of kitchen	anesthetizing any emotions that might surface. Like the windows, the kitchen floor reflects the <u>cleanliness</u> of the house with its <u>spotless white surface, scrubbed and shined</u>, casting off reflections from the <u>bright lights</u> overhead. There is wallpaper on the walls of the kitchen, but it is <u>void of any pattern</u> and lends <u>very little color</u> to the <u>whiteness</u> of the room. Only
	items of importance for the duties of the kitchen are displayed, all in their properly appointed places, with the appropriate covers placed over them to hide them from prying eyes. The only personality the kitchen portrays is a cold, calculating, suspicious one, wary of intruders who may cause unnecessary filth to enter.
Moving to dining room	Around the corner from <u>the kitchen lies the dining room</u>.
Details: formality and whiteness of room	An <u>elegant, dark, formal table</u> sits in the center of the room, the surface of which is smooth as glass under my fingertips. A <u>white centerpiece</u> is carefully placed at the table's center, with two <u>white candles that have never been lit</u> standing
	erect at the centerpiece's ends. The chairs around the table are hard, providing support for the back but lending the body no comfort. Above hangs a crystal chandelier—expensive, elegant, giving the room an artificial brightness. It is made up of many dangling, teardrop-shaped crystals, all <u>cleaned and polished</u>, and is the only object in the dining room that speaks clearly of conspicuous consumption. The drapes covering the tinted windows are a dark color and <u>keep out the sun of the day</u>. This room is <u>often cleaned, often walked through</u>, but never used.
Entering the living room	<u>Having walked through the dining room, I enter the living room</u>. Although this is the only room in the house where

Details:
impersonality of
living room

the family can all converge to spend time together, it is not a cheerful place. The walls are white, like the rest of the house, with the same drapery as the dining room, and the couch and loveseat are velvet, stiff, uncomfortable, and well maintained. A television set is placed in the corner but lies blank with disuse. The air of coldness here seems to hold tension though at the same time it gives the impression of ossification.

I have heard it said that a person's home is a reflection of that person, a sentiment that, with few exceptions, is true of this home. Cleanliness is a priority of the owner, and socializing with people in this house is considered a nuisance that only causes more work because of the dirt that people carry in with them. The walls are kept white because it looks clean and repainting is made easy. And the smell of disinfectant pleases the owner, as it proves to the few who do enter that

Thesis related
and conclusion

the house is clean. This house, the place I am calling home for this period of my life, offers me no comfort but does provide shelter and quiet. And with the dark stillness in its rooms, I can think, read, and plan my escape.

Carol Adams (student),
"An Intruder in the House"

In the introduction to chapter 2, you learned about the difference between writing **objectively** and **subjectively.** Notice, in the previous essay, that although the writer's style is objective, her choice of specific descriptive details and words supports her subjective, negative opinion of the house and its owner.

When brainstorming for a description, it may help to begin by listing all the features of the subject that come to mind and all the details that seem related to those features.

Descriptive details often are combined with other modes of development. The following paragraphs, for example, are from a narrative essay about a young man's visit to the Mexican town that he had left soon after he was born. Notice his descriptions of the people and the Spanish architecture of the town.

Description:
Spanish
architecture

On my arrival at Morelia airport, I was greeted by the   1
most attractive architecture I had ever seen. All the buildings had a very strong Spanish influence. Was it possible I had taken the wrong plane and landed somewhere in Spain?

People and their
clothing

No, indeed; it was Morelia, and what a town! Its people   2
were very plain and small-townlike. I was amused by some very oddly dressed people who wore white cotton clothing. On their heads the men wore straw hats, and the women wore large Spanish scarves called mantillas. I asked a ticket agent about the oddly dressed people. He explained that they were the native people, known as Tarascos. They were

the founders of the land, and even today they are very traditional in their beliefs and ways.

 I took a taxi to El Hotel Virrey de Mendoza, located in the   3
middle of the town square. The hotel was made of hewn
stone that was cut and shaped into the most captivating
three-story building I had ever seen. It was built in the tra-

**Architectural
features**

ditional Spanish style, with a central open patio completely
surrounded by the building. My room had a spacious view
of the town square and its cathedral. The cathedral was built
in the seventeenth century in a baroque style that was popular in Europe. Beside the cathedral was the municipal
palace and other government buildings, all in Colonial
Spanish style. The feeling I had from the view was that I was
back in the days when Spanish viceroys ruled the land, and
the Catholic priests taught religion to the native inhabitants.

Arturo E. Ramirez (student),
"Back to Where the Seed Was Planted"

 Descriptive words and phrases are essential to effective writing. They
can make an object concrete for the reader by describing how it looks,
sounds, tastes, smells, or feels. Such sensory details can create a distinct
impression or **image** of that which is described and thus help the reader
visualize the writer's ideas. You will find specific descriptive words and
details in all the paragraphs and essays that follow. As you read, notice
that experienced writers select revealing details because, as with the incidents in narrative writing, these details produce the most effective
description. In your own writing, select—as the writers of the reading
selections do—the most essential qualities of whatever you describe.

The Hiroshima Museum

Barbara Kingsolver

In this selection from her book High Tide in Tucson, *Barbara King-solver describes her visit to the Peace Memorial Museum in Hiroshima and the items displayed there that speak silently of the impact of an atomic bomb.*

Words to Know

artifacts objects of historical importance
histrionic emotional, theatrical, dramatic
hypocenter surface beneath the center of a nuclear explosion
ideological reflective of an idea, belief, or culture
saki wine made from rice

Getting Started

How do you feel when you look at paintings and exhibits in a museum?

Since that day, I've had the chance to visit another bomb museum of a different kind: the one that stands in Hiroshima. A serene building set in a garden, it is strangely quiet inside, with hushed viewers and hushed exhibits. Neither ideological nor histrionic, the displays stand entirely without editorial comment. They are simply artifacts, labeled: china saki cups melted together in a stack. A brass Buddha with his hands relaxed into molten pools and a hole where his face used to be. Dozens of melted watches, all stopped at exactly eight-fifteen. A white eyelet petticoat with great, brown-rimmed holes burned in the left side, stained with black rain, worn by a schoolgirl named Oshita-chan. She was half a mile from the hypocenter of the nuclear blast, wearing also a blue short-sleeved blouse, which was incinerated except for its collar, and a blue metal pin with a small white heart, which melted. Oshita-chan lived for approximately twelve hours after the bomb.

Questions About the Reading

1. Why do you think the displays in the museum "stand entirely with-out editorial comment"?
2. What do the exhibits tell you about the effect of an atomic bomb?
3. Why do you think the museum visitors are "hushed"?
4. What is the significance of all the watches being "stopped at exactly eight-fifteen"?

Questions About the Writer's Strategies

1. What is the main idea of the paragraph? Is it stated or implied? State the main idea in your own words.
2. What order does the writer use to describe the artifacts in the muse-um? Why do you think she chose that order?
3. Is the paragraph objective or subjective or both? Support your answer with examples.
4. What descriptive details does the writer give about Oshita-chan and her clothing? Do the details provide an image of what happened to Oshita-chan?

Writing Assignments

1. Write a narrative paragraph in which you describe your feelings dur-ing a visit to a museum.
2. Write a narrative paragraph in which you describe a visit to a city you had never been to before.
3. Visit an elder-care center, a church other than your own, or a day-care center for preschoolers, and write a narrative paragraph describing the place.

Mail

Anne Fadiman

Anne Fadiman recalls how her father anticipated receiving the daily mail and disliked any day without a mail delivery.

Words to Know

confirmation   proof, verification
equivalent   equal to, same as
humidor   tobacco jar designed to keep tobacco moist
Muscadet   wine made from Muscat grapes
niche   recess, hollow space
orgies   wild celebrations

Getting Started

Is there something you look forward to that happens every day?

His desk was made of steel, weighted more than a refrigerator, and bristled with bookshelves and secret drawers and sliding panels and a niche for a cedar-lined humidor. (He believed that cigar-smoking and mail-reading were natural partners, like oysters and Muscadet.) I think of it as less a writing surface than a mail-sorting table. He hated Sundays and holidays because there was nothing new to spread on it. Vacations were taxing, the equivalent of forced relocations to places without food. His homecomings were always followed by day-long orgies of mail-opening—feast after famine—at the end of which all the letters were unanswered; all the bills were paid; the outgoing envelopes were affixed with stamps from a brass dispenser heavy enough to break your toe; the books and manuscripts were neatly stacked; and the empty Jiffy bags were stuffed into an extra-large copper wastebasket, cheering confirmation that the process of postal digestion was complete.

Questions About the Reading

1. What does the writer think is the actual purpose of her father's desk?
2. Why did her father hate Sundays, holidays, and vacations?
3. What were vacations like to her father?

4. What was the evidence that her father had "digested" the mail collected during a vacation?

Questions About the Writer's Strategies

1. What is the main idea of the paragraph? Is it stated or implied? If stated, identify the statement.
2. What are the details the writer uses to describe her father's desk?
3. Is there a simile in the paragraph? If so, identify it.
4. Are there statements in the paragraph that are like similes but not identified with the word *like*? If so, identify them.

Writing Assignments

1. Write a descriptive paragraph in which you explain how you sort and handle your mail.
2. Write a paragraph describing a place you like to visit, your neighborhood, your pet dog or cat, or a favorite friend.

My Father

James Baldwin

In this paragraph, James Baldwin describes his father as a man of beauty but of bitterness of spirit.

Words to Know

emanated came from
intolerable unbearable
mementos souvenirs
unabating never ending or ceasing

Getting Started

Have you ever met a person you admired but who also intimidated you?

He was, I think, very handsome. I gather this from photographs and from my own memories of him, dressed in his Sunday best and on his way to preach a sermon somewhere, when I was little. Handsome, proud, and ingrown, "like a toenail," somebody said. But he looked to me, as I grew older, like pictures I had seen of African tribal chieftains: he really should have been naked, with war paint on and barbaric mementos, standing among spears. He could be chilling in the pulpit and indescribably cruel in his personal life and he was certainly the most bitter man I have ever met; yet it must be said that there was something else in him, buried in him, which lent him his tremendous power and, even, a rather crushing charm. It had something to do with his blackness, I think—he was very black—with his blackness and his beauty, and with the fact that he knew that he was black but did not know that he was beautiful. He claimed to be proud of his blackness but it had also been the cause of much humiliation and it had fixed bleak boundaries to his life. He was not a young man when we were growing up and he had already suffered many kinds of ruin; in his outrageously demanding and protective way he loved his children, who were black like him and menaced, like him; and all these things sometimes showed in his face when he tried, never to my knowledge with any success, to establish contact with any of us. When he took one of his children on his knee to play, the child always became fretful and began to cry; when he tried to help one of us with our homework the absolutely unabating tension which

emanated from him caused our minds and our tongues to become paralyzed, so that he, scarcely knowing why, flew into a rage and the child,
not knowing why, was punished. If it ever entered his head to bring a
surprise home for his children, it was, almost unfailingly, the wrong surprise. I do not remember, in all those years, that one of his children was
ever glad to see him come home. From what I was able to gather of his
early life, it seemed that this inability to establish contact with other people had always marked him and had been one of the things which had
driven him out of New Orleans. There was something in him, therefore,
groping and tentative, which was never expressed and which was
buried with him. One saw it most clearly when he was facing new people and hoping to impress them. But he never did, not for long. We went
from church to smaller and more improbable church, he found himself
in less and less demand as a minister, and by the time he died none of
his friends had come to see him for a long time. He had lived and died
in an intolerable bitterness of spirit and it frightened me to see how powerful and overflowing this bitterness could be and to realize that this bitterness now was mine.

Questions About the Reading

1. What was the profession of the writer's father?
2. Was his father successful in his profession?
3. What does the writer think his father looked like?
4. How did the writer's father treat his children?
5. Do you think the writer loves, admires, fears, or dislikes his father?
   Support your answer with statements from the paragraph.

Questions About the Writer's Strategies

1. What is the main idea of the paragraph? Is it stated or implied? If
   stated, where in the paragraph?
2. What are the similes in the paragraph?
3. What order does the writer use in describing his father?
4. Why do you think he chose this order?

Writing Assignments

1. Write a paragraph describing a person you admire and respect.
2. Write a paragraph describing a person you dislike and do not respect.
3. Use the Internet to learn about James Baldwin and write an entry in
   your journal about his career.

Overindulgence

Heidi Hall (student)

In the following paragraph, Heidi Hall, a student at George Fox College, uses descriptive language to make her Aunt Helen's chicken and dumplings seem larger than life. Through language alone, the reader can almost taste what she describes—and feel the aftereffects of too much of a good thing.

Words to Know

celestial heavenly
primordial having to do with the beginning of time
resolve determination
sentry guard; a soldier standing guard

Getting Started

What would make you want to overindulge in a favorite food?

———————————

One of my weaknesses is my Aunt Helen's famous chicken and dumplings. If anything could break my resolve to only have one helping it'd be this celestial dish: Chicken pieces lightly seasoned with herbs and cooked till fork-tender—dumplings floating in the flavorful broth like sentry icebergs in a thick, primordial sea. Never could I stop at just one helping; too many delicious tastes scream, "More! More! This next bite will be even better!" Alas, too often I have staggered from her gracious table a few too many bites past "comfortable," Alka-Seltzer in hand, waistband begging for relief, and my resolve all the firmer to "NEXT time only have one serving."

———————————

Questions About the Reading

1. What are some of the sensory details the writer uses to bring her aunt's chicken and dumplings to life? Do you think the dish Hall describes sounds appetizing? Why or why not?
2. What do you learn about the writer from reading this paragraph?
3. Think about the images Hall uses in this paragraph. Is there anything other than the appearance, taste, and smell of the chicken and dumplings that makes her enjoy them so much?

4. Is there anything that can never be "too much of a good thing"—for instance, a hobby, work, or creative endeavor? If you think there is, why do you think that? If you don't think there is, describe some of the possible negative effects of even the most productive activities.

Questions About the Writer's Strategies

1. Does the writer state the main idea of the paragraph? If so, in which sentence does she state it?
2. The writer uses unusual vocabulary in the second sentence. Why do you think Hall chose to use the words *sentry* and *primordial?*
3. What is the tone of this paragraph? Identify words and expressions that support your answer.
4. Why do you think the writer quotes the food talking to her and then her talking to herself?

Writing Assignments

1. Write a paragraph in which you describe your own favorite—or least favorite—food. Try to use as many unusual but appropriate descriptive words as possible to make the reader imagine vividly what you describe.
2. Write a paragraph describing a family tradition other than a meal. Describe as vividly as possible some of the things that you find comforting about this tradition.

Hush, Timmy—
This Is Like a Church

Kurt Anderson

In this essay, Kurt Anderson, a writer for Time *magazine, describes the Viet Nam Veterans Memorial in Washington, D.C., and the behavior of the people who visit it. (Kurt Anderson, "Hush Timmy—This Is Like a Church" Time, 4/15/85. © 1985 Time Inc. Reprinted by permission.)*

Words to Know

catharsis relief, purification
contemplative thoughtful
liturgical public worship
mandarins officials, authorities
rambunctious boisterous, noisy, unruly
sanctum holy place
stigmatized branded, disgraced
vertex highest point

Getting Started

Is there a place that makes you feel sad or happy?

The veteran and his wife had already stared hard at four particular   1
names. Now the couple walked slowly down the incline in front of the
wall, looking at rows of hundreds, thousands more, amazed at the ros-
ter of the dead. "All the names," she said quietly, sniffling in the early-
spring chill. "It's unreal, how many names." He said nothing. "You have
to see it to believe it," she said.

Just so. In person, close up, the Viet Nam Veterans Memorial—two   2
skinny black granite triangles wedged onto a mount of Washington
sod—is some kind of sanctum, beautiful and terrible. "We didn't plan
that," says John Wheeler, chairman of the veterans' group that raised the
money and built it. "I had a picture of seven-year-olds throwing a
Frisbee around on the grass in front. But it's treated as a spiritual place."
When Wheeler's colleague Jan Scruggs decided there ought to be a monument, he had only vague notions of what it might be like. "You don't
set out and *build* a national shrine," Scruggs says. "It *becomes* one."

Washington is thick with monuments, several of them quite affecting.   3
But as the Viet Nam War was singular and strange, the dark, dreamy,

redemptive memorial to its American veterans is like no other. "It's more solemn," says National Park Service Ranger Sarah Page, who has also worked at the memorials honoring Lincoln, Washington and Jefferson. "People give it more respect." Lately it has been the most visited monument in the capital: 2.3 million saw it in 1984, about 45,000 a week, but it is currently drawing 100,000 a week. Where does it get its power—to console, and also to make people sob?

The men who set up the Viet Nam Veterans Memorial Fund wanted 4 something that would include the name of every American killed in Viet Nam, and would be contemplative and apolitical. They conducted an open design competition that drew 1,421 entries, all submitted anonymously. The winner, Maya Ying Lin, was a Chinese-American undergraduate at Yale: to memorialize men killed in a war in Asia, an Asian female studying at an old antiwar hotbed.

Opposition to Lin's design was intense. The opponents wanted some- 5 thing gleaming and grand. To them, the low-slung black wall would send the same old defeatist, elitist messages that had lost the war in the '60s and then stigmatized the veterans in the '70s. "Creating the memorial triggered a lot of old angers and rage among vets about the war," recalls Wheeler, a captain in Viet Nam and now a Yale-trained government lawyer. "It got white hot."

In the end, Lin's sublime and stirring wall was built, 58,022 names 6 inscribed. As a compromise with opponents, however, a more conventional figurative sculpture was added to the site last fall (at a cost of $400,000). It does not spoil the memorial, as the art mandarins had warned. The three U.S. soldiers, cast in bronze, stand a bit larger than life, carry automatic weapons and wear fatigues, but the pose is not John Wayne-heroic: these American boys are spectral and wary, even slightly bewildered as they gaze southeast toward the wall. While he was planning the figures, sculptor Frederick Hart spent time watching vets at the memorial. Hart now grants that "no modernist monument of its kind has been as successful as that wall. The sculpture and the wall interact beautifully. Everybody won." Nor does Lin, his erstwhile artistic antagonist, still feel that Hart's statue is so awfully trite. "It captures the mood," says Lin. "Their faces have a lost look." Out at the memorial last week, one veteran looked at the new addition and nodded: "That's us."

But it is the wall that vets approach as if it were a force field. It is at 7 the wall that families of the dead cry and leave flowers and mementos and messages, much as Jews leave notes for God in the cracks of Jerusalem's Western Wall. Around the statue, people talk louder and breathe easier, snap vacation photos unselfconsciously, eat Eskimo Pies and Fritos. But near the wall, a young Boston father tells his rambunctious son, "Hush, Timmy—this is like a church." The visitors' processionals do seem to have a ritual, even liturgical quality. Going slowly down toward the vertex, looking at the names, they chat less and less, then fall silent where the names of the first men killed (July 1959) and the last (May 1975) appear. The talk begins again, softly, as they follow the path up out of the little valley of the shadow of death.

For veterans, the memorial was a touchstone from the beginning, and the 1982 dedication ceremony a delayed national embrace. "The actual act of being at the memorial is healing for the guy or woman who went to Viet Nam," says Wheeler, who visits at least monthly. "It has to do with the felt presence of comrades." He pauses. "I always look at Tommy Hayes' name. Tommy's up on panel 50 east, line 29." Hayes, Wheeler's West Point pal, was killed 17 years ago this month. "I know guys," Wheeler says, "who are still waiting to go, whose wives have told me, 'He hasn't been able to do it yet.'" For those who go, catharsis is common. As Lin says of the names, chronologically ordered, "Veterans can look at the wall, find a name, and in a sense put themselves back in time." The war has left some residual pathologies that the memorial cannot leach away. One veteran killed himself on the amphitheatrical green near the wall. A second, ex-Marine Randolph Taylor, tried and failed in January. "I regret what I did," he said. "I feel like I desecrated a holy place." 8

The memorial has become a totem, so much so that its tiniest imperfections make news. Last fall somebody noticed a few minute cracks at the seams between several of the granite panels. The cause of the hairlines is still unknown, and the builders are a little worried. 9

Probably no one is more determined than Wheeler to see the memorial's face made perfect, for he savors the startlingly faithful reflections the walls give off: he loves seeing the crowds of visitors looking simultaneously at the names and themselves. "Look!" he said the other day, gesturing at panel 4 east. "You see that plane taking off? You see the blue sky? No one expected that." 10

Questions About the Reading

1. About how many people a week visited the Viet Nam Veterans Memorial in 1984?
2. How many people a week were visiting the memorial at the time the essay was written (1985)?
3. What did the men who set up the Viet Nam Veterans Memorial Fund want the memorial to include?
4. Who won the contest for the design of the memorial? Why was her design controversial?

5. How many names were inscribed on the wall?
6. What differences are there between people's behavior at the wall and their behavior at the sculpture?

Questions About the Writer's Strategies

1. What is the main idea (thesis) of the essay?
2. Is the main idea directly stated or implied?
3. What is the point of view (person, time, tone) of the essay?
4. What is the impression of the memorial that the writer creates?
5. Is the essay objective, subjective, or both?

Writing Assignments

1. Write a descriptive essay about a place you visited that made you feel particularly sad.
2. Write a descriptive essay about a place you visited that made you feel particularly happy.

3. Use the Internet to research the following historical monuments: the Statue of Liberty in New York City; the Lincoln Memorial in Washington, D.C.; and Mount Rushmore in Keystone, South Dakota. Write an essay describing each monument, who or what it represents, and when and by whom it was built or created. Include a list of the web addresses you use.

   To find helpful web sites, use a search engine—such as Google (**http://www.google.com/**), or Yahoo! (**http://www.yahoo.com/**), and type in keywords, such as "Statue of Liberty" or "national monuments."

Starstruck

Sara Askew Jones

The writer describes a dark, dark night as the best time for lying outside and gazing at the stars.

Words to Know

celestial   heaven, heavenly

constellations   fixed groups of stars, usually named after some mythological being

galaxy   grouping of stars

Leonid meteors   shooting stars, appearing to come from the Leo constellation

solace   relief, comfort

stellar   like a star

Getting Started

Have you ever camped out in a forest or slept overnight in your backyard?

The first time I saw the Milky Way, I stood on a mountain in Western   1
North Carolina and felt the enchantment of our galaxy. Gravity may
have held my feet on terra firma, but the heavens tugged at my heart
and soul. On that winter's night, the stinging cold air sharpened my
senses and magnified the intensity of the moment. Looking at that ribbon of light spilling across the sky, I was absolutely starstruck.

Since that stellar event, I've spent many evenings looking upward.   2
Once on a trampoline with children snuggled up against me, I spent the
night counting shooting stars and satellites until the dew of early dawn
covered us, and the sky faded into morning. My daughter still talks
about those magical hours, spent not in front of a television set or movie
screen, but under the night sky.

I remember my first celestial encounter as a child. My dad showed me   3
the Big and Little Dippers. (When I was older, I learned their more glam-
ourous names—Ursa Major and Ursa Minor.) As a navigator in WW II,
my father had learned to read the constellations like a road map of the
heavens. He conveyed to me a power of the stars that reached beyond
their beauty.

Because so many of my own sky-watching experiences have occurred 4
during the winter, I've always felt this time of year provided the best
stargazing. In truth, dark, dark skies in any season make the celestial
viewing better. Heading out on the night of new moon and getting far
away from city lights help this happen. Also, the higher the altitude, the
better the results.

Still in our colder season, certain planets and stars—such as Jupiter; 5
Saturn; the Pleiades star cluster; and Sirius, the Dog Star—shine more
brilliantly. With longer nights, I have more time to spend outdoors under
a starry blanket.

Last winter produced one of the greatest heavenly shows this cen- 6
tury will ever see. The Leonid meteors showered us for the better part of
several evenings. For me, it meant shooting star bliss. In the middle of a
bitterly cold November night, my husband and I, covered in quilts, lay
upon the grass and watched as falling stars too numerous to count (or
really comprehend) blazed across the sky. I was awed and humbled by
witnessing such a rare spectacle.

A couple of months later, in a field far from my hometown's lights, my 7
husband, nephew, and I joined Danny Cobb, president of the Birming-
ham Astronomical Society on a stargazing adventure. He focused his
telescope on such wonders as the Double Cluster in Perseus, the Crab
Nebula, four of Jupiter's moons, and Castor—a double star. We viewed
these celestial jewels through a large and delicate 10-inch scope, controlled by a computer. The instrument allowed us to see never-imagined
details, and with the telescope's assistance and Danny's knowledge,
stargazing became richer, more complex.

As much as I enjoyed this viewing, I still love the simple joy of lying 8
back on a blanket, picking out familiar constellations, and counting
falling stars. Now that winter is here again, I'll be taking advantage of
every clear evening to settle under the expansive sky. The sprawling
blanket of stars, constellations, planets, and dust particles crisscrossing
the blackness may make some feel insignificant. For me, I find solace in
that—and comfort in the beauty and wonder of the night sky.

Questions About the Reader

1. Where was the writer when she first saw the Milky Way?
2. How did that event affect the writer?
3. What conditions does the writer like best for stargazing?
4. What was the "greatest heavenly" show of this century?
5. How does stargazing make the writer feel?

Questions About the Writer's Strategies

1. What is the thesis of the essay? Is it stated or implied? If stated, identify where and in which sentences.
2. Is the essay objective, subjective, or both? If both, identify at least three objective and three subjective sentences.
3. What is the metaphor the writer uses to describe the Milky Way?
4. What is the order the writer uses?

Writing Assignments

1. Write an essay describing what you saw and felt on a camping trip or sleeping outside overnight.
2. Write an essay describing what you saw on a school field trip.

3. *Working Together* Join with some classmates and, using the Internet, look up at least six of the constellations, planets, or stars the writer identifies in the essay and write an essay describing them.

A Letter from the Desert

Lt. Nicole A. Elwell and Jeff Elwell

A letter from a young U.S. Army lieutenant gives us a true-to-life description of Iraq and its people.

Words to Know

beater dilapidated, rusty car
convoy protective escort for troops
droves crowds, groups of people
emerged came out, appeared
equivalent equal
humbled felt smaller
impoverished poor, needy
regime ruler, controlling authority
sheepish guilty, embarrassed
squelched put down, stopped

Getting Started

Is there an impoverished neighborhood in the city or area in which you live?

This is an excerpt from a letter from my 24-year-old daughter, a U.S. 1
Army first lieutenant somewhere near Baghdad. She is a 1997 graduate of Westlake High School. She's bright, beautiful and highly educated—college classroom educated, that is.

She has just taken the mid-term exam in "Iraq Reality 101." She e- 2
mailed her thoughts and insights to family members. This is the real deal, not a pasteurized CNN–report. It is from a young soldier on the front lines, in an environment far removed from our society, which has no concept of how the Iraqis are living.

I'd say she passed the exam and received a lot more than just a letter 3
grade. She is no longer my little girl; she is my equal.

A few days ago my unit was getting ready to move again. We move 4
often, but most times it is during hours of darkness for obvious reasons. This particular time we moved during daylight hours, and it was the first time I really saw Iraq.

Our convoy rolled out onto one of the few hard-surface roads in the 5
country. As we traveled down the pavement, droves of locals lined the
road as though they were getting ready to watch a parade. The children
ran towards us as fast as their little legs could carry them, not wanting
to miss one truck as it went by.

The houses that the locals emerged from were nothing more than 6
earth and mud huts. Some had bricks cemented together with mud, and
some had a mixture of mud and palm leaves from the few palm trees
along the Euphrates river. These dwellings were far more impoverished
than anything I have ever seen in America.

None had running water, electricity or indoor plumbing; most had 7
fires behind the house for cooking. Most, if not all, families have farm
animals. These animals physically live with the people, generally in the
front yard or on the side of the hut. They do not have pens, and many
children find pleasure in playing with them.

Few people have cars. Most of the people I saw used a donkey and 8
buggy or cart to move goods from place to place. The cars I did see were
equivalent to an American beater—complete with busted windows and
rusted-out quarter panels.

Many times the cars were jammed with people, like the clown car at 9
the circus. I wondered how the car could run at all. As the convoy
passed, the people vigorously waved and smiled. Some gave us the
"thumbs up" sign to convey their support, which is surprising considering that the "thumbs up" sign in the Arab culture is equivalent to giving
someone the finger. (It is amazing to see how quickly the people adapt
to our ways and our customs.)

I happily waved back. The men are like the children. They wave and 10
clap and say "thank you." They even like to catcall at the female soldiers.
Most of these calls are quickly squelched when they see the M4 I carry,
locked and loaded. Their forward demeanor quickly changes to a sheepish grin.

The women are far different. It is evident that they are not allowed to 11
speak. . . . When you pass them on the road, they are usually working in
the fields or tending to the livestock. If they are on the shoulder of the
road, they are carrying heavy loads. They will rarely make eye contact
with you if they are in the presence of a male. If they do make eye contact, it is only for a second, and then they look away. They rarely smile
because they aren't allowed, and there seems to be little in their lives to
smile about.

They hide behind doors (if their dwellings have them), but you can 12
see they are curious about us. Overall, the people are friendly and are
just as interested in us as we are in awe of them.

The children upset me the most. They are dirty and skinny, but they 13
have the most incredible smiles. Their clothes look like hand-me-downs.
I didn't see one child with what appeared to be new clothes.

There was one incident that will stay with me forever. We were driv- 14
ing, and the children were standing on the side of the road. There was a
little boy up ahead of us about 150 meters. He appeared to be blowing
kisses.

I commented to my driver how adorable the little boy was, but as I got 15
closer I realized he wasn't blowing kisses. He was begging for water. His
motion that I mistook for blowing kisses was the sign for food and water.
By the time I realized this, I didn't have time to toss the remaining water
I had in my water bottle out the window. I suddenly felt so guilty. I felt
guilty because I couldn't stop, and I hadn't understood his need in time.

A few hours before, a fellow officer and I were talking about my 16
desire to go to the beach on vacation and eat at the Outback every night
for a week. It seemed greedy and selfish compared to the simple desire
of that one little boy. . . . I will never forget him, and I am humbled by
his struggle and his courage.

As I passed more children, returning their waves and smiles, I realized 17
that this is the only life they know. This is the extent of their prosperity,
their education, their life, unless someone helps them to change it.

The current regime keeps them in poverty. Seeing their faces makes 18
the time away from friends and loved ones worth it. Knowing that in
some way the few months to a year that I spend here will help change
their lives. I might have an indirect hand in helping children learn to
read or to fearlessly express their own opinions.

I even might help the women in this country gain some equality. With 19
Saddam gone, the possibilities are endless.

Knowing this makes not taking a shower every day, sleeping on the 20
ground out in the open or on top of my vehicle, eating MREs and dealing with the constant movement seem unimportant.

Seeing Iraq has changed my outlook on life. I wish that I could share 21
it with you all firsthand—so that you too may experience the people and
appreciate the gift we have in being Americans. . . . I will always remember that little boy each and every time I want to complain about my life
. . . each time I gripe about the bills for my electricity, water, food and
clothing. We are truly the lucky ones.

Questions About the Reading

1. What were the houses and living conditions that the writer saw as the convoy moved along the road?
2. How did the Iraqi people act toward the U.S. Army soldiers?
3. How did the people react when they saw the lieutenant's M4 gun?
4. How did the Iraqi women act as the convoy passed them?
5. What did the little boy want and how did the lieutenant feel about not understanding what he wanted?
6. What does the lieutenant hope will result from her tour of duty in Iraq?

Questions About the Writer's Strategies

1. What is the thesis of the essay? Is it stated or implied? If stated, identify the sentences.
2. Is the essay objective, subjective, or both? If both, identify at least two objective and two subjective sentences.
3. What are some of the details the writer uses to describe the way the Iraqi people treat the soldiers?
4. What are the similes in paragraphs 6, 7, and 11?
5. What order does the writer use? Why do you think she chose the order?

Writing Assignments

1. Write an essay describing the most impoverished neighborhood in your city or the area in which you live.
2. Write an essay describing the people and children of your neighborhood.
3. Write an essay describing the houses and buildings in a rural area.

The Sounds of the City

James Tuite

A sports writer and former sports editor for the New York Times, *James Tuite here describes the sounds of New York City and maintains that visitors hear the sounds but the people who live there do not.*

Words to Know

aviary enclosure for birds
cacophony harsh, discordant sounds
converging coming together
Doppler effect drop in the pitch of a sound
masticate chew
surcease relief, cessation

Getting Started

Have you ever listened to the sounds of your neighborhood or of the town in which you live?

New York is a city of sounds: muted sounds and shrill sounds; shattering sounds and soothing sounds; urgent sounds and aimless sounds. The cliff dwellers of Manhattan—who would be racked by the silence of the lonely woods—do not hear these sounds because they are constant and eternally urban. 1

The visitor to the city can hear them, though, just as some animals can hear a high-pitched whistle inaudible to humans. To the casual caller to Manhattan, lying restive and sleepless in a hotel twenty or thirty floors above the street, they tell a story as fascinating as life itself. And back of the sounds broods the silence. 2

Night in midtown is the noise of tinseled honky-tonk and violence. Thin strains of music, usually the firm beat of rock'n'roll or the frenzied outbursts of the discotheque, rise from ground level. This is the cacophony, the discordance of youth, and it comes on strongest when nights are hot and young blood restless. 3

Somewhere in the canyons below there is shrill laughter or raucous shouting. A bottle shatters against concrete. The whine of a police siren slices through the night, moving ever closer, until an eerie Doppler effect brings it to a guttural halt. 4

There are few sounds so exciting in Manhattan as those of fire appa- 5
ratus dashing through the night. At the outset there is the tentative hint
of the first-due company bullying his way through midtown traffic.
Now a fire whistle from the opposite direction affirms that trouble is,
indeed, afoot. In seconds, other sirens converging from other streets help
the skytop listener focus on the scene of excitement.

But he can only hear and not see, and imagination takes flight. Are the 6
flames and smoke gushing from windows not far away? Are victims
trapped there, crying out for help? Is it a conflagration, or only a trash-
basket fire? Or, perhaps, it is merely a false alarm.

The questions go unanswered and the urgency of the moment dis- 7
solves. Now the mind and the ear detect the snarling, arrogant bickering
of automobile horns. People in a hurry. Taxicabs blaring, insisting on
their checkered priority.

Even the taxi horns dwindle down to a precocious few in the gray and 8
pink moments of dawn. Suddenly there is another sound, a morning
sound that taunts the memory for recognition. The growl of a predatory
monster? No, just garbage trucks that have begun a day of scavenging.

Trash cans rattle outside restaurants. Metallic jaws on sanitation 9
trucks gulp and masticate the residue of daily living, then digest it with
a satisfied groan of gears. The sounds of the new day are businesslike.
The growl of buses, so scattered and distant at night, becomes a
demanding part of the traffic bedlam. An occasional jet or helicopter
injects an exclamation point from an unexpected quarter. When the wind
is right, the vibrant bellow of an ocean liner can be heard.

The sounds of the day are as jarring as the glare of a sun that outlines 10
the canyons of midtown in drab relief. A pneumatic drill frays countless
nerves with its rat-a-tat-tat, for dig they must to perpetuate the city's
dizzy motion. After each screech of brakes there is a moment of suspen-
sion, of waiting for the thud or crash that never seems to follow.

The whistles of traffic policemen and hotel doormen chirp from all 11
sides, like birds calling for their mates across a frenzied aviary. And all
of these sounds are adult sounds, for childish laughter has no place in
these canyons.

Night falls again, the cycle is complete, but there is no surcease from 12
sound. For the beautiful dreamers, perhaps, the "sounds of the rude
world heard in the day, lulled by the moonlight have all passed away,"
but this is not so in the city.

Too many New Yorkers accept the sounds about them as bland parts 13
of everyday existence. They seldom stop to listen to the sounds, to think
about them, to be appalled or enchanted by them. In the big city, sounds
are life.

Questions About the Reading

1. Why do the people who live in Manhattan not hear the sounds of the city?
2. Why does the writer think the sounds tell a "fascinating" story (paragraph 2)?
3. Where is the writer when he is listening to the sounds?
4. What period of time is covered by the writer's description of the sounds of the city?

Questions About the Writer's Strategies

1. What order does the writer use to describe the sounds of the city? Why do you think he chose to use that order?
2. What is the metaphor in paragraph 9?
3. What is the thesis of the essay? Is it stated? State the thesis in your own words.

Writing Assignments

1. Sit outside your house for a while in the morning, afternoon, evening, and night and listen for the sounds of your neighborhood. Write an essay in which you describe the sounds of your neighborhood.
2. Write an essay describing the sounds of your school or of a classroom.
3. In an essay, describe the sounds of your home as everyone gets up in the morning and gets ready to go to school or work.

Limbo

Rhonda S. Lucas (student)

*A new experience, a change in our lives, can make us see familiar objects
in a new light. And a new location can make an old possession—a piece
of furniture, an article of clothing—look strange. Rhonda S. Lucas, a student at East Los Angeles College, discovered both these things one day as
she sat in a garage full of packing boxes and old furniture. In this essay,
she describes what she saw.*

Words to Know

cryptic secret, mystifying

dilapidated fallen into a state of disrepair

elegy a mournful poem or song, often lamenting the dead

futility uselessness

irony the use of words to convey the opposite of their literal
  meaning

limbo an intermediate place or state; a region or condition of
  oblivion or neglect

tubular having the form of a tube

Getting Started

If you had to leave your house tomorrow, what would you miss
most about it?

My parents' divorce was final. The house had been sold and the day 1
had come to move. Thirty years of the family's life were now crammed
into the garage. The two-by-fours that ran the length of the walls were
the only uniformity among the clutter of boxes, furniture, and memories.
All was frozen in limbo between the life just passed and the one to come.

The sunlight pushing its way through the window splattered against 2
a barricade of boxes. Like a fluorescent river, it streamed down the sides
and flooded the cracks of the cold, cement floor. I stood in the doorway
between the house and garage and wondered if the sunlight would ever
again penetrate the memories packed inside those boxes. For an instant,
the cardboard boxes appeared as tombstones, monuments to those
memories.

The furnace in the corner, with its huge tubular fingers reaching out 3
and disappearing into the wall, was unaware of the futility of trying to
warm the empty house. The rhythmical whir of its effort hummed the

elegy for the memories boxed in front of me. I closed the door, sat down on the step, and listened reverently. The feeling of loss transformed the bad memories into not-so-bad, the not-so-bad memories into good, and committed the good ones to my mind. Still, I felt as vacant as the house inside.

A workbench to my right stood disgustingly empty. Not so much as a   4 nail had been left behind. I noticed, for the first time, what a dull, lifeless green it was. Lacking the disarray of tools that used to cover it, now it seemed as out of place as a bathtub in the kitchen. In fact, as I scanned the room, the only things that did seem to belong were the cobwebs in the corners.

A group of boxes had been set aside from the others and stacked in   5 front of the workbench. Scrawled like graffiti on the walls of dilapidated buildings were the words "Salvation Army." Those words caught my eyes as effectively as a flashing neon sign. They reeked of irony. "Salvation—was a bit too late for this family," I mumbled sarcastically to myself.

The houseful of furniture that had once been so carefully chosen to   6 complement and blend with the color schemes of the various rooms was indiscriminately crammed together against a single wall. The uncoordinated colors combined in turmoil and lashed out in the greyness of the room.

I suddenly became aware of the coldness of the garage, but I didn't   7 want to go back inside the house, so I made my way through the boxes to the couch. I cleared a space to lie down and curled up, covering myself with my jacket. I hoped my father would return soon with the truck so we could empty the garage and leave the cryptic silence of parting lives behind.

Questions About the Reading

1. Why is the title of this essay "Limbo"? Between which two stages of life is the writer?
2. How does the writer feel about moving out of the house?
3. Why does the writer view the empty workbench as disgusting (paragraph 4)?
4. Why didn't she want to go back inside the house?
5. What does Lucas mean in the last line by the "cryptic silence" of the house?

Questions About the Writer's Strategies

1. Although she never says it, the writer is saddened by her parents' divorce and the subsequent need to move. What details does she use to convey this feeling?
2. In what ways is this an extremely subjective essay?
3. Give your impression of the writer's life before her parents' divorce. What methods does she use to suggest this impression?
4. What is the thesis statement in the essay? Which paragraphs are used to develop the thesis statement? Is there a concluding paragraph?
5. What is the purpose of the metaphor in the last sentence of paragraph 2? In which sentence of paragraph 3 is the metaphor repeated?

Writing Assignments

1. Write an essay describing your favorite room in the house where you live now or the one where you grew up. Try to use examples from your life to give meaning to the objects you describe.
2. Write an essay describing a walk through your neighborhood or another one with which you are familiar. Describe the things that most interest you or that you think you will remember best in the future.

4

Examples

AN EXAMPLE IS a specific instance or fact that is used to support an idea or a general statement. As you learned in chapter 1, the topic sentence states the main idea of a paragraph, and the thesis statement states the main idea of an essay. Both must be supported through a mode of development, which the writer selects. Writers frequently use **examples** to explain or illustrate a main idea, as in the following paragraph.

Topic sentence	As they had resolved to do, my siblings took any job they could find to survive. In Montreal, Luong went to work at a
Example	plastics factory, mixing resins, until he found a job in the city government. In California, Zuong began working at a hotel,
Example	while his wife Hao started assembling electronics components in a factory; they became self-sufficient so quickly that they never had to resort to welfare. In Australia, Phu took a
Example	job as a cleaning lady until she got a position in the post office. (My nephew Nam went back to school and, after tak-
Example	ing a series of jobs, became a real estate agent.) Tuyet, in
Example	Paris, also started out as a cleaning lady for an office, and eventually found a position in a government agency.

Dugong Van Mai Elliott, *The Sacred Willow,*
Oxford University Press, © 1999, p. 465

Some writers announce their strategy by the transitional words for instance, *to illustrate,* or *for example.* Other times, as in the sentences about the jobs the writer's siblings got, the writer expects the reader to notice that these are examples and that they support the topic of the paragraph.

To make a clear case, the writer usually needs to give several examples. The order in which the examples are presented may be chronological—that is, in sequence according to time. In other cases, **order of importance** may be more effective, with the most important or convincing example presented last. In still other cases, the writer may use an example at the beginning of the essay to capture the reader's interest and to illustrate the **thesis,** which is stated later. The selection that follows illustrates the use of an introductory example.

Example used to introduce essay

1   The red-and-white pickup bounced along a gravel road in north-central Washington State. It was just past midnight on a summer Saturday last year. Two boys and two girls, recent graduates of Tonasket High School, had been "cruising" for a couple of hours, talking and laughing. At a sharp curve, the pickup somehow went off the road, rolled down the steep, rocky mountainside and twisted around a pine tree. All four occupants—none wearing a seat belt—were tossed out of the cab.

2   Driver Joe McDaniel escaped with cuts on his face and arms. Josh Wheeler suffered bruises but was able to cradle Amy Burdick in his arms until help arrived. She died the next day. Katy Watson, a former cheerleader who had won a scholarship to college, was dead at the scene, with massive chest and back injuries.

Thesis statement

3   Motor-vehicle injury is the greatest threat to the lives of adolescents in America. During the 1980s, over 74,000 teenagers were killed in such accidents, more than died from all diseases combined. On average, every two or three weeks the equivalent of a senior class at a typical high school is wiped out on our streets and highways. The National Safety Council (NSC) estimates that the financial toll is at least $10 billion annually for medical and insurance costs, property damage and lost wages resulting from accidents involving teen drivers.

Reader's Digest, June 1991

Examples in an essay can both illustrate and **support** the thesis. That is, if a writer makes a claim or a point in the **thesis statement** and then provides evidence in the form of actual situations that illustrate the thesis, it will help convince the reader that the thesis is valid. When you write, you should also search for examples as a way to test your thesis. For example, if you cannot think of a single specific example that supports your main idea, you will need to rethink your main idea. Or if you think of several examples that support your thesis, but also of several that work against it, you might want to revise your thesis and develop an **objective** essay presenting both sides of the issue.

In addition to providing concrete support for the thesis, examples can be used to enliven and clarify writing. In a description, for instance, examples can supply concrete details that add variety and interest. A single example may also be **extended** throughout an essay to illustrate the thesis, as in the following essay about the Kickapoo Indian Medicine

Company. Notice, too, that minor examples are also used within the essay, as in paragraphs 2 and 3, to support the topic sentences of some paragraphs.

Thesis

By 1880 several hundred medicine shows were traveling in the United States, giving performances varying from simple magic acts to elaborate "med-presentations." Among the largest of such operations from 1880 to 1910 was the Kickapoo Indian Medicine Company, "The King of Road Shows." Founded by two veteran troupers, John E. "Doc" Healy and Charles H. "Texas Charlie" Bigelow, the Kickapoo Company maintained a large headquarters building, "The Principal Wigwam," in New Haven, Connecticut, and from there sent out shows, as many as twenty-five at a time, to cities and villages throughout the country.

Major extended example—from here to end of essay

1

Minor examples of *performers* who were hired

Doc Healy hired performers, both Indian and white— dancers, singers, jugglers, fire-eaters, acrobats, comedians, fiddlers—and Texas Charlie managed the medicine business and trained the "Doctors" and "Professors" who gave "Medical Lectures."

2

Minor examples of *distinctively garbed* troupe members

All troupe members were distinctively garbed. The Indians—including Mohawks, Iroquois, Crees, Sioux, and Blackfeet—billed as "all pure-blooded Kickapoos, the most noted of all Indian Medical People," were adorned with colored beads and feathers and loaded down with primitive weapons; they trailed great strings of unidentified hairy objects. Some lecturers wore western-style leather clothes and boots with silver-capped toes, others fancy silk shirts, frock coats, and high silk hats. One of the most colorful Kickapoo figures was smooth-talking Ned T. Oliver— "Nevada Ned, the King of Gold"—who wore an enormous sombrero from the brim of which dangled 100 gold coins, and a fancy suit loaded with buttons made of gold pieces.

3

The Kickapoo shows were presented under canvas at "Kickapoo Camps" during the summer and in opera houses and town halls in winter. On many nights the show was free to all, on others each adult was charged 10¢. The money poured in from medicine sales.

4

The wonder-working Kickapoo concoctions were "compounded according to secret ancient Kickapoo Indian tribal formulas" from "blood root, feverwort, spirit gum, wild poke berries, sassafras, slippery elm, wintergreen, white oak bark, yellow birch bark, dock root, sarsaparilla, and other Natural Products." The medicines were made in the Connecticut factory in vats so huge the "mixers" had to perch on ladders and wield long paddles. The leader of the Kickapoo line was Sagwa, which sold at 50¢ and $1 per bottle —"Sagwa, the wonderful remedy for catarrh, pulmonary consumption, and all ills that afflict the human body. It is made from roots, barks, gums, leaves, oils, and berries

5

gathered by little Kickapoo children from God's great laboratory, the fertile fields and vast forests. Sagwa, Nature's
own great secret cure, now available to all mankind!"
    Long after the Kickapoo Company was dissolved, a   6
woman who had worked in the medicine factory recalled
that one of the ingredients of Kickapoo Cough Syrup was
Jamaica rum. Could this "cure" have been the inspiration for
the "Kickapoo Joy Juice" Al Capp featured in his popular
comic strip?

Peggy Robbins,
"The Kickapoo Indian Medicine Company"

In this essay, the writer's use of concrete examples gives us a clear picture of the Kickapoo medicine show. In addition, the great number and
the variety of minor examples give us a good idea of the crazy-quilt
nature of medicine shows in general.

    When using examples in your own writing, **brainstorm** for possibili-
ties (as described in chapter 1) and select those that illustrate your idea
most accurately. In choosing among possibilities, select those that you
sense your reader will respond to as convincing and colorful. Several
well-chosen examples will hold your reader's interest and add credibility to your main idea.

Trash Talk

Pete Hamill

The "dissing" or "trash talk" started by Muhammad Ali is now carried on by athletes throughout sports, but not in exactly the same way.

Words to Know

appropriated   taken over, adopted

demean   humble, lower in status

hazard   danger

retaliation   pay back, punishment

Getting Started

Have you ever heard little kids or adults "trash talk" to one another?

In sports, the style established thirty years ago by Muhammad Ali has been appropriated by his inferiors, who emphasize the "dissing" but leave out the irony and the humor. (Only Charles Barkley really gets it.) Prizefighters learn how to demean a man before they've mastered the uppercut. Reggie Miller isn't satisfied with playing better than most men in the NBA; he has to make choke signs and grab his crotch and keep up a torrent of trash talk. No football player seems able to carry a ball for a touchdown without following up with some taunting dance in the end zone. Goodbye, Jim Brown; farewell, Gale Sayers; hello, Neon Deion. No baseball player since Don Baylor has been able to endure the occupational hazard of a knockdown pitch without charging the mound in retaliation. In all sports, grace is treated like a character flaw. Athletes snarl and mock in triumph—and whine in defeat.

Pete Hamill, Position Papers © 1996 by Deidre Enterprises

Questions About the Reading

1. What do you think the writer means by "Only Charles Barkley really gets it"?
2. What do today's players leave out of their trash talk?

3. What do you think is a player's purpose in "dissing" or trash talking an opponent?
4. How does the writer feel about trash talk?

Questions About the Writer's Strategies

1. What is the main idea of the paragraph? Is it stated or implied? If stated, identify the sentences.
2. Is the paragraph objective, subjective, or both?
3. Does the writer use several examples or an extended example? Why do you think he made his choice?
4. What is the order the writer uses? Do you think he had a purpose in the order he uses? If so, what do you think was that purpose?

Writing Assignments

1. Use the Internet to look up Pete Hamill and write a paragraph in which you provide examples of books and other essays by Pete Hamill.
2. Write an example paragraph in which you identify Jim Brown, Gale Sayers, and Neon Deion; discuss the sports they played; and explain what the writer means by "Goodbye, Jim Brown; farewell, Gale Sayers; hello, Neon Deion."

Folk Art in the Barrios

Eric Kroll

In this paragraph, Eric Kroll describes the wall paintings in Santa Fe, New Mexico, that depict a bold and colorful Chicano history and that defy stereotypes.

Words to Know

Aztec   early people of Mexico

disproportionate   not in proportion, not actual size

Father Hidalgo   Miguel Hidalgo y Costilla (1753–1811), a Catholic priest who launched the revolution to free Mexico from Spanish rule

Pancho Villa   Mexican revolutionary leader

Getting Started

Have you ever looked at a painting of a famous person and thought that it wasn't accurate?

On ten Santa Fe walls, the history of the Chicanos, both mythical and actual, is depicted in brilliant colors and disproportionate figures. Aztec medicine figures dance and gods protect peasants, all for the glory of the Chicano in the present. On some walls, the chains of bondage are being broken and the Lady of Justice, depicted as an Indian Maiden, watches over both Indians and Chicanos. On others, Pancho Villa and Father Hidalgo lead the Mexican peasants to freedom. But the clenched fist at the end of the grotesquely muscled arms is the most predominant image. It symbolizes unity, determination, ambition, and pride, all traits that Los Artes believe should be a part of Chicano psychology. The figures they paint are bold, upright, strong, and grasping, far from the stereotype of the Mexican-American with drooping moustache and floppy sombrero lying in the shade of a stucco building.

Questions About the Reading

1. On how many walls in Santa Fe are there paintings of Chicano history?
2. What is the purpose of the paintings?

3. What does the clenched fist in the paintings symbolize?
4. How do the figures in the paintings differ from the stereotype the author describes at the end of the paragraph?

Questions About the Writer's Strategies

1. What is the main idea (topic) of the paragraph?
2. What examples depict the freedom of Mexican peasants?
3. What is the metaphor for the traits that the artists believe the Chicanos should have?
4. What descriptive words are used for the figures in the paintings?
5. What descriptive words are used for the Mexican-American stereotype?

Writing Assignments

1. Write a paragraph in which you use examples to describe the behavior of a television personality.
2. Write a paragraph using examples to illustrate the traditions of different ethnic groups in your city.

Boomtown, U.S.A.

Jeff Glasser

The small town of Bentonville, Arkansas, "booms" after three businesses move into the town.

Words to Know

titan   person of great size or power

spurned   rejected

Xanadu   a place in Mongolia described in the poem "Kubla Khan" by Samuel Taylor Coleridge

Getting Started

Has the town or area in which you live been changed by unemployment, loss of a business, or development of a shopping center?

Sam Walton would not recognize the place. The famously unassuming Wal-Mart founder spurned foreign cars for his red Ford pickup, and he expected his employees to shun a "big showy lifestyle." But today in Mr. Sam's parking lot at Wal-Mart headquarters here, Mercedes Kompressor convertibles shine in the sun alongside BMW M3s. Not far away, Wal-Mart's chief executive and senior vice president live in splendor at Pinnacle, the area's first gated community and its most exclusive country club. Their neighbor, Red Hudson, a retired multimillionaire meat-packer, has built a 17,784-square-foot mansion there—complete with Italian marble and Minnesota stone—for a much-gossiped-about $10 million. Across the new Interstate 540 from Pinnacle, trucking titan J. B. Hunt is trying to erect his own Xanadu, with a dozen deluxe office and condominium towers, a hospital, and, in a first for the region, a skyline. "Everything's a poppin'," says the 74-year-old Hunt as he tools around the site in his tan GMC Sierra truck. "In the next five years, the weeds will be a city."

Questions About the Reading

1. Why would Sam Walton "not recognize the place"?
2. What is Red Hudson's business?
3. What is J. B. Hunt's business? Why is he called a "titan"?
4. What is the "first for the region"?
5. What does J. B. Hunt mean when he says, "In the next five years, the weeds will be a city"?

Questions About the Writer's Strategies

1. What is the main idea of the paragraph? State it in your own words.
2. What are the examples that support the main idea?
3. What is the metaphor in the paragraph?

Writing Assignments

1. Write a paragraph giving specific examples of the effect on your town of unemployment or loss of a business.
2. Interview some residents who were displaced by a building project in your town and write a paragraph using examples of how it changed their lives.
3. These are the first two lines of the poem "Kubla Khan."

   "In Xanadu did Kubla Khan
   A stately pleasure-dome decree"

Write a paragraph explaining the relation of Xanadu to J. B. Hunt's building project.

My Suit

Ricardo Galvez (student)

Ricardo Galvez, a student at Los Angeles Harbor College in California, shows us with examples that the way people dress influences the way they are treated by others.

Words to Know

drenching   soaking, saturating
merit   value, worth

Getting Started

Have you ever felt you were treated better or worse because of the clothes you were wearing?

I had once been told that people are treated primarily according to the way they dress. With this in mind, I gathered all of my suits and selected the best one. I wore it to church that Sunday. To my surprise, I found this statement to have some merit. After mass I went to lunch with the singles' group from church. Wearing a tie made my neck feel as if I had been hanging at the end of a rope. I was beginning to perspire quite heavily under the miserably hot sun and drenching humid air. The dress shoes were also uncomfortable and I almost fell as I slipped on a slice of banana near the buffet table. Nevertheless, it was well worth the sacrifice. Usually I had to wait fifteen minutes for a table for two. That day I was tended to immediately, and I even reserved a large table for all of the singles while they found parking spaces outside. More important, I met a sweet, attractive young lady who asked me to accompany her to a dance. The next fourteen months of courtship that followed made me aware of the fact that to feel miserable didn't have to mean that I had to be miserable. Being with her made me forget all discomfort.

Questions About the Reading

1. Did the writer have several suits? If so, which of his suits did the writer select to wear?
2. Whom did the writer go to lunch with after church?
3. How did wearing a tie make the writer feel?

4. Did the writer feel it was worthwhile to be uncomfortable in his suit and shoes? Why?

Questions About the Writer's Strategies

1. What is the main idea of the paragraph? Does the writer state the main idea directly? If so, in which sentence?
2. What are the examples the writer uses to prove his main idea?
3. What is the order in which the writer tells us about his experience?
4. What is the point of view of the paragraph in person, time, and tone?

Writing Assignments

1. Write a paragraph in which you use examples to tell about an experience you had that was related to the clothes you were wearing.
2. Assume you have had an interview for a job you want. Write a paragraph in which you give examples of what you wore and how you think your clothes influenced the success or failure of the interview.

The Social Meaning of T-Shirts

Diana Crane

The T-shirt has become popular for expressing the wearer's support for an organization or a cause.

Words to Know

cachet   approval
coopted   used, taken

Getting Started

What T-shirts are in your closet and what do they say about you?

The use of a specific type of clothing—the T-shirt—to communicate   1
other types of information began in the late 1940s, when faces and political slogans appeared on T-shirts and, in the 1960s, with commercial
logos and other designs. Technical developments in the 1950s and 1960s,
such as plastic inks, plastic transfers, and spray paint, led to the use of
colored designs and increased the possibilities of the T-shirt as a means
of communication. Approximately one billion T-shirts are purchased
annually in the United States (McGraw 1996).

The T-shirt performs a function formerly associated with the hat, that   2
of identifying an individual's social location instantly. Unlike the hat in
the nineteenth century, which signaled (or concealed) social class status,
the T-shirt speaks to issues related to ideology, difference, and myth: politics, race, gender, and leisure. The variety of slogans and logos that
appear on T-shirts is enormous. Much of the time, people consent to
being coopted for "unpaid advertising" for global corporations selling
clothes, music, sports, and entertainment in exchange for the social
cachet of being associated with certain products (McGraw 1996). Some
of the time, people use T-shirts to indicate their support for social and
political causes, groups, or organizations to which they have made a
commitment. Occasionally, the T-shirt becomes a medium for grass-
roots resistance. Bootlegged T-shirts representing characters on the television show *The Simpsons* appeared in response to T-shirts marketed by
the network that produced the show (Parisi 1993). The bootlegged T-
shirts represented the Simpson family as African Americans. Bart
Simpson was shown as Rastabart, with dreadlocks and a red, green, and

gold headband, as Rasta-dude Bart Marley, and as black Bart, paired with Nelson Mandela. Using clothing behavior as a means of making a statement, the T-shirts appeared to be intended as an affirmation of African Americans as an ethnic group and as a commentary on the narrow range of roles for black characters in the show. Victims of gender-related violence, such as rape, incest, battering, and sexual harassment, have used T-shirts as venues for statements about their experiences that are exhibited in clotheslines in public plazas (Ostrowski 1996). By contrast, some young men use T-shirts to express hostile, aggressive, or obscene sentiments denigrating women or to display pictures of guns and pistols (Cose 1993; *Time* 1992). Teens of both sexes use them as a means of expressing their cynicism about the dominant culture, particularly global advertising (Sepulchre 1994b).

The significance of the T-shirt in Western culture, as a means of social   3 and political expression, is seen by comparing its roles in Western countries with the response to it in a nondemocratic country, the People's Republic of China (Barmé 1993). In 1991, a young Chinese artist created T-shirts bearing humorous statements, some of which could be interpreted as having mild political implications. The T-shirts were enormously successful with the public but were perceived as "a serious political incident" by the Chinese authorities. The artist was arrested and interrogated, and the T-shirts were officially banned. Thousands of them were confiscated and destroyed, although many Chinese continued to wear them.

Questions About the Reading

1. When did T-shirts begin to be used to communicate information?
2. What developments increased the use of T-shirts to communicate?
3. How does the use of the T-shirt to communicate differ from the use of the hat?
4. What "statement" did the Bart Simpson T-shirt seem to make?
5. What happened to the Chinese artist and the T-shirts he created? Why?

Questions About the Writer's Strategies

1. What is the thesis of the essay? State it in your own words.
2. What are the specific examples the writer uses to support her thesis?
3. What is each example meant to communicate?

4. Could the second paragraph be made into more than one paragraph? If so, how? What would be the topic sentence of each paragraph?

Writing Assignments

1. Write an essay using examples of each T-shirt you own that has lettering on it and explain what it "says" about you.
2. ***Working Together*** Join with some classmates and write an essay using examples of the T-shirts each of you owns and explain what each T-shirt communicates about the wearer.

The Internet Instills Family Values—Really

Alcestis "Cooky" Oberg

Alcestis "Cooky" Oberg, a science and technology writer and member of the contributing board of USA Today, *counters the claim that people spend too much time on the Internet.*

Words to Know

cosmic   vast, grandiose
guttural   rasping, throaty
intergalactic   between the galaxies
monosyllables   single-syllable words
primal   primitive
sanctuary   safe place
virtual   not actual

Getting Started

What do you use the Internet for and how much time do you spend each day on the Internet?

When the study came out last month claiming that some people are spending too much time on the Internet and not enough time living real life, I laughed. 1

Not 10 minutes before, I had rounded up my herd for dinner with the usual cattle call: "Join the land of the living!" Out from behind their computers, they emerged—answering the primal call of hunger and of Mom. 2

I have noticed that family life takes on a zombie-esque quality when the computers are on. I dislike television for the same reason. I always wondered whether family life would be richer if we just shut everything off. A poet-friend of mine actually tried it with his young family: no television, no computers, just books. 3

Unfortunately, after a while, the adults exhibited that out-of-touch aura bookish people get—and the kids would sneak out to watch *Sesame Street* at the neighbor's house almost as soon as they could walk. 4

Let's face it: Real life is hard work. There are all of those disagreeable chores such as earning a living, paying taxes, cleaning windows and toilets, not to mention puzzling out what your significant other, your 5 spouse, your kids and your parents want from you—all of these things that put the *real* into real life. Tuning all of that out and going to that "better place" on the Internet is like dying and going to heaven, only you're still alive. Sort of.

In the right hands, though, that computer mouse can actually take you 6 over the rougher bumps on real life's road. Take adolescence. When kids hit that uncommunicative, "I don't know those people who call themselves my parents" stage, you can reach your kids by e-mail. For instance, even though we lived under the same roof, I found I could get a good, long, sometimes funny e-mail response from my teenager during "the surly years." I never would have gotten beyond monosyllables and guttural utterances in face-to-face real life.

And the Internet has turned out to be a new, fairly wholesome vehicle 7 for socializing teens—safer than fast cars and seedy hangouts. One shy boy I know set up a virtual drama club on the Net, with 150 kids across the nation.

They took on the roles of various science-fiction characters and played 8 out cosmic dramas they wrote themselves. One night, they simulated an incredibly detailed and clever intergalactic battle—one the Pentagon would envy. In high school, these gentle kids didn't particularly fit in with the body-piercing gang or the fast-car crowd. The Internet provided them with a social sanctuary where they met their real peers and made very real friends.

Then there's our own Virtual Granny. When my husband's mom vis- 9 ited us last year, he introduced her to the joys of e-mail, file-attach photos, eBay, Amazon and the virtual portfolio. She took to it all like a born nerd. She found old pals, communicated with nieces and grandchildren, bought stuff to be delivered to her doorstep at the click of a mouse. It was midnight before I got past her and sent out my business e-mail. "You created a monster," I confided to my husband, "and it's your mother!"

Let's face it: Anyone who accuses the Internet of taking too much time 10 away from "real life" must first consider what that real life is. The elderly, for instance, are often shut in and isolated by their health. Sometimes, they are "retired" to a different city, uprooted from their old hometowns where they spent most of their lives and raised their families. These seniors are a fast-growing population of Internet users, not because they're fleeing attachments, but because they are seeking them. They can connect with old friends and feel a part of the lives of their far-flung children and grandchildren, which they couldn't possibly do without physically living in the same town or under the same roof.

In our family, the Internet didn't isolate Granny further, didn't stop 11 her from doing charity work, going to church or seeing her nearby friends. It didn't stop my kids from taking out the garbage, doing their

chores or having real-life friends. The Internet just became one more
social avenue in our lives.

Indeed, we're not far from the day when whole intellectual and cul- 12
tural communities are established on the Net, like that teenage virtual-
drama club: People who are separated by accident of geography but
have common interests and circumstances can finally meet and form a
circle of their own—beyond the circle of the family they were born into,
the jobs they go to and the cities where they live.

And it doesn't mean that at some point our Net life and our "real" life 13
can't meet face to face. My Net life and my real life meet every month—
on my Visa bill. And I still have to pay for my virtual merchandise with
very, very real money.

Questions About the Reading

1. How does the writer call her family to dinner?
2. What happened to the family that turned off its televisions and
   computers?
3. How did the writer reach her teenagers during their "surly years"?
4. What club did the shy boy set up through the Internet?
5. What advantages does the Internet provide for elderly people?

Questions About the Writer's Strategies

1. What is the main idea of the essay? Is there a thesis statement? If so,
   where is it located?
2. What specific examples does the writer use?
3. What order does the writer use in presenting the examples? Why do
   you think she chose that order?
4. Besides examples, what modes of development does the writer use?
5. Is the essay objective or subjective?

Writing Assignments

1. *Working Together* Join with some classmates to write an essay that
   illustrates your different uses of the Internet with examples.
2. *Working Together* Join with some classmates to write an essay
   about the advantages and disadvantages of using the Internet. Use
   examples to support each position.

3. Write an essay about three web sites that provide career information.
   Include the address for each site, describe the kind of information each
   site provides, and use examples to show which site is the most useful.

Foreign Flavors, Mainstream Taste

Debra Aho Williamson

Ethnic foods are going mainstream because a taste for them is shared by all of us.

Words to Know

demographically diverse statistically different as to race, ethnicity, and other factors

emporium large store, marketplace

gelatinous like gelatin, jellylike

Getting Started

What ethnic foods are available in your neighborhood grocery store?

To understand how the changing tastes of the U.S. consumer are 1 affecting food marketing, pay a visit to the Uwajimaya supermarket in downtown Seattle.

This is no tiny, cluttered store on a side street in Chinatown. A 50,000- 2 square-foot retail emporium a few blocks from Safeco Field, Uwajimaya carries everything you could imagine for Asian cooking. There's an entire aisle of nothing but noodles. A produce section with so many exotic-looking vegetables that the clerks have created handwritten signs describing what they are. There's sushi-grade seafood, several varieties of Chinese black bean sauce and frozen mochi desserts—ice cream balls rolled in a gelatinous coating, sold individually or in six-packs.

On a busy recent afternoon before a Mariners home game, you notice 3 something else unusual. Yes, there are people of Asian descent here, but there also are a striking number of non-Asians. In fact, a full 30% of Uwajimaya's customers are not Asian, and the store has even become a tourist destination.

"Mainstreaming is the name of the game," says Tomoko Moriguchi- 4 Matsuno, Uwajimaya's VP-retail. "It's food. It's not Chinese, Japanese, Korean. People are more interested in food, and they're more open to different things."

That, in a nutshell, is what many in the food business believe is the 5 future of food marketing. As the U.S. has become more demographically diverse, food and restaurant marketers have expanded their palates to reach growing Hispanic and Asian populations. But at the same time, marketers are broadening their offerings to the general market to include new flavors and stronger tastes.

Even chicken soup stalwart Campbell Soup Co. is getting in the game. 6 Its Stockpot subsidiary, a supplier to restaurants, is planning to launch a three-item line of Asian-flavor sauces and soup bases, including a Vietnamese broth called pho. So far there's no indication that the red-and-white label will include pho, but Stockpot acknowledges that Campbell's foodservice units serve as test kitchens for future grocery products.

"The Away from Home division is a way for Campbell to keep its eye 7 on new flavor trends, so as these trends emerge there is always an opportunity to incorporate them into retail products," says Kathleen Horner, Stockpot's president.

Unilever recently introduced a five-item line of Lipton Asian-flavor 8 side dishes, including beef lo mein noodles and sweet and sour noodles. And General Mills' Pillsbury Co. markets a flavor of Haagen-Dazs ice cream called Dulce de Leche, a caramel and cream confection inspired by a Latin American dessert.

There also are growing efforts to market more directly to Hispanics. 9 Gatorade Co.'s new Xtremo sports drink features flavors like mango and tropical punch. PepsiCo sibling Frito-Lay recently launched a new version of Doritos aimed at Hispanics in the U.S. And Doctor's Associates' Subway Restaurants has been steadily ramping up a Hispanic ad campaign from Havas' MVBMS Hispanic, New York, that launched last year. The campaign now accounts for about 5% to 10% of Subway's overall ad budget, says Chris Carroll, director of marketing for the Subway Franchisee Advertising Board.

All this activity is coming about because the census is showing a dra- 10 matic rise in the Hispanic and Asian populations in the U.S. In 1990, 9% of the U.S. population identified themselves as Hispanic and 2.9% as Asian or Pacific Islander. By 2007, nearly 15% of the U.S. will be of Hispanic ethnicity and nearly 5% Asian, according to projections from market researcher SRC.

Some marketers, like Kraft Foods, have used the new census data to 11 confirm what they already know. "Fundamentally, the country is changing, and to be where consumers want to be, you've got to change with it," says Linda Crowder, director of multicultural marketing. Kraft products like Mayonesa con Limon (mayo with lemon) and Gelatina par Leche (Jell-O with milk), both introduced in the past year, aim squarely at U.S. Hispanic tastes.

Hispanic consumers spend nearly 25% more than other consumer 12 groups on food consumed at home, according to researcher Packaged Facts. That's because Latino families tend to be larger and there's more focus on eating a meal at home.

Ethnic groups are "your biggest growth market," says Thomas Tseng, 13 director of marketing for Cultural Access Group, a Los Angeles ethnic market researcher.

While the black population is expected to remain flat, representing 14 about 12% of the population in 2007, according to SRC, it carries great weight. Among all U.S. ethnic groups, Mr. Tseng says African Americans possess the greatest purchasing power at $572 billion. "This consumer group often gets overlooked or is lumped in together with the general market since language is not an issue—most marketers think they reach this group with their general-market strategies, but they don't," he says. "African Americans possess distinct cultural attributes and affinities that translate into distinct food preferences and shopping behaviors. They shop more frequently, spend more money on food purchased at home, and are responsive to advertising aimed at them."

Questions About the Reading

1. What kind of foods are carried in the Uwajimaya supermarket in Seattle?
2. What is meant by "the future of food marketing"?
3. Which ethnic group is expected to become nearly 15 percent of the United States population by 2007?
4. Which ethnic group spends "more than other consumer groups on food consumed at home"? Why?
5. Which population group has "the greatest purchasing power"? Why? Why is this group often overlooked?

Questions About the Writer's Strategies

1. What is the thesis of the essay? Is it stated or implied? If stated, identify the sentences.
2. Does the writer use several examples or an extended example to support the thesis?
3. What is the writer's purpose in including the quoted information?

Writing Assignments

1. *Working Together*   Join with some classmates and write an essay citing examples of the ethnic composition of the streets on which each of you lives.
2. Visit at least three supermarkets or neighborhood grocery stores and write an essay including examples of the various ethnic foods that each store carries.

Between Two Wars, 1913–1945

Kathryn VanSpanckeren

The writer details the changes that took place in the United States between World War I and World War II and provides examples of writers and novels in which the changes are depicted.

Words to Know

edifice   large, imposing building

Freudian psychology   psychoanalysis; treatment of mental disorders, based on the method developed by Sigmund Freud, an Austrian physician and psychiatrist

proliferated   grew by multiplying

prophetically   forecast the future

Getting Started

What changes have taken place in your life since September 11, 2001? What changes do you think will take place in the United States following the end of the war on terrorism?

Many historians have characterized the period between the two world wars as the United States' traumatic "coming of age," despite the fact that U.S. direct involvement was relatively brief (1917–1918) and its casualties many fewer than those of its European allies and foes. John Dos Passos expressed America's postwar disillusionment in the novel *Three Soldiers* (1921), when he noted that civilization was a "vast edifice of sham, and the war, instead of its crumbling, was its fullest and most ultimate expression." Shocked and permanently changed, Americans returned to their homeland but could never regain their innocence.

Nor could soldiers from rural America easily return to their roots. After experiencing the world, many now yearned for a modern, urban life. New farm machines such as planters, harvesters, and binders had drastically reduced the demand for farm jobs; yet despite their increased productivity, farmers were poor. Crop prices, like urban workers' wages, depended on unrestrained market forces heavily influenced by business interests: Government subsidies for farmers and effective workers' unions had not yet become established. "The chief business of the American people is business," President Calvin Coolidge proclaimed in 1925, and most agreed.

In the postwar "Big Boom," business flourished, and the successful 3
prospered beyond their wildest dreams. For the first time, many
Americans enrolled in higher education—in the 1920s college enroll-
ment doubled. The middle-class prospered; Americans began to enjoy
the world's highest national average income in this era, and many people purchased the ultimate status symbol—an automobile. The typical
urban American home glowed with electric lights and boasted a radio
that connected the house with the outside world, and perhaps a telephone, a camera, a typewriter, or a sewing machine. Like the business-
man protagonist of Sinclair Lewis's novel *Babbitt* (1922), the average
American approved of these machines because they were modern and
because most were American inventions and American-made.

Americans of the "Roaring Twenties" fell in love with other modern 4
entertainments. Most people went to the movies once a week. Although
Prohibition—a nationwide ban on the production, transport, and sale of
alcohol instituted through the 18th Amendment to the U.S.
Constitution—began in 1919, underground "speakeasies" and night-
clubs proliferated, featuring jazz music, cocktails, and daring modes of
dress and dance. Dancing, moviegoing, automobile touring, and radio
were national crazes. American women, in particular, felt liberated.
Many had left farms and villages for homefront duty in American cities
during World War I, and had become resolutely modern. They cut their
hair short ("bobbed"), wore short "flapper" dresses, and gloried in the
right to vote assured by the 19th Amendment to the Constitution, passed
in 1920. They boldly spoke their mind and took public roles in society.

Western youths were rebelling, angry and disillusioned with the sav- 5
age war, the older generation they held responsible, and difficult postwar
economic conditions that, ironically, allowed Americans with dollars—
like writers F. Scott Fitzgerald, Ernest Hemingway, Gertrude Stein, and
Ezra Pound—to live abroad handsomely on very little money. Intellectual
currents, particularly Freudian psychology and to a lesser extent
Marxism (like the earlier Darwinian theory of evolution), implied a "god-
less" world view and contributed to the breakdown of traditional values.
Americans abroad absorbed these views and brought them back to the
United States where they took root, firing the imagination of young writers and artists. William Faulkner, for example, a 20th-century American
novelist, employed Freudian elements in all his works, as did virtually all
serious American fiction writers after World War I.

Despite outward gaiety, modernity, and unparalleled material pros- 6
perity, young Americans of the 1920s were "the lost generation"—
so named by literary portraitist Gertrude Stein. Without a stable,
traditional structure of values, the individual lost a sense of identity. The
secure, supportive family life; the familiar, settled community; the natu-

ral and eternal rhythms of nature that guide the planting and harvesting on a farm; the sustaining sense of patriotism; moral values inculcated by religious beliefs and observations—all seemed undermined by World War I and its aftermath.

Numerous novels, notably Hemingway's *The Sun Also Rises* (1926) and Fitzgerald's *This Side of Paradise* (1920), evoke the extravagance and disillusionment of the lost generation. In T. S. Eliot's influential long poem *The Waste Land* (1922), Western civilization is symbolized by a bleak desert in desperate need of rain (spiritual renewal). 7

The world depression of the 1930s affected most of the population of the United States. Workers lost their jobs, and factories shut down; businesses and banks failed; farmers, unable to harvest, transport, or sell their crops, could not pay their debts and lost their farms. Midwestern droughts turned the "breadbasket" of America into a dust bowl. Many farmers left the Midwest for California in search of jobs, as vividly described in John Steinbeck's *The Grapes of Wrath* (1939). At the peak of the Depression, one-third of all Americans were out of work. Soup kitchens, shanty towns, and armies of hobos—unemployed men illegally riding freight trains—became part of national life. Many saw the Depression as a punishment for sins of excessive materialism and loose living. The dust storms that blackened the midwestern sky, they believed, constituted an Old Testament judgment: the "whirlwind by day and the darkness at noon." 8

The Depression turned the world upside down. The United States had preached a gospel of business in the 1920s; now, many Americans supported a more active role for government in the New Deal programs of President Franklin D. Roosevelt. Federal money created jobs in public works, conservation, and rural electrification. Artists and intellectuals were paid to create murals and state handbooks. These remedies helped, but only the industrial build-up of World War II renewed prosperity. After Japan attacked the United States at Pearl Harbor on December 7, 1941, disused shipyards and factories came to bustling life massproducing ships, airplanes, jeeps, and supplies. War production and experimentation led to new technologies, including the nuclear bomb. Witnessing the first experimental nuclear blast, Robert Oppenheimer, leader of an international team of nuclear scientists, prophetically quoted a Hindu poem: "I am become Death, the shatterer of worlds." 9

Questions About the Reading

1. What does the writer mean by "civilization was a 'vast edifice of sham, and the war, instead of its crumbling, was its fullest and most ultimate expression'"?
2. What was the effect on colleges and American families of the post-war boom in business?
3. What is the 19th Amendment to the Constitution, when was it passed, and whom did it benefit? What is the 18th Amendment to the Constitution and what was its effect?
4. What changed in people's attitudes toward business and government after the 1930s? What caused the change in attitudes?

Questions About the Writer's Strategies

1. What is the thesis of the essay? State it in your own words.
2. What is the main idea of each paragraph? Is it stated or implied? If stated, in which sentence or sentences? If implied, state it in your own words.
3. Could any of the paragraphs be combined? If so, which ones? Why?

Writing Assignments

1. Write an essay using examples to explain the major changes that have taken place in the United States since the end of World War II.
2. Write an essay using examples to explain the significant changes that have taken place in the United States since the September 11, 2001 terror attack.
3. Write an essay using examples to explain how September 11, 2001 affected your life or a relative's or friend's life.

My Mother Never Worked

Bonnie Smith-Yackel

Bonnie Smith-Yackel's family survived on a farm during the Great Depression, a time when both the weather and the economy made the hardships of farm life nearly overwhelming. In this personal essay, Smith-Yackel uses the example of her mother's life to illustrate the unfairness in American attitudes toward women and the work they do to keep their families intact.

Words to Know

cholera a contagious, often fatal disease, usually restricted to farm animals in this country

reciprocated returned

sustenance nourishment, support for life

widow's pension the Social Security payments made to a widow, based on her deceased husband's eligibility

Getting Started

What do you think about our government's policy that home-makers are not legally workers?

"**S**ocial Security Office." (The voice answering the telephone sounds very self-assured.) 1

"I'm calling about . . . I . . . my mother just died . . . I was told to call you and see about a . . . death-benefit check, I think they call it . . ." 2

"I see. Was your mother on Social Security? How old was she?" 3

"Yes . . . she was seventy-eight . . ." 4

"Do you know her number?" 5

"No . . . I, ah . . . don't you have a record?" 6

"Certainly. I'll look it up. Her name?" 7

"Smith. Martha Smith. Or maybe she used Martha Ruth Smith . . . Sometimes she used her maiden name . . . Martha Jerabek Smith." 8

"If you'd care to hold on, I'll check our records—it'll be a few minutes." 9

"Yes . . ." 10

Her love letters—to and from Daddy—were in an old box, tied with ribbons and stiff, rigid-with-age leather thongs: 1918 through 1920; hers written on stationery from the general store she had worked in full-time and managed, single-handed, after her graduation from high school in 11

1913; and his, at first, on YMCA or Soldiers and Sailors Club stationery dispensed to the fighting men of World War I. He wooed her thoroughly and persistently by mail, and though she reciprocated all his feelings for her, she dreaded marriage . . .

"It's so hard for me to decide when to have my wedding day—that's 12 all I've thought about these last two days. I have told you dozens of times that I won't be afraid of married life, but when it comes down to setting the date and then picturing myself a married woman with half a dozen or more kids to look after, it just makes me sick . . . I am weeping right now—I hope that some day I can look back and say how foolish I was to dread it all."

They married in February, 1921, and began farming. Their first baby, 13 a daughter, was born in January, 1922, when my mother was 26 years old. The second baby, a son, was born in March, 1923. They were renting farms; my father, besides working his own fields, also was a hired man for two other farmers. They had no capital initially, and had to gain it slowly, working from dawn until midnight every day. My town-bred mother learned to set hens and raise chickens, feed pigs, milk cows, plant and harvest a garden, and can every fruit and vegetable she could scrounge. She carried water nearly a quarter of a mile from the well to fill her wash boilers in order to do her laundry on a scrub board. She learned to shuck grain, feed threshers, shuck and husk corn, feed corn pickers. In September, 1925, the third baby came, and in June, 1927, the fourth child—both daughters. In 1930, my parents had enough money to buy their own farm, and that March they moved all their livestock and belongings themselves, 55 miles over rutted, muddy roads.

In the summer of 1930 my mother and her two eldest children 14 reclaimed a 40-acre field from Canadian thistles, by chopping them all out with a hoe. In the other fields, when the oats and flax began to head out, the green and blue of the crops were hidden by the bright yellow of wild mustard. My mother walked the fields day after day, pulling each mustard plant. She raised a new flock of baby chicks—500—and she spaded up, planted, hoed, and harvested a half-acre garden.

During the next spring their hogs caught cholera and died. No cash 15 that fall.

And in the next year the drought hit. My mother and father trudged 16 from the well to the chickens, the well to the calf pasture, the well to the barn, and from the well to the garden. The sun came out hot and bright, endlessly, day after day. The crops shriveled and died. They harvested half the corn, and ground the other half, stalks and all, and fed it to the cattle as fodder. With the price at four cents a bushel for the harvested crop, they couldn't afford to haul it into town. They burned it in the furnace for fuel that winter.

In 1934, in February, when the dust was still so thick in the Minnesc air that my parents couldn't always see from the house to the barn, their fifth child—a fourth daughter—was born. My father hunted rabbits daily, and my mother stewed them, fried them, canned them, and wished out loud that she could taste hamburger once more. In the fall the shotgun brought prairie chickens, ducks, pheasant, and grouse. My mother plucked each bird, carefully reserving the breast feathers for pillows.

In the winter she sewed night after night, endlessly, begging cast-off 18 clothing from relatives, ripping apart coats, dresses, blouses, and trousers to remake them to fit her four daughters and son. Every morning and every evening she milked cows, fed pigs and calves, cared for chickens, picked eggs, cooked meals, washed dishes, scrubbed floors, and tended and loved her children. In the spring she planted a garden once more, dragging pails of water to nourish and sustain the vegetables for the family. In 1936 she lost a baby in her sixth month.

In 1937 her fifth daughter was born. She was 42 years old. In 1939 a 19 second son, and in 1941 her eighth child—and third son.

But the war had come, and prosperity of a sort. The herd of cattle had 20 grown to 30 head; she still milked morning and evening. Her garden was more than a half acre—the rains had come, and by now the Rural Electricity Administration and indoor plumbing. Still she sewed— dresses and jackets for the children, house dresses and aprons for herself, weekly patching of jeans, overalls, and denim shirts. Still she made pillows, using the feathers she had plucked, and quilts every year— intricate patterns as well as patchwork, stitched as well as tied—all necessary bedding for her family. Every scrap of cloth too small to be used in quilts was carefully saved and painstakingly sewed together in strips to make rugs. She still went out in the fields to help with the haying whenever there was a threat of rain.

In 1959 my mother's last child graduated from high school. A year 21 later the cows were sold. She still raised chickens and ducks, plucked feathers, made pillows, baked her own bread, and every year made a new quilt—now for a married child or for a grandchild. And her garden, that huge, undying symbol of sustenance, was as large and cared for as in all the years before. The canning, and now freezing, continued.

In 1969, on a June afternoon, mother and father started out for town 22 so that she could buy sugar to make rhubarb jam for a daughter who lived in Texas. The car crashed into a ditch. She was paralyzed from the waist down.

In 1970 her husband, my father, died. My mother struggled to regain 23 some competence and dignity and order in her life. At the rehabilitation institute, where they gave her physical therapy and trained her to live usefully in a wheelchair, the therapist told me: "She did fifteen pushups today—fifteen! She's almost seventy-five years old! I've never known a woman so strong!"

From her wheelchair she canned pickles, baked bread, ironed clothes, 24 wrote dozens of letters weekly to her friends and her "half dozen or more kids," and made three patchwork housecoats and one quilt. She made balls and balls of carpet rags—enough for five rugs. And kept all her love letters.

"I think I've found your mother's records—Martha Ruth Smith; mar- 25 ried to Ben F. Smith?"

"Yes, that's right."　　　　　　　　　　　　　　　　　　　　26
"Well, I see that she was getting a widow's pension . . ."　　　　　27
"Yes, that's right."　　　　　　　　　　　　　　　　　　　　28
"Well, your mother isn't entitled to our $255 death benefit."　　　29
"Not entitled! But why?"　　　　　　　　　　　　　　　　　　30
The voice on the telephone explains patiently:　　　　　　　　　31
"Well, you see—your mother never worked."　　　　　　　　　　32

Questions About the Reading

1. Why didn't the writer's mother want to get married?
2. How old was the writer's mother when she had her eighth child? How old was she when she was paralyzed?
3. In her later years, how do you think Mrs. Smith's attitude had changed from the one she expressed in the letter quoted in paragraph 12? What had become of her fears of marriage?
4. Why did Mrs. Smith do the pushups, and why did she continue to work in her final years, when she really didn't have to?
5. Speculate about why Mrs. Smith kept her love letters. Why do you think the writer mentions the fact in paragraph 24?

Questions About the Writer's Strategies

1. What is the thesis in this essay? Where is it expressed?
2. How well do the writer's examples support her thesis?
3. Aside from the extended example of her mother's life, what other mode of development does the writer use in the essay?
4. Describe the writer's point of view in the essay. How does she use time? Does her tone change during the essay?
5. Why does the writer provide so few details about her father and the family's children?

Writing Assignments

1. Write an essay giving examples of the obstacles women have to overcome in today's society.
2. Think of an extraordinary person you know, and write an essay using examples to show what makes that person extraordinary and why he or she is important to others.
3. Write an essay using examples, or one extended example, to show what the word *sacrifice* means.

5

Classification and Division

SUPPOSE YOU ARE looking over the clothing in your closet, trying to sort out the confusion. You decide to classify your clothing into several categories: good clothes for looking your best on the job; older clothes for weekends and informal occasions; and very old clothes that have some stains and holes (but that you can still use when you wash the car or the dog). You have now classified all your clothes into three orderly categories, according to their various uses. You may even want to expand your classification by adding a fourth category: clothes that are no longer useful and should be thrown away. You may have washed the dog in them once too often.

The purpose of **classification** is to take many of the same type of thing—for example, clothing, school papers, presidents, recipes, or music—and organize this large, unsorted group into categories. You may decide to classify your group of similar things, such as music, into the categories of classical, jazz, and rock and roll. Or you might classify recipes into main dishes, salads, and desserts.

You should determine your categories by a quality or characteristic that the items have in common. In each case, you will have to search for the categories that will help you classify an unsorted group of items.

In the following example, the writer classifies mothers of handicapped children in three categories of attitudes.

Topic sentence ⌐ Researchers note three frequent attitudes among mothers of   1
⌐ handicapped children. The first attitude is reflected by those

Category 1: rejection

mothers who reject their child or are unable to accept the child as a handicapped person. Complex love-hate and acceptance-rejection relationships are found within this group. Rejected children not only have problems in adjusting to themselves and their disabilities, but they also have to contend with disturbed family relationships and emotional insecurity. Unfortunately, such children receive even less encouragement than the normal child and have to absorb more criticism of their behavior.

Category 2: overcompensation

A second relationship involves mothers who overcompensate in their reactions to their child and the disorder. They tend to be unrealistic, rigid, and overprotective. Often, such parents try to compensate by being overzealous and giving continuous instruction and training in the hope of establishing superior ability. 2

Category 3: acceptance

The third group consists of mothers who accept their children along with their disorders. These mothers have gained the ability to provide for the special needs of their handicapped children while continuing to live a normal life and tending to family and home as well as civic and social obligations. The child's chances are best with parents who have accepted both their child and the defects. 3

Janet W. Lerner,
Learning Disabilities, Fifth Edition

A **division** paper requires taking one thing—a man's suit, for example—and dividing it into its component parts or characteristics: jacket, pants, and vest (maybe).

Classification and division are often used together. For example, you might want to *divide* your neighborhood into sections (north, south, east, west). You might then *classify* the sections by how much noise and traffic are present in each—noisy, relatively quiet, and quiet. The purpose of classification and division is to categorize a complex whole into simple, useful categories or subdivisions.

In the following example, the writer classifies three police officer positions and then divides each position by the duties required.

Classification

Division 1

Division 2

Division 3

The presidential crime commission offered a partial solution to overworked police forces: Split up the policeman's job three different ways. Under this plan, a "community service officer," often a youth from the ghetto, would perform minor investigative chores, rescue cats, and keep in touch with combustible young people. A police officer, one step higher, would control traffic, hold back crowds at parades, and investigate more serious crimes. A police agent, the best-trained, best-educated man on the ladder, would patrol high-crime areas, respond to delicate racial situations, and take care of tense confrontations.

"The Police Need Help," *Time* (October 4, 1968), p. 27

Whether using classification or division, you should be sure the categories are logical and appropriate, with as little overlap between categories as possible. If you are classifying chocolate desserts, you should not add vanilla custard to your list. You should also make your categories reasonably complete. You would not want to leave out chocolate cake in your classification of chocolate desserts.

If you are groping for a method of classification, you may want to try *several* ways of categorizing the same information. If you are classifying your clothes based on how attractive they look in your closet, you might sort them by color. But if you want to make the best use of the space in your closet, you might sort your clothes by type of garment—jackets, pants, shirts, and so forth. In short, you should choose your method of classifying any group of items based on the idea or point you want to support.

In the following paragraph, the writer uses classification to recommend ways to categorize book owners.

Topic sentence: classification	There are three kinds of book owners. The first has all the standard sets and best-sellers—unread, untouched. (This deluded individual owns woodpulp and ink, not books.)
Category 1: nonreaders	
Category 2: occasional readers	The second has a great many books—a few of them read through, most of them dipped into, but all of them as clean and shiny as the day they were bought. (This person would probably like to make books his own, but is restrained by a false respect for their physical appearance.) The third has a few books or many—every one of them dog-eared and dilapidated, shaken and loosened by continual use, marked and scribbled in from front to back. (This man owns books.)
Category 3: devoted readers	

Mortimer J. Adler,
"How to Mark a Book"

Notice, too, that the transitional words *first, second,* and *third* are used to identify the book owner according to how much each owner reads books. The words *first, second,* and *third* also help move the reader from one point to another. Some other transitional words and phrases that often are used in classification and division are *one, two, three;* and *for one thing, for another thing, finally.* As you write and revise your paragraphs and essays, you will want to think about using transitions to help maintain the **unity** and logical flow, or **coherence,** of your writing.

Like Adler, author of the paragraph on book owners, writers often use topic sentences such as "A safe city street has three main qualities" (see chapter 1, pp. 6–7) or "The treatment prescribed for the disease was aspirin, bed rest, and fluids" to indicate the categories that will follow in the body of a paragraph or essay. Following "A safe city street has three main qualities," the writer would explain the three specific qualities that make a city street safe. Following "The treatment prescribed for the disease was aspirin, bed rest, and fluids," the writer would probably explain the reasons for prescribing aspirin, bed rest, and fluids.

Usually, too, writers will *follow the same order* in discussing the divisions (or categories) that they used in first introducing them. For instance, suppose the topic is "Four methods can be used to cook fish: broiling, baking, poaching, and frying." Ordinarily the writer would explain (1) broiling, then (2) baking, (3) poaching, and (4) frying. Listing the categories and explaining them in order can make the composition easier for the reader to follow. In the revised student essay that follows, the three students who collaborated in writing it initially classified students as "unconcerned," "ambitious," and "inconsistent." Although they did not follow this order in their first draft, in **revising** the essay, the students changed the order to unconcerned, inconsistent, and ambitious. This order—which followed an undesirable-to-desirable pattern—was then used as the basis for the order of the paragraphs.

Thesis statement: classification

Students come in all ages, races, and genders. You can find the unconcerned, inconsistent, and ambitious in any group of students.

Category 1: unconcerned students

First, Ralph, a student in my English class, is an example of a student who has an unconcerned attitude. He has a negative outlook on life, and at times his attitude is downright hostile. He enters the classroom late and disrupts the class by slamming the door or by talking to other students while the teacher is giving a lecture. He does not care at all about the importance of an education. Ralph is more interested in watching sports, enjoying some form of entertainment, or going to parties.

Category 2: inconsistent students

Second, an inconsistent student can be described as a person whose attitude toward education changes or varies. For example, a first grader's grades have gone up and down. She has been in school for only two semesters, but she has shown a big change in her grades. The first semester she received an E (Excellent) in reading and an S (Satisfactory) in math. The second semester she received an N (Not satisfactory) in reading and an E in math. When asked why her reading grade dropped, she said because she no longer liked reading. After her teacher taught her how to have fun doing her math, she no longer concentrated on reading. As a result, she would only take her math homework out of her book bag when it came time to do her homework.

Last, there are many ambitious students who are eager to do well in their studies and to achieve degrees. Their priorities have been set, and they have made plans for reaching their goals. Their sole ambition is to excel and succeed. Many students can be classified as ambitious. Valerie, who is pursuing a degree in nursing, is a classic example. She

Category 3:
ambitious
students

attends class eagerly and regularly, even though she has two children and a home to care for. Recently, she had an illness that caused her to be absent for two weeks and to fall behind in her assignments. She returned and, with her usual ambition, soon caught up with her overdue assignments and achieved Bs or better grades in her courses.

Conclusion:
restatement
of thesis

In conclusion, the attitudes exemplified above can be found in students of any age, race, or gender. Whether they are attending grade school, high school, or college, students can be found who are unconcerned, inconsistent, or ambitious.

As with any piece of writing, a useful practice is to jot down many ideas and make rough lists as part of your **brainstorming** and prewriting. Do not skimp on your planning, and do expect to revise—perhaps several times—to produce a clear, understandable, and effective paragraph or essay.

The Mad Dog's Hair: Alcoholism

Gustave Simons

The writer classifies drinkers under three categories and tells us which kind of drinker is the most dangerous.

Word to Know

recollection   memory

Getting Started

Do you know anyone who is addicted to alcohol, smoking, or dieting? Are you trying to quit smoking or trying to break some other habit?

There are three categories under which drinkers can be classified: moderate drinkers, who take two cocktails before dinner; heavy drinkers, who take two or three cocktails before lunch, two more cocktails before going home, and another two at home before dinner; and alcoholics, whose intake may begin with a shot or two of bourbon in their morning coffee and continue through the morning, lunch, the afternoon, and evening until they fall into bed with no recollection whatever the next morning as to where they have been or to what they have done during the day before. These are the problems, the dangerous ones; these are the alcoholics, a constant danger not only to themselves, but to their families, their business associates, and possibly to the community where they live.

Questions About the Reading

1. What are the categories by which the writer classifies drinkers?
2. What are the drinking behaviors of the moderate and heavy drinkers?
3. Who is the most dangerous drinker?
4. How is the alcoholic affected by his drinking?

Questions About the Writer's Strategies

1. What is the main idea of the paragraph? Is it stated or implied? If stated, state it in your own words.
2. What is the order the writer uses in classifying drinkers?

Writing Assignments

1. Write a paragraph in which you classify your friends or relatives who smoke.
2. Write a paragraph in which you classify friends or relatives who are dieting.
3. Write a paragraph in which you classify friends or relatives according to their exercise programs.

Graffiti

Susan A. Phillips

*The writer spent time in Los Angeles among gang members and learned
how they classified graffiti.*

Words to Know

affirmative positive

discontinuous not continual, not constant

graffiti painting or inscriptions, usually on walls or buildings

RIPs rest in peace, a memorial

Getting Started

What kinds of graffiti do you find in your neighborhood or city?

———

Gang members identify basically four interrelated but distinct types of
graffiti: hitting up, crossing out, roll calls, and RIPs (memorial graffiti).
They correspond roughly to the categories with which Ley and
Cybriwsky (1974) designated Philadelphia graffiti: affirmative and
aggressive. Through "hitting up" and "roll calls," gang members make
positive statements about group belonging and membership (what Ley
and Cybriwsky indicate to be roughly affirmative). Through "crossing
out" or "challenging," they engage other gangs in discontinuous dia-
logues that are ritual struggles for power and recognition within their
community (what Ley and Cybriwsky indicate to be aggressive).
Constituting the last category are the memorial markers gang members
make for homies lost during the course of these struggles; generally they
are called "RIPs." These categories relate to different elements of gang
life and membership.

———

Questions About the Reading

1. What are the categories of graffiti identified by the Los Angeles gang
   members?
2. What kind of statements are being made by "hitting up" and "roll
   calls"?
3. What category of graffiti engages other gangs in struggles for power?

4. What is the purpose of RIPs?
5. What are the different kinds of graffiti depicting?

Questions About the Writer's Strategies

1. What is the main idea of the paragraph? State it in your own words.
2. Although the writer groups "hitting up" and "roll calls" as "positive statements," how do they differ?
3. What is the order the writer uses? Why do you think she chose that order?

Writing Assignments

1. Drive around your town to observe the graffiti on fences and buildings. Write a paragraph in which you classify the graffiti according to your own criteria.
2. Write a paragraph in which you classify the billboard ads in your town.
3. *Working Together* Join with some classmates and choose a specific time and date for watching different television stations. Write a paragraph in which you classify the different ads you saw.

4. *Working Together* Join with some classmates and set a time and date to be on the Internet. Write a paragraph classifying the ads or spam you saw.

Fans

Paul Gallico

Paul Gallico is known for his sports writing and for his books, including
Mrs. 'Arris Goes to New York *and* The Snow Goose. *In the following paragraph he classifies sports fans.*

Words to Know

aristocratic   upper-class
commiseration   sympathy
incandescents   very bright, shining lights
lurks   lies in wait

Getting Started

How would you classify the people who attend a rock concert, a
musical play, a symphony, and an opera performance?

The fight crowd is a beast that lurks in the darkness behind the fringe
of white light shed over the first six rows by the incandescents atop the
ring, and is not to be trusted with pop bottles or other hardware. The
tennis crowd is always preening and shushing itself. The golf crowd is
the most unwieldy and most sympathetic, and is the only horde given to
mass production of that absurd noise written generally as "tsk tsk tsk
tsk," and made between tongue and teeth with head-waggings to denote
extreme commiseration. The baseball crowd is the most hysterical, the
football crowd the best-natured and the polo crowd the most aristocratic. Racing crowds are the most restless, wrestling crowds the most
tolerant, and soccer crowds the most easily incitable to riot and disorder.
Every sports crowd takes on the characteristics of the individuals who
compose it. Each has its particular note of hysteria, its own little cruel-
ties, mannerisms, and bad mannerisms, its own code of sportsmanship
and its own method of expressing its emotions.

Questions About the Reading

1. What are the classifications of sports fans that the writer discusses?
2. Which crowd is the most likely to be disorderly?

3. What determines the characteristics of each sports crowd?
4. What do you think happens to make a golf crowd go "tsk tsk tsk tsk" to show "extreme commiseration"?
5. Which crowd is the most hysterical?

Questions About the Writer's Strategies

1. What is the main idea (topic) of the paragraph?
2. Which sentence(s) state the topic of the paragraph?
3. Where are the topic sentence(s) located in the paragraph?
4. What is the metaphor the writer uses for the fight crowd?
5. What appears to determine the order in which the writer discusses the different crowds? If you were writing the paragraph, would you use a different order? If so, explain how you might change the order.

Writing Assignments

1. Write a paragraph in which you classify the crowds at three different musical events.
2. Write a paragraph in which you classify the cars in a parking lot.

Brain Power

Lester C. Thurow

The writer identifies the inventions that led to our first and second industrial revolutions but maintains that the third, the "information revolution," is not based on information.

Words to Know

biotechnology   application of technology to biology
denominator   controlling or common term
misnomer   incorrect name or term

Getting Started

How would you classify the changes that have taken place in your life as a result of the invention of the computer?

Future economic historians looking back will probably see the end of the 20th century as the third industrial revolution. In the first industrial revolution, at the beginning of the 19th century, the steam engine brought 8,000 years of agricultural dominance to an end and created the modern industrial era. At the end of the 19th century, electrification caused the second industrial revolution. Electrical power generation and distribution quickly became a big industry. The telephone could be invented. Electric lights made work or leisure into nighttime as well as daytime activities. People slept less. The third industrial revolution is sometimes called an information revolution, but that is a misnomer since many of the industries involved in the revolution, such as biotechnology and new designer-made materials, are not information industries. Its key distinguishing characteristic and common denominator is not information, but rather a world in which skills and knowledge are the dominant sources of wealth. Bill Gates, now the world's richest man, is the best symbol of this shift.

Questions About the Reading

1. What was the first industrial revolution and what did it replace as our dominant industry?
2. What inventions led to the first and second industrial revolutions?

3. What is the third revolution called? Why does Thurow say this is a misnomer?
4. What does Thurow say is the third revolution's characteristic? Why? Who is the best symbol of this revolution?

Questions About the Writer's Strategies

1. What is the main idea of the paragraph? State it in your own words.
2. What order does the writer use?
3. In addition to classification, what other modes of development does the writer use?
4. If you wanted to divide the paragraph into more than one paragraph, where would you divide it? What would be the main idea and topic sentence of each paragraph?

Writing Assignments

1. Write a paragraph in which you classify the ways in which the computer has changed or influenced your life.
2. Write a paragraph in which you classify the inventions you use for doing your household tasks and explain how they have changed your way from the way your parents or grandparents did these tasks.

The ABCs
of the U.S.A.

Michael Dobbs

*Michael Dobbs, a Briton, finds America a strange experience and classi-fies American characteristics—from the open display of "Ambition" to the invention of "Zillion." ("The ABCs of the U.S.A." by Michael Dobbs, The Washington Post, June 21, 1987. © **1987, The Washington Post, reprinted with permission.**)*

Words to Know

arteriosclerosis   hardening or thickening of the arteries

bemused   confused, puzzled

Hechinger   garden superstore company located in the Washington, D.C., area

injunction   directive or order

la linea Italiana   literally, the Italian line

la queue Française   literally, the French line

queue   line of people

visa   authorization to visit and travel within a country

Getting Started

Do you think there are characteristics that are unique to the American people?

$\mathbf{A}$merica can be a strange experience for a foreigner. My wife and I   1
arrived in the United States in January after seven years overseas—four in France, three in Poland. From the jumble of first impressions, we compiled an A-to-Z explanation of why America can be such a foreign country to those who arrive here from Europe.

I should explain at the outset that I am from Britain, but my Florida-   2
born wife, Lisa, is as American as apple pie. In this alphabet, however, A does not stand for apple pie. It stands for:

Ambition. In the Old World, people are taught to hide it. An exception   3
was Macbeth who (Shakespeare tells us) nurtured "an ambition that o'er-leaps itself and falls on the other side"—and look what happened to him. Here, it seems quite proper to announce that you are after the boss's job or want to make a million dollars by the age of 30.

Breakfast. The American habit of conducting business at breakfast has 4 reached Europe, but I doubt that it will ever really catch on. In France and Britain, breakfast is too much a family affair. Here, it has become part of the power game.

Credit cards. You really can't leave home without them. It is interest- 5 ing, and somewhat infuriating, to discover that bad credit is better than no credit at all: I was refused a Visa card on the grounds that I did not have a credit profile. Speaking of credit cards, we are bemused by the relatively new fad of destroying the carbons. Back in Europe, people prefer to keep their fingers clean.

Dreams. The American Dream, dented though it's been recently, is still 6 very much alive. Dreaming great dreams is what keeps American society going—from the waitress who wants to become a car dealer to the street kid who wants to become a basketball star. Europeans dream dreams too, but don't seem to believe in them so much. See *Ambition.*

Exercise. A couple of years ago, I came to Washington in the slip- 7 stream of French President François Mitterrand. A cheer went up from the French press corps as our bus passed a fitness center—and we saw body-conscious Americans bending, stretching and leaping from side to side. America's fetish for fitness amuses—and puzzles—Europeans.

First names. In Europe, there is a natural and orderly progression from 8 the use of last names to the use of first names. Here, it's first names at first sight. This can create confusion. I have one acquaintance who calls me Bill—and I am not quite sure how to correct him.

Gadgets. These can be addictive. It is difficult to imagine now how we 9 survived for so long without the cruise control, the automatic ice dispenser, the microwave and the cordless telephone.

Hechinger. If I were in charge of arranging the programs of visiting del- 10 egations from communist countries, I would include a compulsory visit to Hechinger. We know Polish farmers who have to wait months to buy fencing for their livestock. Their eyes would pop out of their heads in this temple of American capitalism.

Insurance. Americans have a policy to cover every risk, both conceiv- 11 able and inconceivable. So far, we have refused rental reimbursement insurance for our car, death insurance for our mortgage and supplementary title insurance for our house. It gives us a feeling of living dangerously.

Junk food. Anyone who wants to understand why Americans suffer 12 from higher rates of cancer and arteriosclerosis only has to look at what they eat.

Ketchup. I had to come to America to discover that it can be eaten with 13 anything—from french fries to French cheese.

Lines. American lines—beginning with the yellow line at immigration 14 control—are the most orderly and organized in the world. The British queue, once internationally renowned, has begun to fray at the edges in recent years. *La queue Française* was never very impressive, and *la linea Italiana* is simply a mob.

Money. In Europe, money is something that everybody likes to have— 15 but is careful not to flaunt. Unless it has been in the family for several generations, there is often an assumption that it has been acquired dishonestly. In America, the green justifies the means.

No smoking. No longer just a polite injunction in America, almost an 16 evangelical campaign. Nobody would dare ask a Frenchman to put out his Gauloises in a restaurant.

Ollie North. What other major western democracy would allow a lieu- 17 tenant colonel to make foreign policy? A hero for some, a traitor for others, Ollie (see *First names*) is a wonderful example of the American go-for-it attitude that both awes and alarms foreigners.

Patriotism. Exists everywhere, of course, but the American version is 18 brasher, louder, and more self-conscious than the European. In Britain, it is taken for granted that a citizen or politician loves his country. Here, he is expected to prove it.

Quiet. American cities are quieter than European cities—thanks to 19 noise controls on automobiles and the recent spate of environmental legislation. This was a major surprise for someone brought up to assume that America was a noisy place.

Religion. It's difficult, somehow, to imagine an English version of Jim 20 and Tammy Bakker. When my parents came to visit recently, they were startled at the sight of a fire-breathing Jimmy Swaggart denouncing the Bakkers on live TV. That's not the kind of way they behave in our dear old Church of England.

Sales. Ever since arriving in Washington, we have been hurrying to 21 take advantage of this week's unrepeatable *offer*—only to discover that it is usually repeated next week. We are just catching on that there is always an excuse for a sale.

Television. How grown-ups can watch game shows and sitcoms at 11 22 A.M. mystifies me—but the national habit, day or night, is contagious. I recently found myself nodding in full agreement with a professional type who was saying that American kids watch too much television. It was only later that I realized that I was watching him say this on television.

Ulcers. See *Work.*   23

Visas. Americans don't need visas to visit Britain (or most European 24 countries, for that matter). To get my entry permit for the United States, I had to sign a document promising that I would not overthrow the government by force, had never been a member of the Communist Party, and was not wanted for war crimes. I had to provide details of my affiliation to labor unions as well as affidavits from four countries stating that I had no criminal record. All this for cruise control and a cordless telephone.

Work. A leading Polish sociologist, Jan Szczepanski, once told me that 25 many Poles imagine that they will become rich simply by emigrating to America. He tries to persuade whoever will listen that America became a rich society through work, work and more work. It is still true.

X-rated movies. We have them in Europe too, but not on motel room 26 TVs and not in most small towns.

Yuppies. The European counterpart remains a pale shadow of the all- 27 American original. The animal seems more driven, more ubiquitous on this side of the Atlantic.

Zillion. What other nation would have invented a number that is infi- 28 nitely more than a billion? America may not always be the best, but it is certainly the biggest.

Questions About the Reading

1. How long had the writer lived overseas before arriving in the United States?
2. What is the writer's nationality?
3. How does the writer feel about Americans' use of first names?
4. What is the writer's opinion of what Americans eat?
5. How does the European attitude toward money differ from the American attitude?

Questions About the Writer's Strategies

1. What is the tone of the essay? How does the writer achieve it?
2. What is the thesis of the essay?
3. What is the point of view in person of the essay? Is it consistent throughout the essay? If not, identify the paragraphs in which it differs.
4. In addition to classifying American characteristics, what other strategies does the writer use to support his thesis?

Writing Assignments

1. Write an essay in which you classify and explain the characteristics of a city you have visited.

2. Visit your college web site and the sites of several other colleges. Write an essay in which you classify the sites based on their effectiveness in explaining the academic programs the colleges offer. Include a list of the web site addresses you use.

3. *Working Together*   Join with some classmates to write an essay in which you classify and explain the characteristics that are common either to people in a particular profession or to the students in your school.

"Ever Et Raw Meat?"

Stephen King

Stephen King, best known for such horror novels and movies as Carrie *and* Misery, *classifies readers according to the questions they ask him.*

Words to Know

blasphemous   irreverent, profane
E. E. Cummings   American poet known for experimenting with form, punctuation, spelling, and syntax in his poetry
enumerate   name one by one
flagellate   beat, whip
kleptomaniac   a person who has an impulse or compulsion to steal
laconic   concise expression; expressed in few words
modicum   small amount
self-abnegation   self-denial, giving up of one's rights
Zen   Buddhist sect

Getting Started

What questions would you like to ask Stephen King?

————————————————

It seems to me that, in the minds of readers, writers actually exist to 1 serve two purposes, and the more important may not be the writing of books and stories. The primary function of writers, it seems, is to answer readers' questions. These fall into three categories. The third is the one that fascinates me most, but I'll identify the other two first.

The One-of-a-Kind Question

Each day's mail brings a few of these. Often they reflect the writer's field 2 of interest—history, horror, romance, the American West, outer space, big business. The only thing they have in common is their uniqueness. Novelists are frequently asked where they get their ideas (see category No. 2), but writers must wonder where this relentless curiosity, these really strange questions, come from.

There was, for instance, the young woman who wrote to me from a 3 penal institution in Minnesota. She informed me she was a kleptomaniac.

She further informed me that I was her favorite writer, and she had stolen every one of my books she could get her hands on. "But after I stole *Different Seasons* from the library and read it, I felt moved to send it back," she wrote. "Do you think this means you wrote this one the best?" After due consideration, I decided that reform on the part of the reader has nothing to do with artistic merit. I came close to writing back to find out if she had stolen *Misery* yet but decided I ought to just keep my mouth shut.

From Bill V. in North Carolina: "I see you have a beard. Are you mor- 4
bid of razors?"

From Carol K. in Hawaii: "Will you soon write of pimples or some 5
other facial blemish?"

From Don G., no address (and a blurry postmark): "Why do you keep 6
up this disgusting mother worship when anyone with any sense knows a MAN has no use to his mother once he is weaned?"

From Raymond R. in Mississippi: "Ever et raw meat?" (It's the la- 7
conic ones like this that really get me.)

I have been asked if I beat my children and/or my wife. I have been 8
asked to parties in places I have never been and hope never to go. I was once asked to give away the bride at a wedding, and one young woman sent me an ounce of pot, with the attached question: "This is where I get my inspiration—where do you get yours?" Actually, mine usually comes in envelopes—the kind through which you can view your name and address printed by a computer—that arrive at the end of every month.

My favorite question of this type, from Anchorage, asked simply: 9
"How could you write such a why?" Unsigned. If E. E. Cummings were still alive, I'd try to find out if he'd moved to the Big North.

The Old Standards

These are the questions writers dream of answering when they are col- 10
lecting rejection slips, and the ones they tire of quickest once they start to publish. In other words, they are the questions that come up without fail in every dull interview the writer has ever given or will ever give. I'll enumerate a few of them:

Where do you get your ideas? (I get mine in Utica.)   11

How do you get an agent? (Sell your soul to the Devil.)   12

Do you have to know somebody to get published? (Yes; in fact, it 13
helps to grovel, toady, and be willing to perform twisted acts of sexual depravity at a moment's notice, and in public if necessary.)

How do you start a novel? (I usually start by writing the number 1 in 14
the upper right-hand corner of a clean sheet of paper.)

How do you write best sellers? (Same way you get an agent.)   15

How do you sell your book to the movies? (Tell them they don't 16
want it.)

What time of day do you write? (It doesn't matter; if I don't keep busy 17
enough, the time inevitably comes.)

Do you ever run out of ideas? (Does a bear defecate in the woods?) 18

Who is your favorite writer? (Anyone who writes stories I would have 19
written had I thought of them first.)

There are others, but they're pretty boring, so let us march on. 20

The Real Weirdies

Here I am, bopping down the street, on my morning walk, when some 21
guy pulls over in his pickup truck or just happens to walk by and says,
"Hi, Steve! Writing any good books lately?" I have an answer for this;
I've developed it over the years out of pure necessity. I say, "I'm taking
some time off." I say that even if I'm working like mad, thundering
down homestretch on a book. The reason why I say this is because no
other answer seems to fit. Believe me, I know. In the course of the trial
and error that has finally resulted in "I'm taking some time off," I have
discarded about 500 other answers.

Having an answer for "You writing any good books lately?" is a good 22
thing, but I'd be lying if I said it solves the problem of *what the question
means.* It is this inability on my part to make sense of this odd query,
which reminds me of that Zen riddle—"Why is a mouse when it
runs?"—that leaves me feeling mentally shaken and impotent. You see,
it isn't just *one* question; it is a *bundle* of questions, cunningly wrapped
up in one package. It's like that old favorite, "Are you still beating your
wife?"

If I answer in the affirmative, it means I may have written—how 23
many books? two? four?—(all of them good) in the last—how long?
Well, how long is "lately"? It could mean I wrote maybe three good
books just last week, or maybe two *on this very walk up to Bangor
International Airport and back!* On the other hand, if I say no, what does
that mean? I wrote three or four *bad* books in the last "lately" (surely
"lately" can be no longer than a month, six weeks at the outside)?

Or here I am, signing books at the Betts' Bookstore or B. Dalton's in 24
the local consumer factory (nicknamed "the mall"). This is something I
do twice a year, and it serves much the same purpose as those little bun-
dles of twigs religious people in the Middle Ages used to braid into
whips and flagellate themselves with. During the course of this exercise
in madness and self-abnegation, at least a dozen people will approach
the little coffee table where I sit behind a barrier of books and ask
brightly, "Don't you wish you had a rubber stamp?"

I have an answer to this one, too, an answer that has been developed 25
over the years in a trial-and-error method similar to "I'm taking some
time off." The answer to the rubber-stamp questions is: "No, I don't
mind."

Never mind if I really do or don't (this time it's my own motivations 26
I want to skip over, you'll notice); the question is, Why does such an
illogical query occur to so many people? My signature is actually
stamped on the covers of several of my books, but people seem just as
eager to get these signed as those that aren't so stamped. Would these
questioners stand in line for the privilege of watching me slam a rubber
stamp down on the title page of *The Shining* or *Pet Sematary?* I don't
think they would.

If you still don't sense something peculiar in these questions, this one 27
might help convince you. I'm sitting in the cafe around the corner from
my house, grabbing a little lunch by myself and reading a book (reading
at the table is one of the few bad habits acquired in my youth that I have
nobly resisted giving up) until a customer or maybe even a waitress
sidles up and asks, "How come you're not reading one of your own
books?"

This hasn't happened just once, or even occasionally; it happens *a lot.* 28
The computer-generated answer to this question usually gains a chuckle,
although it is nothing but the pure, logical and apparent truth. "I know
how they all come out," I say. End of exchange. Back to lunch, with only
a pause to wonder why people assume you want to read what you
wrote, rewrote, read again following the obligatory editorial conference
and yet again during the process of correcting the mistakes that a good
copy editor always prods, screaming, from their hiding places (I once
heard a crime writer suggest that God could have used a copy editor,
and while I find the notion slightly blasphemous, I tend to agree).

And then people sometimes ask in that chatty, let's-strike-up-a- 29
conversation way people have, "How long does it take you to write a
book?" Perfectly reasonable question—at least until you try to answer it
and discover there is no answer. This time the computer-generated
answer is a total falsehood, but it at least serves the purpose of advanc-
ing the conversation to some more discussable topic. "Usually about
nine months," I say, "the same length of time it takes to make a baby."
This satisfies everyone but me. I know that nine months is just an average, and probably a completely fictional one at that. It ignores *The
Running Man* (published under the name Richard Bachman), which was
written in four days during a snowy February vacation when I was
teaching high school. It also ignores *It* and my latest, *The Tommyknockers.*
It is over 1,000 pages long and took four years to write. *The Tommyknockers* is 400 pages shorter but took five years to write.

Do I mind these questions? Yes . . . and no. Anyone minds questions ₃₀
that have no real answers and thus expose the fellow being questioned
to be not a real doctor but a sort of witch doctor. But no one—at least no
one with a modicum of simple human kindness—resents questions from
people who honestly want answers. And now and then someone will
ask a really interesting question, like, Do you write in the nude? The
answer—not generated by computer—is: I don't think I ever have, but if
it works, I'm willing to try it.

Questions About the Reading

1. According to King, what seems to be the primary function of writers?
2. What do the one-of-a-kind questions have in common?
3. What does the writer mean when he says he gets his inspiration from
    what "comes in envelopes—the kind through which you can view
    your name and address printed by computer—that arrive at the end
    of every month"?
4. What are the writer's definitions of "old standards" and "real
    weirdies"?
5. What are the four "real weirdies" the writer has been asked?

Questions About the Writer's Strategies

1. What are the different modes of development that the writer uses in
    the essay?
2. What is the point of view in person and time? Are they consistent
    throughout the essay?
3. What is the tone of the essay? Is it consistent throughout?
4. What organizational pattern and modes of development does the
    writer use in describing "one-of-a-kind questions" and "old
    standards"?
5. What organizational pattern does the writer use in describing "real
    weirdies"?

Writing Assignments

1. Choose three or more famous writers and write an essay about the
    questions you would like to ask them.
2. *Working Together* Join with some classmates to write an essay
    about the questions you would like to ask Babe Ruth, Michael Jordan,
    and Martina Navratilova.

Eggs, Twinkies and Ethnic Stereotypes

Jeanne Park

Jeanne Park, an Asian American, found herself labeled as intelligent while in elementary school. In high school, she learned her intelligence did not set her apart in the classroom, but that outside the classroom her ethnic background did.

Words to Know

condescending patronizing
metamorphose change in nature

Getting Started

At lunchtime, do the students at your school segregate themselves according to their racial or ethnic background?

Who am I? 1

For Asian-American students, the answer is a diligent, hardworking 2
and intelligent young person. But living up to this reputation has secretly haunted me.

The labeling starts in elementary school. It's not uncommon for a 3
teacher to remark, "You're Asian, you're supposed to do well in math."
The underlying message is, "You're Asian and you're supposed to be smarter."

Not to say being labeled intelligent isn't flattering, because it is, or not 4
to deny that basking in the limelight of being top of my class isn't ego-boosting, because frankly it is. But at a certain point, the pressure became crushing. I felt as if doing poorly on my next spelling quiz would stain the exalted reputation of all Asian students forever.

So I continued to be an academic overachiever, as were my friends. By 5
junior high school I started to believe I was indeed smarter. I became condescending toward non-Asians. I was a bigot; all my friends were Asians. The thought of intermingling occurred rarely if ever.

My elitist opinion of Asian students changed, however, in high 6
school. As a student at what is considered one of the nation's most competitive science and math schools, I found that being on top is no longer an easy feat.

I quickly learned that Asian students were not smarter. How could I 7 ever have believed such a thing? All around me are intelligent, ambitious people who are not only Asian but white, black and Hispanic.

Superiority complexes aside, the problem of social segregation still 8 exists in the schools. With a few exceptions, each race socializes only with its "own kind." Students see one another in the classroom, but outside the classroom there remains distinct segregation.

Racist lingo abounds. An Asian student who socializes only with 9 other Asians is believed to be an Asian Supremacist or, at the very least, arrogant and closed off. Yet an Asian student who socializes only with whites is called a "twinkie," one who is yellow on the outside but white on the inside.

A white teenager who socializes only with whites is thought of as 10 prejudiced, yet one who socializes with Asians is considered an "egg," white on the outside and yellow on the inside.

These culinary classifications go on endlessly, needless to say, leaving 11 many confused, and leaving many more fearful than ever of social experimentation. Because the stereotypes are accepted almost unanimously, they are rarely challenged. Many develop harmful stereotypes of entire races. We label people before we even know them.

Labels learned at a young age later metamorphose into more visible 12 acts of racism. For example, my parents once accused and ultimately fired a Puerto Rican cashier, believing she had stolen $200 from the register at their grocery store. They later learned it was a mistake. An Asian shopkeeper nearby once beat a young Hispanic youth who worked there with a baseball bat because he believed the boy to be lazy and dishonest.

We all hold misleading stereotypes of people that limit us as individ- 13 uals in that we cheat ourselves out of the benefits different cultures can contribute. We can grow and learn from each culture whether it be Chinese, Korean or African American.

Just recently some Asian boys in my neighborhood were attacked by 14 a group of young white boys who have christened themselves the Master Race. Rather than being angered by this act, I feel pity for this generation that lives in a state of bigotry.

It may be too late for our parents' generation to accept that each per- 15 son can only be judged for the characteristics that set him or her apart as an individual. We, however, can do better.

Questions About the Reading

1. How did it affect the writer to be labeled as intelligent?
2. What did the writer learn about other students when she went to the competitive high school?
3. What is an Asian Supremacist? A "twinkie"? An "egg"?
4. According to the writer, how do the culinary classifications influence people's behavior?
5. According to the writer, how should we judge people?

Questions About the Writer's Strategies

1. Is the essay developed using classification or using division?
2. What mode of development does the writer use in paragraph 4?
3. What is the topic of paragraph 12? What mode of development does the writer use in the paragraph?
4. What are some transitional words the writer uses?
5. What is the thesis of the essay? Is it stated or implied?
6. Is the essay objective, subjective, or both?

Writing Assignments

1. Write an essay in which you classify the people in your neighborhood according to the cars they drive.
2. Write an essay in which you classify the students in your school according to what they eat for lunch.
3. Write an essay in which you divide a house, a car, or an item of clothing into its parts.

Conservation

Daniel Yergin

Most of us probably think the meaning of conservation *is clear—driving less, turning the thermostat down, using human power instead of machine power. But Daniel Yergin wants us to know that there is more than one way to conserve a barrel of oil.*

Words to Know

curtailment   decrease in amount, cutting back

entailing   involving

ideological   having to do with ideas

imagery   figurative language

implement   to put into effect

nondisruptive   not interrupting

petrodollar   money or currency held by a country that exports oil

prosaic   dull

semantically   having to do with the meaning of languages or words

widget   small mechanical part, gadget

Getting Started

How do you and your family try to conserve energy? What else could you do to conserve energy?

There is a source of energy that produces no radioactive waste, nothing in the way of petrodollars, and very little pollution. Moreover, the source can provide the energy that conventional sources may not be able to furnish. Unhappily, however, it does not receive the emphasis and attention it deserves. 1

The source might be called energy efficiency, for Americans like to think of themselves as an efficient people. But the energy source is generally known by the more prosaic term *conservation*. To be semantically accurate, the source should be called conservation energy, to remind us of the reality—that conservation is no less an energy alternative than oil, gas, coal, or nuclear. Indeed, in the near term, conservation could do more than any of the conventional sources to help the country deal with the energy problem it has. 2

Three Types of Conservation

One can pick up a piece of coal, hold it in one's hand, and say, "This is   3
coal." Conservation is far harder to grasp and comprehend. While it
involves a host of different things—heat pumps, insulation, new engines—
it also involves changes in methods, and even more important, an ongoing
commitment to promote and implement it. To clarify matters, we can identify three categories of energy conservation, although the boundaries
among them are fuzzy. The first two are not desirable. The third is.

The first category of conservation is out-and-out *curtailment*. When   4
supplies are suddenly interrupted, energy saving is forced as factories
are closed and working days lost. This is what happened when interstate
natural gas ran short in 1976 and 1977, and during the coal strike of 1977
and 1978. The country can expect more curtailment in the future if sensible actions are not taken now.

A second category is *overhaul*, dramatically changing the way   5
Americans live and work. An extreme example would be the outlawing
of further suburbanization, forcing people to move into the urban center
and live in tall buildings not equipped with places to park a car. Very few
people would willingly accept that kind of energy conservation program.

To many people, energy conservation means only curtailment or   6
overhaul—something repressive and most un-American, involving cutting back, rationing, and unemployment. They see it as the product of an
anti-growth crusade led by the granola-chomping children of the afflu-
ent. Unhappily, some of the language of the Carter Administration—
such as the President's insistence on "sacrifice"—has strengthened this
unpleasant and misleading imagery in the mind of the public.

But there is a third way to think about conservation: as a form of   7
adjustment, entailing such things as insulating the house, making automobiles, industrial processes, and home appliances more efficient, and
capturing waste heat. This can be called *productive conservation*, which
encourages changes in capital stock and daily behavior that promote
energy savings in a manner that is economically and socially nondisruptive. Its aim is to use less energy than has been the habit to accomplish some task—whether it be to heat a home or to make a widget—in
order to prevent disruption later. Conservation, therefore, is not a theo-
logical or ideological issue. It should be pursued not as an end in itself,
but as a means toward greater social and economic welfare, as a way to
promote the well-being of the citizenry. As two prominent analysts, Lee
Schipper and Joel Darmstadter, have expressed it, "The most impelling
factor in encouraging conservation actions is the cost of not conserving."

Questions About the Reading

1. Why does the writer say curtailment and overhaul of our energy use are not desirable? Support your answer with statements from the reading.
2. What does conservation involve? Support your answer with details from the reading.

Questions About the Writer's Strategies

1. What is the thesis of the essay? Is it stated? If so, in which sentences?
2. What is the dominant mode of development used by the writer?
3. Does the writer use any other modes? If so, identify them in the reading.
4. What is the point of view (person, time, tone) in the reading? Identify words and statements in the reading to support your answer.
5. Which paragraphs develop the thesis? What are their main ideas and topic sentences?
6. Could paragraph 7 be divided into more than one paragraph? If so, where would you divide it?

Writing Assignments

1. Write a paper in which you identify and explain at least three categories of conservation that you and your family could contribute to by being less wasteful.
2. Write a paper in which you identify and explain at least three categories of resources that are limited and must be conserved. Then indicate what you and your family could do to conserve them.

Secrets of Man's Unspoken Language

Desmond Morris

A distinguished scientist offers a classification of the gestures that we experience in our lives and tells us what they mean.

Words to Know

aborigines   natives, earliest known inhabitants of a region
doffed   removed, took off
effigies   likeness or replica of, usually, a person
maligned   disliked, spoke negatively of
relic   souvenir
repertoire   stock, group, or knowledge of
salutation   greeting, acknowledgment

Getting Started

What gestures do you and your friends use to greet or say good-bye to each other?

If a Norwegian, a Korean and a Masai were suddenly marooned to- 1
gether on a desert island, communication would still be possible: they could easily convey their basic moods and intentions to one another without words, because all humanity shares a large repertoire of common visual signals. The true origin of many of these gestures is no longer known. But students of human behavior can trace certain actions that we take for granted today. Most are centuries old and steeped in history.

The nod. The vertical head nod, always a yes sign, occurs almost 2
everywhere in the world. Remote tribes, from the Australian aborigines to the natives of Tierra del Fuego, were found to be nodding for yes when first encountered by white men. It has even been recorded in people born deaf and blind. This strongly suggests that affirmative nodding may be an inborn action for the human species—a pattern programmed by our genes. Essentially, it is the beginning of a bow—a way of lowering the body to show submission.

The head shake. This, too, is virtually global in range and is always a 3
negative sign. Like many important gestures, it is thought to be a relic

from our personal past—from our early infancy when we were nursed at the breast or the bottle. The baby who is not hungry rejects the breast by turning the head sharply to the side. From this beginning, it is argued, has come our adult sign for negation. When a parent warns a child not to do something by wagging a forefinger, he is using the finger in imitation of the shaken head—often adding speed and vigor to the signal.

Crossing the fingers. When we say, "Keep your fingers crossed," we 4 are, historically speaking, requesting an act of Christian worship. Crossing oneself—making the sign of the cross by moving the arm downward and then sideways in front of the body—is an ancient protective device of the Christian Church. In earlier times, crossing the second finger tightly over the first was the secret version of this, and was done with the hand carefully hidden from view. But lacking any obvious religious character, the action easily slid into everyday use, even by non-Christians, as a casual wish for good fortune. Although still done secretly to protect oneself from the consequences of lying, as a "good luck" sign it has now come out into the open.

Thumbing the nose. The origin of this gesture—one of the most com- 5 mon and widespread insults in the world—is uncertain. It is usually thought to represent the hostile, erect comb of a fighting cock. (Animal signs are a favorite form of insult; the mocking, hands-to-ears flapping action popular among children, for example, mimics the long ears of the much-maligned donkey.) But the "cockscomb" sign has also been explained as a deformed salute, an imitation of grotesque, long-nosed effigies, or the mock firing of a catapult.

The OK sign. When an American wants to signal that something is 6 OK, fine, perfect, he raises his hand and makes a circle with his thumb and forefinger. This sign derives from a gesture people all over the world make unconsciously when speaking about some fine point. To say that something is precise or exact, we go through the motions of holding something very small between the tips of our thumb and forefinger, which then automatically form a ring. In America this unconscious movement became a deliberate signal meaning "perfect." But be careful with this one: in other countries the circle sign can mean something quite different. In Japan, it means money (because coins are circular); in France it means "nothing" or "worthless" (the circle meaning zero); in Malta, Sardinia and Greece it is an obscene insult.

Clasped hands raised above the head. This traditional posture 7 adopted by boxers and wrestlers after winning a fight is one of the many "triumph displays" that grow out of the surge of feeling following a victory. In nearly all triumphant moments, the victor expresses his sudden increase in status by raising his height in some way. Young children are likely to jump up and down excitedly. Among adults, the display differs from context to context, but there is often a raising of the arms high above the head.

Triumphant arm-raising may be amplified by raising the victorious 8 individual on the shoulders of his supporters, or parading him on top of some kind of vehicle. Without realizing it, the modern sports or political hero who parades through the streets of his hometown in an open car is recreating the ancient Roman Triumph, in which a conquering general entered Rome at the head of his army in a four-horse chariot decorated with laurel, a golden crown held above his head by a slave, and his face reddened with vermilion to simulate the blood of sacrificial victims.

The salute began as an act of token submission: removing the hat as 9 part of a formal bow. In earlier centuries the bow was so deep that the doffed hat almost touched the floor. This was abbreviated into the modern military salute in which the hand is brought smartly up to touch the temple. The same gesture survives as a friendly greeting: casually touching the brim of the hat, or the temple, with the fingers.

Thumbs up, thumbs down. When a Roman gladiator was defeated in 10 combat in the arena, he might be spared, or killed on the spot by his victor; the spectators could influence the decision by the position of their thumbs. The gesture for death was thrusting the thumb downward— apparently an imitation of thrusting the sword into the victim. It is popularly believed that the life sign was thumbs up, but this appears to be a misinterpretation. The phrase used in ancient writings, *pollice compresso*, literally means "thumbs compressed"; the spectators held out their hands with the thumbs hidden inside their closed fingers, meaning do *not* make the sword thrust.

The modern thumbs-up sign meaning "OK, fine, good," like the V- 11 for-Victory sign made famous by Sir Winston Churchill, was spread across much of the world by the British during World War II. Many Italians refer to it as the "English OK" signal. So a popular gesture which started out as a mistranslation from the literature of ancient Rome is now "returning" to the city from which it never really came.

Tapping the temple. Many people understand this as a sign for stu- 12 pidity. To make the meaning more precise, you might instead twist your forefinger against your temple, indicating "a screw loose," or rotate your forefinger close to your temple, signaling that the brain is going round and round. but even these actions would be confusing to some people. In Saudi Arabia, for example, stupidity can be signaled by touching the lower eyelid with the tip of the forefinger. Other local stupidity gestures include tapping the elbow of the raised forearm, flapping the hand up and down in front of half-closed eyes, rotating a raised hand or laying one forefinger flat across the forehead.

The salutation. People seem almost incapable of beginning or ending 13
any kind of encounter without some type of salutation. Man appears to
have needed such "salutation displays" for many thousands of years.
Early man established a major division of labor, with the male hunters
leaving the group at specific times, then returning to home base with the
kill. The importance of success or failure on the hunt meant that these
were vital moments in the life of the primeval tribe, so elaborate rituals
of greeting and farewell were developed.

The main moment of greeting was—and is—when actual body con- 14
tact is made; at full intensity this consists of a total embrace, with much
hugging, patting, squeezing, kissing, laughing and even weeping. But
before this, comes the moment when friends recognize each other from
a distance. Apparently some form of arm action at the moment of first
sighting is global for mankind. Clearly, the vertical, up-and-down wave
of the hand is a way of patting the friend's body at a distance in anticipation of the embrace to come.

The handshake, too, is a salutation display. Different cultures have 15
formalized, in different ways, the body contact which comes at the key
moment of greeting.

Some emphasize head-to-head contact as in nose-rubbing or stylized 16
mutual cheek-kissing. Westerners use a whole range of body contacts of
decreasing strength, right down to the formal handshake. But they are all
variations on a basic theme—the body embrace. This is the fundamental
human-contact action, the one we all know as babies, infants and growing children, and to which we return whenever the rules permit and we
wish to demonstrate feelings of attachment for another individual.

Questions About the Reading

1. How can people who speak different languages communicate with
   one another?
2. What are the global signals for "yes" and "no"?
3. What is the historical meaning of crossed fingers?
4. What does the crossed fingers signal usually mean now?
5. Why should you be careful about using the OK sign in other countries?

Questions About the Writer's Strategies

1. What is the thesis of the essay? State it in your own words.
2. Besides classification, what other modes of development does the
   writer use?

3. What are the divisions of salutations the writer provides in paragraphs 14 through 17?
4. How would you change paragraphs 14 through 17 to clarify the salutation divisions?

Writing Assignments

1. *Working Together*   Join with some classmates and write an essay in which you classify any special or unique gestures each person uses.
2. Write an essay in which you classify the gestures that are used by the police before and after a large sports event.

Comparison
and Contrast

To COMPARE IS to show how items are alike. To **contrast** is to show how items are different. Thus comparison and contrast involve pointing out the similarities or differences between two (or more) items. Birdwatchers, for instance, may compare bird A with bird B according to their common color, but contrast them according to their difference in size.

In the preceding chapter, you learned about the **modes of development** called **classification** and **division.** The comparison and contrast modes are related to those modes. In deciding what to compare or contrast, you will want to make sure that the items share points in common. Thus the items are usually the same kind or **class** of thing, and in comparing or contrasting them, you essentially establish at least two categories, showing the differences or similarities between them. For instance, you can compare two passenger cars—a Ford and a Chevrolet—with more precision than you can a Ford and a helicopter. Fords are compared with Chevrolets because they have many features in common—features that you can pinpoint. Similarly, you can usually compare two paintings more precisely than you can a novel and a painting.

Once you have selected the closely related items, you will want to explain as clearly as possible the ways in which the items are alike or different. In any one piece of writing, you may want to use comparison only—or contrast only. Or you may decide to use both in the same essay. These three possibilities are illustrated in the following paragraphs. Notice, in each case, how the writer compares or contrasts *specific* points.

Comparison

A Buick and a Cadillac, both built by General Motors, are alike in many ways. A Buick, which measures over 200 inches in length and weighs over 3,000 pounds, is large and holds the road well. A Cadillac is similar in length and weight. Like a Buick, a Cadillac gets relatively low gas mileage compared with smaller economy cars made by the same manufacturer. The Buick provides an unusually comfortable ride, especially on cross-country trips on the highway, as does a Cadillac. And both cars enjoy a certain status as a luxury automobile.

Contrast

The twins are as different as two people can be. Sally, who is always hoping someone will have a party, has black hair, brown eyes, and an outgoing personality. She wants to be an actress or a popular singer. Susan, more serious and studious, has blonde hair, blue eyes, and a somewhat shy manner. Since she has done well in all her classes in graphic arts and math, she plans to become an architect or an engineer.

Mixed Comparison and Contrast

Most Americans would say it is not really possible to establish an ideal society. But time after time, a small dedicated group of people will drop out of the mainstream of American society to try, once more, to live according to the group's concept of an ideal society. Most of these groups have believed in holding their property in common. Most have used the word *family* to refer to all members of the group. Many of these groups, however, have differed widely in their attitudes toward sex and marriage.

Notice that all three of these paragraphs supply information but do not try to claim that one of the compared items is better or worse than the other. Notice, too, the **objective** tone of these paragraphs. However, writers also use comparison and contrast to support their opinions about subjects or to show how a certain thing or idea is superior to others in the same class. The writer of the paragraph about twins, for instance, could have used her information to support an opinion, as in the following revised paragraph.

Opinion

The twins are as different as two people can be. Sally, who has black hair, brown eyes, and an outgoing, flighty personality, is always hoping someone will have a party. She fritters away her time and money shopping for the latest clothes, and she dreams of being an actress or a popular singer. But until she settles down and applies her energy to something useful, she will probably not be successful at anything. Susan, more serious and studious, has blonde hair,

blue eyes, and a somewhat shy manner. Since she works
hard and makes good use of her time, she has done well in

Opinion   ⌈ all her classes in graphic arts and math. She plans to become
⌊ an architect or an engineer and will no doubt be a good one.

As you plan a comparison-and-contrast composition, it is very useful
to **brainstorm** for items of comparison. That is, as described in chapter
1, think about the subjects of your composition and briefly jot down
whatever comes to mind about them. You can then use your list in deciding on the content of your paragraph.

Organization

You should organize your comparison (or contrast) by whichever
method suits your material best. One simple method is to explain a characteristic of item A, perhaps its cost, and then immediately compare it
with the same characteristic of item B—and then go on to compare the
two items point by point. For example, in contrasting two chocolate
cakes, you may first want to say cake A is more expensive to prepare
than cake B. Second, you may say that cake A, which requires more steps
and ingredients, takes more time to make than cake B. Third, cake A is
richer—almost too rich—and sweeter than cake B. You may conclude by
saying that you recommend cake B. In this manner, you move back and
forth, mentioning the specific differences between cake A and cake B in
an orderly manner.

When the writer compares (or contrasts) two objects item by item, it
is called the **alternating** or **point-by-point method.** The following diagram shows how this method works in the paragraph comparing Buicks
and Cadillacs.

Alternating (or point-by-point) method
Topic sentence: "A Buick and a Cadillac . . . are alike in many ways."

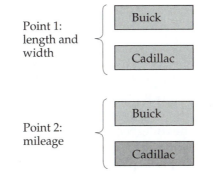

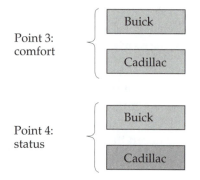

If the writer prefers a second type of organization, the **block method,** he or she explains all the characteristics of the first item together in a block and then explains all the characteristics of the second item in the same order in a corresponding block. The paragraphs contrasting the twins Sally and Susan (pages 146–147) are organized in this block method.

Block method

Topic sentence: "The twins are as different as two people can be."

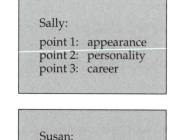

A third method, the **mixed method,** is useful when the writer wants to both compare and contrast in the same paragraph. All the similarities of the two items may first be explained and then all the differences. (Or, if the writer chooses, the differences may be explained first and then the similarities.) The following diagram shows this third method of organization, which was used in the paragraph on ideal societies (page 146).

Mixed comparison-and-contrast method

Topic sentence: "people . . . drop out of the mainstream of American society . . . to live according to the group's concept of an ideal society."

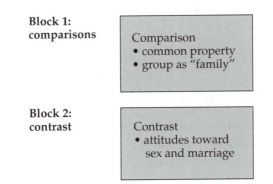

Block 1: comparisons

> Comparison
> • common property
> • group as "family"

Block 2: contrast

> Contrast
> • attitudes toward sex and marriage

You will want to use these same three methods—alternating, block, and mixed—in writing longer essays. In the following essay, the writer uses the alternating method of organization to contrast types of people.

There are only two types of people in the world, Type A and Type Z. It isn't hard to tell which type you are. How long before the plane leaves do you arrive at the airport?

Point 1: catching a plane

Early plane-catchers, Type A, pack their bags at least a day in advance, and they pack neatly. If they're booked on a flight that leaves at four in the afternoon, they get up at 5:30 that morning. If they haven't left the house by noon, they're worried about missing the plane.

Late plane-catchers, Type Z, pack hastily at the last minute and arrive at the airport too late to buy a newspaper.

Point 2: reading a book

What do you do with a new book? Type A reads more carefully and finishes every book, even though it isn't any good.

Type Z skims through a lot of books and is more apt to write in the margins with a pencil.

Point 3: eating breakfast

Type A eats a good breakfast; Type Z grabs a cup of coffee.

Point 4: turning off lights

Type As turn off the lights when leaving a room and lock the doors when leaving a house. They go back to make sure they've locked it, and they worry later about whether they left the iron on or not. They didn't.

Type Zs leave the lights burning and if they lock the door at all when they leave the house, they're apt to have forgotten their keys.

Point 5: seeing the dentist

Type A sees the dentist twice a year, has an annual physical checkup and thinks he may have something.

Type Z has been meaning to see a doctor.

Point 6: using toothpaste

> Type A squeezes a tube of toothpaste from the bottom, rolls it very carefully as he uses it and puts the top back on every time.
> Type Z squeezes the tube from the middle, and he's lost the cap under the radiator.

Point 7: other characteristics

> Type Zs are more apt to have some Type A characteristics than Type As are apt to have any Type Z characteristics.

Point 8: marriage

> Type As always marry Type Zs.
> Type Zs always marry Type As.

Andy Rooney,
"Types"

The comparison and contrast mode of development gives Rooney a framework for making use of **irony**. Irony is a device used by writers to imply something different or the opposite from what is actually stated. Here, Rooney uses irony for its humorous effect, with the ultimate irony being that Type As and Type Zs always marry their opposites.

Comparison and contrast, like classification and division, is a useful mode of development for writing on the academic subjects you will study in college courses. You will encounter it in textbooks, with comparison indicated by such transitional words as *similarly* and *by comparison* and contrast by *however, on the other hand,* and *on the contrary*. If you become comfortable with this mode, it will come in handy in your writing for other courses. Be alert, for example, to essay assignments and exam questions that begin "Compare and contrast . . ."

In the readings that follow, you will find the alternating, block, and mixed methods of comparison-and-contrast development. You will also see the variety of ideas that writers express through comparison and contrast.

Dogs and Cats

Konrad Lorenz

Konrad Lorenz tells us what our dogs and cats have in common and how they differ.

Words to Know

carnivores   meat-eating animals
domesticated   tamed
servitude   in service or bondage to another person
sphere   range
uncompromising   firm, unchanging

Getting Started

What pets do you have or have you had in the past?

Only two animals have entered the human household otherwise than as prisoners and become domesticated by other means than those of enforced servitude: the dog and the cat. Two things they have in common, namely, that both belong to the order of carnivores and both serve man in their capacity of hunters. In all other characteristics, above all in the manner of their association with man, they are as different as the night from the day. There is no domestic animal that has so radically altered its whole way of living, indeed its whole sphere of interests, that has become domestic in so true a sense as the dog; and there is no animal that, in the course of its centuries-old association with man, has altered so little as the cat. There is some truth in the assertion that the cat, with the exception of a few luxury breeds, such as Angoras, Persians and Siamese, is no domestic animal but a completely wild being. Maintaining its full independence it has taken up its abode in the houses and outhouses of man, for the simple reason that there are more mice there than elsewhere. The whole charm of the dog lies in the depth of the friendship and the strength of the spiritual ties with which he has bound himself to man, but the appeal of the cat lies in the very fact that she has formed no close bond with him, that she has the uncompromising independence of a tiger or a leopard while she is hunting in his stables and barns, that she still remains mysterious and remote when she is rubbing herself gently against the legs of her mistress or purring contentedly in front of the fire.

Questions About the Reading

1. What do a dog and a cat have in common?
2. How do a dog and a cat differ?
3. Why does a cat want to live in houses and outhouses?
4. How do a dog and a cat differ in their association with their owners?

Questions About the Writer's Strategies

1. What method of comparison and contrast does the writer use?
2. Could the paragraph be made into more than one paragraph? If so, how?
3. What is the main idea of the paragraph? Is it stated or implied? If stated, identify the sentences. If implied, state it in your own words.

Writing Assignments

1. Write a paragraph in which you compare and contrast the behavior of your pets or those of your friends. Identify the method or methods you used.
2. Visit a zoo and watch two different animals. Write a paragraph in which you explain the behaviors they have in common and those in which they differ. Identify the method or methods you used.

Yin and Yang

Mary Paumier Jones

The yin-yang symbol comes from ancient Chinese cosmology. It represents both the dark and the light, or shaded and sunlit, sides of a mountain. The "yin" represents the female or shaded aspects of the symbol such as the earth, darkness, and passivity. The "yang" represents the male aspects of the symbol, such as light, sun, and activity. In this paragraph from her essay, "The Opposite of Saffron," Mary Paumier Jones explains that the yin and yang movements in T'ai Chi, a Chinese form of exercise, form a perfect balance. (Adapted from **http://www2.cybernex .net/~jefkirsh/symbol.html.***)*

Words to Know

inscrutably   obscurely, mysteriously

intercourse   communication

simultaneous   at the same time

Getting Started

How are walking and running alike? How are they different?

In T'ai Chi class Dr. Young talked about yin and yang. In the beginning square form, each movement is followed by a pause: the movement is yin, the pause yang. To my Western ears this smacks of sexism; the masculine principle acting, the feminine doing nothing. But I eventually begin to learn the pause is not nothing. Given its proper weight, gravity, and time, the pause does its work, its stretch, its subtle modification of the quality of the move before and the one to come. Later in the round form, the movement is continuous. Yin and yang, though still opposite, are inscrutably simultaneous, engaged in an ancient abstract intercourse.

Questions About the Reading

1. What is yin and what is yang in the beginning square form of T'ai Chi?
2. Why does the writer think yin and yang "smacks of sexism"?
3. What is the purpose of the pause?
4. How does the round form of T'ai Chi differ from the square?

Questions About the Writer's Strategies

1. What is the main idea of the paragraph? Is it stated or implied?
2. What is the point of view (person, time, tone) of the paragraph?
3. Is the point of view consistent throughout the paragraph? If not, where and in what way does it change?
4. If the point of view in the paragraph changes, is the change acceptable? Why or why not?

Writing Assignments

1. Write an essay about two sports you have played, explaining how the sports are alike and how they are different.
2. Write an essay about two subjects you have studied in school and explain how they are alike and how they are different.

Good Girl, Bad Girl

Anna Quindlen

Understanding why two people become friends is sometimes difficult. In this paragraph, essayist Anna Quindlen provides a candid assessment of an unbalanced friendship from her days at a boarding school for girls.

Words to Know

dialectical   having to do with two opposite or contradictory forces

naïve   innocent

refectory   cafeteria, dining hall

Getting Started

What is it that attracts two friends to each other?

She was my best friend, and hard as it may have been to figure by the looks of us, she was the good girl, I the bad. I suppose everyone has at least one friendship like this in their lives. We were dialectical, she the thesis, I the antithesis. She was direct, trustworthy, kind, and naïve; I was manipulative, selfish, and clever. She laughed at all my jokes, took part in all my schemes, told everyone that I was the smartest and the funniest and the best. Like a B movie of boarding school life, we stole peanut butter from the refectory, short-sheeted beds, called drugstores and asked them if they had Prince Albert in a can. Whenever I hear a mother say, "If so-and-so told you to jump off the Brooklyn Bridge, would you do it?" I think of her. On my order, she would have jumped.

Questions About the Reading

1. How do you imagine the author and her friend looked? Reread the first sentence before you describe the two girls.
2. What does the writer mean when she says that her exploits were "like a B movie of boarding school life"?
3. Does the writer believe she and her friend had a healthy relationship? Why or why not?

Questions About the Writer's Strategies

1. Is the writer's mode of development comparison, contrast, or a combination of the two?
2. What other mode of development does the writer use?
3. What words does the writer use to describe herself? What words does she use to describe how her friend thought of her?
4. What simile does the author use to describe the friendship?

Writing Assignments

1. Write a narrative paragraph that compares your personality with that of one of your closest friends.
2. Write a paragraph in which you compare and contrast a childhood friendship with a current friendship.
3. In a paragraph, compare and contrast a relationship between friends with one between brothers and sisters. Use examples from your own experience to illustrate similarities and differences.

Two Diversities

Peter Wood

*In the following two paragraphs, Peter Wood explains the relation
between Diversity I and Diversity II.*

Words to Know

approximated   came close or near to
diversiphile   a person who supports diversity
profound   deep

Getting Started

Did you visit other colleges before you chose the one you now
attend?

———————

Among the many meanings of diversity, let's for the moment distin-   1
guish two: the actual racial and ethnic condition of America, which I will
call *diversity I,* and the diversiphile ideal of how American society should
recognize and respond to its racial and ethnic composition, which I will
call *diversity II.* In principle, it ought to be easy to distinguish between
them. One refers to the facts, the other to hopes or wishes. *Diversity I* is
the sort of thing that we might expect could be counted, or at least
approximated with wide agreement. We know with reasonable certainty, for example, that about 13 percent of the U.S. population consid-
ers itself of African descent. We can and do argue with one another over
the significance of this fact, but the fact itself is not seriously in dispute.

Diversity II by contrast, is an ideal. It expresses a vision of society in   2
which people divide themselves into separate groups, each with profound traditions of its own, but held together by mutual esteem, respect,
and tolerance. It would be futile, however, to look for general agreement
about the exact details of this ideal. Many Americans do not share it, and
even among those who do profess a favorable view, opinions vary as to
what precisely a truly *diverse* society should be. *Diversity II* supporters
do, however, often translate their ideal into numerical "goals" for particular situations—and they do so by invoking *diversity I.* So, for example, we hear that because 13 percent of Americans are of African descent,
13 percent of TV anchormen should be of African descent. The basic
political program of *diversity II* advocates (the diversiphiles) is to create
a society in which the real diversity of society at large is *proportionally*

represented in schools, colleges, the workplace, government, the arts, and all other positively valued social contexts. Thus *diversity II*, the ideal, depends—at least in principle—on *diversity I*, the facts.

———————

Questions About the Reading

1. What are the distinctions the writer makes between the two diversities?
2. According to the writer, what is *diversity I* based on?
3. What is the "vision" of society under *diversity II*?
4. What are the "goals" of supporters of *diversity II*?

Questions About the Writer's Strategies

1. What is the main idea of the paragraphs?
2. What method or methods of comparison and contrast does the writer use?
3. Besides comparison and contrast, what other modes of development does the writer use?
4. Are the paragraphs objective or subjective?

Writing Assignments

1. Write one or two paragraphs in which you compare and contrast two or more colleges you have visited. Identify the methods you have used.
2. Write one or more paragraphs in which you compare and contrast the neighborhoods in your town. Identify the methods you have used.
3. Write one or more paragraphs in which you compare and contrast two sports events you have attended or have watched on TV. Identify the methods you used.

Neat People vs. Sloppy People

Suzanne Britt

In this essay from her book Show and Tell, *Suzanne Britt explains the differences between neat and sloppy people, claiming—surprisingly—that neat people are lazier and meaner than sloppy people.*

Words to Know

cavalier   easygoing, offhand
meticulously   excessively
métier   occupation
rectitude   character, principles

Getting Started

How would you characterize neat people and sloppy people?

I've finally figured out the difference between neat people and sloppy people. The distinction is, as always, moral. Neat people are lazier and meaner than sloppy people.

Sloppy people, you see, are not really sloppy. Their sloppiness is merely the unfortunate consequence of their extreme moral rectitude. Sloppy people carry in their mind's eye a heavenly vision, a precise plan, that is so stupendous, so perfect, it can't be achieved in this world or the next.

Sloppy people live in Never-Never Land. Someday is their métier. Someday they are planning to alphabetize all their books and set up home catalogs. Someday they will go through their wardrobes and mark certain items for tentative mending and certain items for passing on to relatives of similar shape and size. Someday sloppy people will make family scrapbooks into which they will put newspaper clippings, postcards, locks of hair, and the dried corsage from their senior prom. Someday they will file everything on the surface on their desk, including the cash receipts from coffee purchases at the snack shop. Someday they will sit down and read all the back issues of *The New Yorker*.

For all these noble reasons and more, sloppy people never get neat. They aim too high and wide. They save everything, planning someday to file, order, and straighten out the world. But while these ambitious plans take clearer and clearer shape in their heads, the books spill from the shelves onto the floor, the clothes pile up in the hamper and closet, the family mementos accumulate in every drawer, the surface of the desk is buried under mounds of paper, and the unread magazines threaten to reach the ceiling.

Sloppy people can't bear to part with anything. They give loving 5 attention to every detail. When sloppy people say they're going to tackle the surface of the desk, they really mean it. Not a paper will go unturned; not a rubber band will go unboxed. Four hours or two weeks into the excavation, the desk looks exactly the same, primarily because the sloppy person is meticulously creating new piles of papers with new headings and scrupulously stopping to read all the old book catalogs before he throws them away. A neat person would just bulldoze the desk.

Neat people are bums and clods at heart. They have cavalier attitudes 6 toward possessions, including family heirlooms. Everything is just another dust-catcher to them. If anything collects dust, it's got to go and that's that. Neat people will toy with the idea of throwing the children out of the house just to cut down on the clutter.

Neat people don't care about process. They like results. What they 7 want to do is get the whole thing over with so they can sit down and watch the rasslin' on TV. Neat people operate on two unvarying principles: Never handle any item twice, and throw everything away.

The only thing messy in a neat person's house is the trash can. The 8 minute something comes to a neat person's hand, he will look at it, try to decide if it has immediate use and, finding none, throw it in the trash.

Neat people are especially vicious with mail. They never go through 9 their mail unless they are standing directly over a trash can. If the trash can is beside the mailbox, even better. All ads, catalogs, pleas for charitable contributions, church bulletins and money-saving coupons go straight into the trash can without being opened. All letters from home, postcards from Europe, bills and paychecks are opened, immediately responded to, then dropped in the trash can. Neat people keep their receipts only for tax purposes. That's it. No sentimental salvaging of birthday cards or the last letter a dying relative ever wrote. Into the trash it goes.

Neat people place neatness above everything, even economics. They 10 are incredibly wasteful. Neat people throw away several toys every time they walk through the den. I knew a neat person once who threw away a perfectly good dish drainer because it had mold on it. The drainer was too much trouble to wash. And neat people sell their furniture when they move. They will sell a La-Z-Boy recliner while you are reclining in it.

Neat people are no good to borrow from. Neat people buy everything 11 in expensive little single portions. They get their flour and sugar in two-pound bags. They wouldn't consider clipping a coupon, saving a leftover, reusing plastic non-dairy whipped cream containers or rinsing off tin foil and draping it over the unmoldy dish drainer. You can never borrow a neat person's newspaper to see what's playing at the movies. Neat people have the paper all wadded up and in the trash by 7:05 A.M.

Neat people cut a clean swath through the organic as well as the inorganic world. People, animals, and things are all one to them. They are so insensitive. After they've finished with the pantry, the medicine cabinet, and the attic, they will throw out the red geranium (too many leaves), sell the dog (too many fleas), and send the children off to boarding school (too many scuff marks on the hardwood floors). 　12

Questions About the Reading

1. What is the reason, according to the writer, that people are sloppy?
2. What do sloppy people intend to do with everything they keep?
3. Why do sloppy people never get neat?
4. Why are people neat?
5. How do neat people handle their mail?

Questions About the Writer's Strategies

1. What is the comparison/contrast method used by the writer?
2. What is the topic of each paragraph, beginning with the second?
3. Is each topic stated in a sentence? If so, what are the topic sentences?
4. What is the tone of the essay? Is it consistent throughout?

Writing Assignments

1. Write an essay in which you compare/contrast shopping in different grocery stores.
2. *Working Together* Join with some classmates to compare/contrast how people in different neighborhoods keep their yards.

Conversational Ballgames

Nancy Masterson Sakamoto

The difference between Western and Japanese conversation styles is like the difference between tennis or volleyball and bowling, according to Nancy Sakamoto in this essay from her book Polite Fictions. *She is an American married to a Japanese man and is a professor of American Studies at a Japanese university.*

Words to Know

elaboration   further information; additional details
indispensable   necessary, essential
unconsciously   unknowingly

Getting Started

Is there a difference between the way you talk to a friend and the way you talk to a teacher, a stranger, or an older person?

———————————

After I was married and had lived in Japan for a while, my Japanese 1
gradually improved to the point where I could take part in simple conversations with my husband and his friends and family. And I began to notice that often, when I joined in, the others would look startled, and the conversational topic would come to a halt. After this happened several times, it became clear to me that I was doing something wrong. But for a long time, I didn't know what it was.

Finally, after listening carefully to many Japanese conversations, I dis- 2
covered what my problem was. Even though I was speaking Japanese, I was handling the conversation in a western way.

Japanese-style conversations develop quite differently from western- 3
style conversations. And the difference isn't only in the languages. I realized that just as I kept trying to hold western-style conversations even when I was speaking Japanese, so my English students kept trying to hold Japanese-style conversations even when they were speaking English. We were unconsciously playing entirely different conversational ball games.

A western-style conversation between two people is like a game of 4
tennis. If I introduce a topic, a conversational ball, I expect you to hit it back. If you agree with me, I don't expect you simply to agree and do nothing more. I expect you to add something—a reason for agreeing,

another example, or an elaboration to carry the idea further. But I don't expect you always to agree. I am just as happy if you question me, or challenge me, or completely disagree with me. Whether you agree or disagree, your response will return the ball to me.

And then it is my turn again. I don't serve a new ball from my origi- 5
nal starting line. I hit your ball back again from where it has bounced. I carry your idea further, or answer your questions or objections, or challenge or question you. And so the ball goes back and forth, with each of us doing our best to give it a new twist, an original spin, or a powerful smash.

And the more vigorous the action, the more interesting and exciting 6
the game. Of course, if one of us gets angry, it spoils the conversation, just as it spoils a tennis game. But getting excited is not at all the same as getting angry. After all, we are not trying to hit each other. We are trying to hit the ball. So long as we attack only each other's opinions, and do not attack each other personally, we don't expect anyone to get hurt. A good conversation is supposed to be interesting and exciting.

If there are more than two people in the conversation, then it is like 7
doubles in tennis, or like volleyball. There's no waiting in line. Whoever is nearest and quickest hits the ball, and if you step back, someone else will hit it. No one stops the game to give you a turn. You're responsible for taking your own turn.

But whether it's two players or a group, everyone does his best to 8
keep the ball going, and no one person has the ball for very long.

A Japanese-style conversation, however, is not at all like tennis or vol- 9
leyball. It's like bowling. You wait for your turn. And you always know your place in line. It depends on such things as whether you are older or younger, a close friend or a relative stranger to the previous speaker, in a senior or junior position, and so on.

When your turn comes, you step up to the starting line with your 10
bowling ball, and carefully bowl it. Everyone else stands back and watches politely, murmuring encouragement. Everyone waits until the ball has reached the end of the alley, and watches to see if it knocks down all the pins, or only some of them, or none of them. There is a pause, while everyone registers your score.

Then, after everyone is sure that you have completely finished your 11
turn, the next person in line steps up to the same starting line, with a different ball. He doesn't return your ball, and he does not begin from where your ball stopped. There is no back and forth at all. All the balls run parallel. And there is always a suitable pause between turns. There is no rush, no excitement, no scramble for the ball.

No wonder everyone looked startled when I took part in Japanese 12
conversations. I paid no attention to whose turn it was, and kept snatch-

ing the ball halfway down the alley and throwing it back at the bowler. Of course the conversation died. I was playing the wrong game.

This explains why it is almost impossible to get a western-style con- 13 versation or discussion going with English students in Japan. I used to think that the problem was their lack of English language ability. But I finally came to realize that the biggest problem is that they, too, are play- ing the wrong game.

Whenever I serve a volleyball, everyone just stands back and watches 14 it fall, with occasional murmurs of encouragement. No one hits it back. Everyone waits until I call on someone to take a turn. And when that person speaks, he doesn't hit my ball back. He serves a new ball. Again, everyone just watches it fall.

So I call on someone else. This person does not refer to what the pre- 15 vious speaker has said. He also serves a new ball. Nobody seems to have paid any attention to what anyone else has said. Everyone begins again from the same starting line, and all the balls run parallel. There is never any back and forth. Everyone is trying to bowl with a volleyball.

And if I try a simpler conversation, with only two of us, then the other 16 person tries to bowl with my tennis ball. No wonder foreign English teachers in Japan get discouraged.

Now that you know about the difference in the conversational ball- 17 games, you may think that all your troubles are over. But if you have been trained all your life to play one game, it is no simple matter to switch to another, even if you know the rules. Knowing the rules is not at all the same thing as playing the game.

Even now, during a conversation in Japanese I will notice a startled 18 reaction, and belatedly realize that once again I have rudely interrupted by instinctively trying to hit back the other person's bowling ball. It is no easier for me to "just listen" during a conversation, than it is for my Japanese students to "just relax" when speaking with foreigners. Now I can truly sympathize with how hard they must find it to try to carry on a western-style conversation.

If I have not yet learned to do conversational bowling in Japanese, at 19 least I have figured out one thing that puzzled me for a long time. After his first trip to America, my husband complained that Americans asked him so many questions and made him talk so much at the dinner table that he never had a chance to eat. When I asked him why he couldn't talk and eat at the same time, he said that Japanese do not customarily think that dinner, especially on fairly formal occasions, is a suitable time for extended conversation.

Since westerners think that conversation is an indispensable part of 20 dining, and indeed would consider it impolite not to converse with one's dinner partner, I found this Japanese custom rather strange. Still, I could accept it as a cultural difference even though I didn't really understand it. But when my husband added, in explanation, that Japanese consider it extremely rude to talk with one's mouth full, I got confused. Talking with one's mouth full is certainly not an American custom. We think it very rude, too. Yet we still manage to talk a lot and eat at the same time. How do we do it?

For a long time, I couldn't explain it, and it bothered me. But after I discovered the conversational ballgames, I finally found the answer. Of course! In a western-style conversation, you hit the ball, and while someone else is hitting it back, you take a bite, chew, and swallow. Then you hit the ball again, and then eat some more. The more people there are in the conversation, the more chances you have to eat. But even with only two of you talking, you still have plenty of chances to eat.   21

Maybe that's why polite conversation at the dinner table has never been a traditional part of Japanese etiquette. Your turn to talk would last so long without interruption that you'd never get a chance to eat.   22

Questions About the Reading

1. How did the writer's Japanese husband, family, and friends react to her participation in conversations?
2. What does the writer say was wrong with how she was handling the conversations?
3. How does the writer characterize Western-style conversation? To what does she compare Western-style conversation?
4. How does the writer characterize Japanese-style conversation? To what does she compare Japanese-style conversation?
5. What did the writer's Japanese husband complain about after his first trip to America?

Questions About the Writer's Strategies

1. What is the thesis of the essay?
2. What method of comparison-and-contrast organization does the writer use?
3. What is the simile the writer uses for a Western-style conversation between two people? What simile does she use for a conversation among several people?
4. What simile does the writer use for a Japanese-style conversation?
5. How do Westerners manage to carry on a conversation while they are eating and not talk with their mouths full?

6. Does the writer use any mode of development in addition to contrast? If so, what is it and in which paragraphs is it found?

Writing Assignments

1. Write an essay in which you contrast the way you talk to your best friends with the way you talk to neighborhood or school friends. Use dialogue to illustrate the differences.
2. Go to a shopping mall and listen to the people who are walking around or working in the stores. Classify the different people you see and write an essay in which you compare and/or contrast their conversations.

Aiming for Success?

Marvin Olasky

Marvin Olasky, a professor at the University of Texas, uses two sports figures—Kevin Mitchell and Michael Jordan—to advise incoming students about what it takes to succeed. He shared his advice in this article, written in the fall of 1997.

Words to Know

exhilaration   excitement
predestining   deciding in advance

Getting Started

What do you think you need to do to successfully reach your career goal? What do you need not to do?

Students will be heading off to college soon, and as a professor I know 1
the pattern. For the first few weeks, the exhilaration of new beginnings
reigns. Then the grind commences. I know a little about sports, so when
they start muttering about their workload, I'm ready to ask, "Who do
you want to be—Kevin Mitchell or Michael Jordan"?

I've encountered each of those talented athletes twice, once up close 2
and once from afar. Each time, I was impressed with the difference.

My first encounters came in 1993 and 1994, when I was visiting 3
spring-training camps with my sons, interviewing players and writing
magazine articles about what they believed concerning God.

Kevin Mitchell (no longer a household name) was so out of shape that 4
the other players made jokes about him. He said, "Whatever I do, the Big
Man Upstairs takes care of me." Mitchell had been the 1989 National
League Most Valuable Player, and his raw talent was the stuff of legend.
Often he took no batting practice. Before a 1994 game in Chicago, his
coaches gave him a scouting report on the pitcher. He didn't even look
at it. He just walked to the plate and hit a home run.

Also in 1994, history's greatest basketball player tried to transform 5
into a baseball player. Michael Jordan took batting practice for hours on
end, just as he'd taken shots at the basket. He said, "Every time I read
something negative about my being here, I think about God giving me
the opportunity to do something that I really like to do. I want to work

hard." In basketball, natural ability plus hard work helped Jordan excel. In baseball, despite hard work, he just couldn't hit.

My next encounter with them was this past June. Millions saw Jordan 6 play a game of hard-charging basketball with the flu as he led the Chicago Bulls to another championship. He told reporters, "It's a great feeling, I'm tired, I'm weak. I have a whole summer to recuperate."

Kevin Mitchell, meanwhile, was being released by the Cleveland 7 Indians. This spring they signed him for a half-million dollars, plus another $100,000 if he stayed under 240 pounds, plus another million if he played regularly. The goal was to get the 5-foot-11 player in shape, but he showed up at spring training weighing 270 and was unable to complete a half-mile training run. Jordan played championship basketball with a high temperature, but Mitchell missed game after game of relatively stationary baseball with minor complaints. (Once, predestining himself, he showed up at the ballpark wearing slippers and pajamas.)

A *Sports Illustrated* story about Mitchell early this year played his saga 8 for laughs. "Oft-injured Kevin Mitchell," Tom Verducci wrote, "loves toys and clubhouse high jinks." The overweight Mitchell, we were told, "Showed up late for spring training because he needed emergency dental work after munching on a microwaved chocolate donut."

The Mitchell story, however, is a tragedy of talent wasted. Former 9 manager Davey Johnson used to tell him, "Kevin, don't put on too much weight. . . . It will take a toll on your legs. Make a few sacrifices now." Mitchell did not make any sacrifices. His extra poundage made him vulnerable. He played in at least 150 games only once, the year he was voted MVP. As teams were awed by his talent and then frustrated by his sloth, Mitchell had a total of 10 stops, including one in Japan.

He went to Japan out of shape in 1995, hit the first pitch for a grand 10 slam, and then twisted his knee and was done. He joined the Boston Red Sox in 1996, sat out 10 days with a strained hamstring, had three hits, including a home run in his first game back, then reinjured the hamstring in the same game and spent six weeks on the disabled list.

Sports Illustrated excused some of his conduct: poor background, abu- 11 sive father; what can you expect? Puh-leeze: Mitchell had great opportunity—now he's not only out of shape but also out of baseball. My students have great opportunity: They are in the state's top university with time to learn and hours to burn. Some may have talent like Michael Jordan's in particular spheres, but they'll never make full use of it unless, in their work habits, they kick out the Kevin and be like Mike.

Questions About the Reading

1. What was the fundamental cause of Kevin Mitchell's failure?
2. Why does the writer tell his students about Mitchell and Michael Jordan?
3. When did the writer interview the players and what was he interviewing them for? How did the players answer the writer?
4. What did Mitchell do that caused his release by the Cleveland Indians?
5. What does the writer mean when he says his students need to "kick out the Kevin and be like Mike"?

Questions About the Writer's Strategies

1. What method(s) of comparison and contrast does the writer use?
2. Does the writer use any other modes of development in the essay? If so, what are they? Identify sentences and paragraphs to support your answer.
3. What is the thesis of the essay? Is it stated? If so, identify it; if not, state the thesis in your own words.
4. What is the tone of the essay?
5. Is the essay objective, subjective, or both? Support your answer with examples.

Writing Assignments

1. Write an essay in which you compare and/or contrast the work habits of two of your friends.
2. Write an essay in which you compare and/or contrast what you must and must not do to meet your career goals.

Super Bowl vs. the Oscars

Marc Levine

The writer claims that the Super Bowl and the Oscars tell us what we want to believe about ourselves.

Words to Know

ambivalence conflicting feelings
anonymous nameless, unknown
archetypal model, pattern
capricious changeable, unpredictable
exploited used
poignancy pain

Getting Started

What television programs do you watch on a regular basis?

They are the yin and yang of American public life, the moon and sun 1
of our communal rituals. Together, more Americans watch them than
attend church or vote in presidential elections. One is a festival of cul-
mination, a final day of revelry before packing it in for the rest of the
long, dark winter. The other is a rite of spring, featuring a parade of
latter-day fertility gods and goddesses clad in outlandish designer garb.

They are, of course, the Super Bowl and the Oscars. Like it or not, they 2
are America's preeminent means of announcing itself to the world; we
can share our ideals with hundreds of millions of our friends (and enemies) around the planet.

In tandem, the two events unfold the larger-than-life story that we 3
most want to believe about ourselves: that we love fame but reward dili-
gence; that we are ferocious but fair; and that we worship fleeting
beauty and enduring courage, glamour and self-effacement, in equal
measure. If the Super Bowl and the Oscars did not already exist, surely
we would have to create them.

Both are the domain of those with extraordinary physical attributes— 4
those who are stronger, or more beautiful, or more adept, or less averse
to pain than we are. One emphasizes the spirit of collective effort, by
gathering anonymous men in identical uniforms—even their faces are
largely concealed—to sacrifice themselves for the shared ideals of the
tribe. The other glorifies the exceptional individual, who is celebrated for

the very beauty and talent that sets him or her apart from lesser members of the species. Virtually anywhere there is a television—in Afghanistan, in Uruguay—these grand pageants are watched.

The grip they have on our collective imagination is hardly accidental. 5 It's deeply rooted in mythology. The Super Bowl tells the tale of a final battle. Although great men—the Joe Montanas and the Emmitt Smiths— shine under such circumstances, it is forever a contest between archetypal hordes, the Buccaneers and Raiders, the Cowboys and Steelers. Our attention may get diverted by peripheral narratives—this year, there was the issue of loyalty (coach John Gruden's) and a clash of two generations (Keyshawn Johnson vs. Jerry Rice).

But the dominant theme of the Super Bowl is that justice is best meted 6 out on the battlefield. Not surprisingly the theatrics of the event have a way of being exploited for political purposes—particularly during wartime. When President Nixon started a tradition of placing a congratulatory postgame phone call to the winning coach, U.S. involvement in Vietnam was dividing the country, much as the question of war against Iraq hung over this year's contest, lending a special poignancy to the countless shots of troops watching the game from remote stations.

No doubt, part of the Super Bowl's appeal is its ability to make us feel 7 more united than we actually are. After all, football is at its core a war game—a struggle in the trenches for turf between an offense and a defense—and the spectacle arouses enthusiasm for battle and assures us that the task can be done efficiently and reasonably.

Above all, the Super Bowl offers us a model of the kind of moral clar- 8 ity that can be elusive on the playing fields of our lives. Its scores are settled on neutral territory, and its teams are governed by inflexible rules. There is little room for favoritism or sentimentality or emotional nuance. Football knows right from wrong. The field is the great equalizer. Ivy League education and good looks will not save you when you are in the path of a steamrolling linebacker. The Super Bowl shows us a world we all can agree on—one in which, far removed from the messiness of everyday life, strength and skill and practical intelligence prevail. Its champions earn their trip to Disneyland, because they prove themselves to be rulers of a magical kingdom.

The Oscars, on the other hand, restore us to the ferment of the social 9 world. On Oscar night, we are voyeurs, luxuriating in desire, envy and scorn for those from whom we have been cordoned off. Oscar's realm of mythology allows charm, money, fame and influence to matter. Sex and youth count above all, which is why, to Oscar's disgrace, women over 40 (unless your name is Meryl Streep) are rarely on display. The identity of George Clooney's date is of great importance, and Julia Roberts' gown always will be a topic of conversation.

The results of the balloting may be certified by the folks at 10
PricewaterhouseCoopers—and who would distrust an accountant?—
but the voting itself is done in private, where the familiar traits of petti-
ness, jealousy, love and allegiance run amok. We practically expect an
undeserving nominee or two to walk away with an Oscar, because the
Academy Awards are played in the arena of human judgment and sub-
jectivity, and there are no referees.

Like Greek gods, the stars of the show are magnifications of the best 11
and worst in all of us. No matter that they arrive bedecked with jewels
or with a supermodel on their arm or with a complexion whose glow is
suspiciously youthful; at the Oscars they are stripped to their most vulnerable selves, utterly at the mercy of the unpredictable. Oscar is
unapologetically capricious. Sometimes he punishes worldly success
(Spielberg waited almost two decades to be called to the podium); sometimes he exalts it, absurdly, and treats it like art (*Titanic*). The Oscars give
us unfiltered human spectacle, in which one is either called to the stage
to meet with approval or forced to sit and contend with feelings of neglect and disappointment.

To call the Oscars an industry awards show is like calling the Super 12
Bowl a weekend football game. True, statuettes are handed out, and
plays are executed or botched. But the real distinction of these events is
that they bring us together, give us something to talk about and get us
caught up in a drama whose outcome is almost beside the point. (For
many of us, a friendly workplace wager is needed to help us decide
which team, or nominees, we favor.)

Although the Super Bowl and Oscars invariably are the most-watched 13
shows of the year—this year's game drew 88.6 million viewers, and
about half that many will struggle to stay awake into the wee hours for
next Sunday's Oscars—in most cases, we don't watch because we're
football fans or film buffs. Do you remember who played in last year's
Super Bowl? Will you be able to name the best foreign film two weeks
from now? We watch for the same reason we eat yams and marshmal-
lows on Thanksgiving: for the consoling sensation of tradition and
togetherness, as well as the shared experience of forging ahead into
changing times.

When Doug Williams became the first black quarterback to lead his 14
team in a Super Bowl—the year was 1988, the team was Washington,
and Williams was the MVP of the game—we all broke a racial barrier
together. Likewise last year, when Halle Berry and Denzel Washington
were the first African Americans to walk off with top acting prizes on the
same night, and it seemed possible that stardom, wealth and extrava-
gant sex appeal—oh, and talent, too—were finally colorblind. How can
we not care about Oscar and the Super Bowl? We live in America.

Super Bowl and Oscars: These twin phenomena, so much more than 15
simply sports and celebrity, hold up a fun-house mirror to us. At one
moment they show us the people we wish to be (judicious and strong, if
somewhat unemotional), and at the next they show us the people we
often are (fallible and impulsive, but deeply feeling). Both images are
powerful, because both are us—what advertisers would call the "core
attributes" of the American brand. Our typical ambivalence about mixing idealism with consumerism is allowed, thankfully, to be put on hold
for these two events. The commercialism is embraced because the Super
Bowl and the Oscars are the most stunning and persuasive commercials
for America that our culture produces. They are the Home Shopping
Network of us, and by tuning in, we express our passion as avid
consumers—of ourselves.

Questions About the Reading

1. What do the Super Bowl and the Oscars have in common?
2. What is the dominant theme of the Super Bowl?
3. How do the Oscars differ from the Super Bowl?
4. What is the disgrace of the Oscars?
5. According to the writer, why do we watch the Super Bowl and the
   Oscars?

Questions About the Writer's Strategies

1. What are the metaphors in the first paragraph?
2. What method of comparison and contrast does the writer use? Is the
   method consistent throughout the essay?
3. What is the thesis of the essay? State it in your own words.

Writing Assignments

1. *Working Together*   Join with some classmates and identify at least
   two television programs your group watches regularly. Write an
   essay in which you compare and contrast the programs. Identify the
   methods you have used.
2. Write an essay in which you compare and contrast two books (novels or nonfiction) or poems you have read recently. Identify the methods you have used.

Southern Comforts

Ann Patchett

The writer explains why Elvis Presley, Dale Earnhardt, and Eudora Welty are idolized by Southerners.

Words to Know

anthology   collection of written works
fundamental   basic, required

Getting Started

What historical landmarks are there in your town or state?

———————————

Had Elvis been from Detroit, he would have still had a brilliant career.   1
The difference between Northern Elvis and Southern Elvis would have come after the time of his death. In the North, his house would have been cleaned, sold, and bought by other people who would have actually lived there. Perhaps they would occasionally say to guests at dinner parties, "Did you know that Elvis Presley once lived in this house?" But Elvis was from the South, which means that for a price of a ticket you can stand behind velvet ropes at Graceland and look at the sad shag carpet in the Jungle Room or drive down to Tupelo, Miss., and tour the little house where he was born. He was, after all, a poor country boy who drove a delivery truck, loved his mother, and ate bad food, which means he had all the fundamental elements of Southern heroism. It takes a certain amount of storytelling to make a person into a myth, and that's something we've specialized in down here since Davy Crockett first cut his name into a tree. But as any good storyteller knows, the heroes we are most likely to root for are the ones who look like us.

Examining our collective regional affection for Dale Earnhardt and   2
Eudora Welty, you see a man who was like us and a woman who knew how to capture people like us. They were not people of whom you might say, "They remembered where they came from." That is a phrase that could be applied to Jerry Hall, who pays tribute to her Texas roots while running with the Rolling Stones in London. Earnhardt and Welty never left where they came from. Somehow, even while achieving their respective greatness, they did not outgrow us.

This does not mean that their appeal was limited to states that fought   3
for the Confederacy. Certainly they had legions of fans stretching from

Anaheim to Long Island City, but they were each particularly identified
with the region they came from and with the Southerners who loved
them and claimed them. However unlikely it may seem that a woman
who was considered the modern-day Chekhov and the man who was
the king of NASCAR could be embraced as cultural icons of a region, it
is true. They spoke for us, and in return we worshiped them.

You will never be Michael Jordan, no matter how much you practice. 4
He stays above us with his perfect combination of work, talent, and
genetic superiority, and we look on his splendor with awe. But the glory
of Dale Earnhardt felt somehow obtainable. Here was a guy who liked
to hunt and fish. A guy who would play cards and have a beer.

If Dale Earnhardt was able to be both a great NASCAR driver and one 5
of the guys, Eudora Welty used her brilliance and humanity to show us
the guys we thought we already knew, the ones who worked in post
offices and public schools, poor people and traveling salesmen. Every
school-age child in the south has read a Eudora Welty story in a literature anthology, and most of them have felt a twinge of recognition. She
did not live in New York and go to the right kinds of parties. She stayed
at home and took care of her mother, and we loved her for her stories.

It is a little-known fact that what Miss Welty loved was driving. What 6
people in Jackson remember is seeing her in her car, getting smaller and
smaller behind the wheel as the years went by. Late in her life, there was
talk that she had always wanted a Mercedes convertible, and we should
have bought her one, even if all she could have done at that point was
look at it parked out in the driveway.

While the country blurs together in an unbroken string of Gap T-shirts 7
and Filet-O-Fish sandwiches, the South is still hanging onto its regional
identity. Whether this has to do with the old scars of the Civil War, the
combination of heat and humidity, or the deep entrenchment of poverty,
I can't say. We feel separate, apart from the country we live in, and so we
love the people to whom we can point to and say, There, she is different
the way I am different. His daring acceleration, her fearless imagination
catches the corner of our identity.

I saw a car recently with a long metal street sign filling up its back 8
window. "Dale Earnhardt Ave.," it said. Meanwhile, Eudora Welty's
house is being made into a historic landmark, like Faulkner's house, like
Elvis's. They spoke for us. They were like us. How fortunate we are to
have their enormous legacies to point to when, in the future, we try to
explain who we are.

Questions About the Reading

1. How would Elvis Presley's house been treated if he had been from Detroit?
2. Why have Elvis's houses been treated as they have been?
3. What has the South specialized in? Why?
4. Why are Dale Earnhardt and Eudora Welty idolized in the South?

Questions About the Writer's Strategies

1. What is the main idea of the essay? State it in your own words.
2. In addition to comparison and contrast, what other modes of development does the writer use?
3. What is the metaphor in paragraph 7?
4. Is the essay objective or subjective? Identify sentences to support your answer.
5. What method of comparison and contrast does the writer use? Is the method consistent throughout the essay?

Writing Assignments

1. Identify at least two historical landmarks in your town or state and write an essay comparing and contrasting the landmarks and why they are important. Identify the method or methods you used.
2. Write an essay in which you compare and contrast neighborhoods or schools in your town. Identify the methods you use.

Process

IF YOU WANT to hook up your new computer, you will probably follow the directions, or a **process,** provided by the manufacturer. A **process** is a method of doing a task or a job, usually in orderly steps, to achieve a desired result. For example, directions and recipes are both detailed explanations of processes. So are all articles and essays that tell how to prepare for a job interview, assemble a stereo system, dress for success, or operate a personal computer. So, too, are essays that describe how someone else used a process to accomplish something or complete a task.

In an essay explaining how to carry out a process, the writer needs to give clear and accurate guidance or directions, making the steps as simple as possible for the reader to follow. To do this, the writer must decide exactly what the reader already knows and what he or she needs to be told. The burden is on the writer to provide complete information to enable the reader to perform the task. If the writer forgets to mention how long the cookies should bake, the cook may be left with burned chocolate-chip cookies and disappointed friends.

The written explanation of such a process must be organized with particular care. Each step or part of the directions should be discussed in the same order as it occurs in the process. The following sample paragraph is a recipe for shrimp—one you might want to try. Notice that the writer begins with the purchase of the shrimp and then proceeds, step by step, through preparing, cooking, and serving the shrimp.

Topic sentence   When fresh shrimp can be had, have it. What size? Medium
for reasons of economy and common sense. Huge shrimps

Step 1:
choose size

Step 2:
choose quantity

Step 3: shell
shrimp

Step 4: cooking
directions

are magnificently expensive while small ones come in such numbers per pound that shelling them becomes slave labor. Buy two pounds of fresh shrimp and shell them. First, with a thumbnail pinch the tail shell hard crosswise (so the tail segments will come out intact), then handle the headless animals like so many pea pods; split them lengthwise, save the contents, and throw the husks away. Sauté the shrimp with three crushed garlic cloves in two-thirds of a stick of butter. When the shrimp turn pink, add a 12-ounce can of Italian tomatoes (which taste better than the fresh super-market kind), two bay leaves, a teaspoon of dried oregano, a half-cup of dry white wine, and the juice of a lemon. Simmer for ten minutes, sprinkle with chopped parsley and serve with rice.

Philip Kopper,
"Delicacies de la Mer"

Because this paragraph is telling the reader what to do, the **point of view** is **second person** (you), and it is in the present tense (*come, buy, save, throw,* and so forth). But the word *you* is unstated, which makes the paragraph seem to address the reader even more directly. This **tone** is commonly used in process writing that instructs the reader.

Not all process essays are such clear-cut models of process writing as the previous example. In some cases, a paragraph or essay describing a process may serve a purpose similar to that of a **narrative** or a **description.** That is, whereas strictly process writing is intended primarily to **instruct,** process writing also can be adapted to situations in which the writer mainly wants to **inform** or **describe.** In such cases, a process is often combined with narration and description, as in the following example. Notice that in describing the process—the way the woman packs her suitcases and leaves the house—the writer describes her character. You also know, by the contrast between her habits and those of her husband, that her basic character differs sharply from his. By detailing the process of packing and combining it with other narrative details, the writer tells you indirectly what has previously happened in the woman's life.

Introduction—
narrative

Step 1:
preparation

Step 2: finding
suitcases

He slammed the door angrily behind him, and she heard the squeal of the tires as he raced off in the car. For a moment, she felt her usual fear. She knew he shouldn't drive after he'd been drinking heavily.   1

But then she turned, went to the linen closet, and took out a clean towel. She spread the towel out on her neatly made bed.   2

Next, she got her overnight bag and a larger suitcase from the closet and put them carefully on the towel on her bed.   3

Step 3: packing
suitcases

⌐ Methodically, she took neatly folded underwear, stockings, and nightgowns from her drawers and packed them in neat rows in the two bags. One set in the overnight bag, and five in the larger suitcase. She laid aside a nightgown with a matching robe to pack last.

Next, she lifted dresses and suits, carefully hung on the   4
hangers and buttoned up so they wouldn't wrinkle, from her closet and folded them into the larger suitcase. Two extra blouses and a dress went into the overnight bag. She'd wear the suit she had on.

She brought plastic bags from the kitchen and put her   5
shoes into them. One pair went into the overnight bag; two pairs, one for the dresses and one for the suits, went into the larger bag. Then she put her bedroom slippers and the nightgown with the matching robe on top of the other clothes in the overnight bag. She would take only the overnight bag into her parents' house, at least at first. No need for them to know right away that this time was for more than one night. They'd always said that she wasn't going to change him and that the marriage wouldn't last.

Step 4: final
check and look
around

⌐ She sighed again, closed the suitcases, carried them out to   6
her car, and then went back into the house for one last look around. Almost ready, she took her coat from the hall closet, folded it carefully over her arm, and took a last look at his shoes and socks left beside his chair and the newspaper flung across the couch where it would leave newsprint on the upholstery. She left the shoes and socks but couldn't resist folding the newspaper and putting it on a table. Finally, she went out, closed the door silently behind her, got into her car, and drove quietly and slowly away.

As you started reading this essay, you probably realized right away that it would be more narrative and descriptive than instructive of a process. Two signals that alerted you are that the point of view is **third person** (*she*) and past tense (*took, packed, lifted, laid,* and so on). Think, for a minute, about writing a clear process explanation using that person and tense. Experienced writers may use varying **points of view** in process writing, but for clear point-by-point process explanations, the **second person** (*you*), the present tense (*take, pour, measure*), and a straightforward tone are the most common.

Although a process approach can sometimes be useful in writing narratives and descriptions that deal with significant activities or accomplishments, you usually will use process for giving directions, describing how a mechanical gadget works, or reporting on science experiments. In these situations you may combine process with other modes like **definition** (chapter 9), **examples** (chapter 4), and **cause and effect** (chapter 8). Always remember that three factors are essential to an effective process essay. First, be sure that the steps or procedures are carefully organized, step by step—usually in the same order as they should be carried out—so that the reader can understand and follow your explanation. Second, be sure that you include any information that the reader needs about any special materials or preliminary steps. And, third, include *all* the specific steps in the process.

Brewing Beer

Grace Lichtenstein

It's a lengthy and exacting process to produce a bottle of Coors beer.

Words to Know

amber   brownish gold color
fermentation   breakdown of molecules in a compound

Getting Started

What is your favorite dessert? What is the process in making that dessert?

Like other beers, Coors [Beer] is produced from barley. Most of the big Midwestern brewers use barley grown in North Dakota and Minnesota. Coors is the single American brewer to use a Moravian strain, grown under company supervision, on farms in Colorado, Idaho, Wyoming and Montana. At the brewery, the barley is turned into malt by being soaked in water—which must be biologically pure and of a known mineral content—for several days, causing it to sprout and producing a chemical change—breaking down starch into sugar. The malt is toasted, a process that halts the sprouting and determines the color and sweetness (the more the roasting, the darker, more bitter the beer). It is ground into flour and brewed, with more pure water, in huge copper-domed kettles until it is the consistency of oatmeal. Rice and refined starch are added to make mash; solids are strained out, leaving an amber liquid malt extract, which is boiled with hops—the dried cones from the hop vine which add to the bitterness, or tang. The hops are strained, yeast is added, turning the sugar to alcohol, and the beer is aged in huge red vats at near-freezing temperatures for almost two months, during which the second fermentation takes place and the liquid becomes carbonated, or bubbly. (Many breweries chemically age their beer to speed up production; Coors people say only naturally aged brew can be called a true "lager."). Next, the beer is filtered through cellulose filters to remove bacteria, and finally is pumped into cans, bottles or kegs for shipping.

Questions About the Reading

1. What is different about the grain used by Coors from that of other brewers?
2. What are the products used in making beer?
3. What is special about the water used in producing beer?
4. What are the steps followed in making beer?
5. What makes beer carbonated or bubbly? What is necessary to make a beer called "lager"?

Questions About the Writer's Strategies

1. What is the writer's purpose in explaining the beer-making process?
2. What is the point of view in the paragraph? Is it consistent?
3. In addition to process, what other modes of development are used by the writer?

Writing Assignments

1. Write a paragraph in which you explain the process of making your favorite dessert.
2. Write a paragraph in which you explain the process of registering for classes.

The Marginal World

Rachel Carson

The shoreline of the sea is ever-changing, and Rachel Carson explains the process that causes the changes.

Words to Know

receded   fell back

warps   bends, twists

Getting Started

What is the process you follow in getting ready for school, doing your grocery shopping, or cleaning your bedroom?

―――――――――――――

The edge of the sea is a strange and beautiful place. All through the long history of Earth it has been an area of unrest where waves have broken heavily against the land, where the tides have pressed forward over the continents, receded, and then returned. For no two successive days is the shore line precisely the same. Not only do the tides advance and retreat in their eternal rhythms, but the level of the sea itself is never at rest. It rises or falls as the glaciers melt or grow, as the floor of the deep ocean basins shifts under its increasing load of sediments, or as the earth's crust along the continental margins warps up or down in adjustment to strain and tension. Today a little more land may belong to the sea, tomorrow a little less. Always the edge of the sea remains an elusive and indefinable boundary.

―――――――――――――

Questions About the Reading

1. What is the process that causes the shoreline of the sea to change?
2. What actions cause the level of the sea to change?

Questions About the Writer's Strategies

1. What is the main idea of the paragraph? Is it stated or implied? If stated, identify the sentences. If implied, state the idea in your own words.

2. What is the writer's purpose?
3. Has the writer used any modes of development in addition to process? If so, what are they?
4. What is the tone of the paragraph?

Writing Assignments

1. Write a paragraph in which you explain the process you follow in getting ready for school.
2. Write a paragraph in which you explain the process you follow in doing your grocery shopping.
3. Write a paragraph in which you explain the process you follow in cleaning your bedroom.

The Right Way to Eat an Ice-Cream Cone

L. Rust Hills

Rust Hills was fiction editor of Esquire *and the* Saturday Evening Post, *and is now a free-lance writer. In this paragraph, taken from his book* How To Do Things Right, *he explains his technique, which was perfected through years of taking his children to ice-cream cone stands. Having told us the preliminary pitfalls—melted ice cream on car upholstery, choosing a flavor, holding more than one cone—he delivers the ultimate instructions on eating the cone.*

Words to Know

forgoing   deciding against
jostling   bumping together
molecules   very small particles
stance   way of standing

Getting Started

What is the best or right way to eat spaghetti?

Grasp the cone with the right hand firmly but gently between thumb and at least one but not more than three fingers, two-thirds of the way up the cone. Then dart swiftly away to an open area, away from the jostling crowd at the stand. Now take up the classic ice-cream-cone-eating stance: feet from one to two feet apart, body bent forward from the waist at a twenty-five-degree angle, right elbow well up, right forearm horizontal, at a level with your collarbone and about twelve inches from it. But don't start eating yet! Check first to see what emergency repairs may be necessary. Sometimes a sugar cone will be so crushed or broken or cracked that all one can do is gulp at the thing like a savage, getting what he can of it and letting the rest drop to the ground, and then evacuating the area of catastrophe as quickly as possible. Checking the cone for possible trouble can be done in a second or two, if one knows where to look and does it systematically. A trouble spot some people overlook is the bottom tip of the cone. This may have been broken off. Or the flap of the cone material at the bottom, usually wrapped over itself in that funny spiral construction, may be folded in a way that is imperfect and leaves an opening. No need to say that through this opening—in a matter of perhaps thirty or, at most, ninety seconds—will begin to pour

hundreds of thousands of sticky molecules of melted ice cream. You
know in this case that you must instantly get the paper napkin in your
left hand under and around the bottom of the cone to stem the forth-
coming flow, or else be doomed to eat the cone far too rapidly. It is a
grim moment. No one wants to eat a cone under that kind of pressure,
but neither does anyone want to end up with the bottom of the cone
stuck to a messy napkin. There's one other alternative—one that takes
both skill and courage: Forgoing any cradling action, grasp the cone
more firmly between thumb and forefinger and extend the other fingers
so that they are out of the way of the dripping from the bottom, then
increase the waist-bend angle from twenty-five to thirty-five degrees,
and then eat the cone, *allowing* it to drip out of the bottom onto the
ground in front of you! Experienced and thoughtful cone-eaters enjoy
facing up to this kind of sudden challenge.

Questions About the Reading

1. How many ways are there to eat an ice-cream cone?
2. Despite all of the problems with ice-cream cones, does the writer like
   to eat them?

Questions About the Writer's Strategies

1. When faced with having to write a clear and easy-to-understand
   description of a complicated process (how to prepare income-tax
   returns, do minor home repairs, or operate a computer), writers must
   use very precise language. Which words or phrases in this paragraph
   have a technical precision that makes this process clear to the reader?
2. The writer describes a number of problems associated with ice-cream
   cones. Which words or phrases does he use to help the reader know
   when he is about to identify these problems?

Writing Assignments

1. Choose another popular yet sometimes hard-to-eat food, e.g.,
   spaghetti and meatballs, and imagine that you have to write directions for eating this food for someone who is wearing a new white
   suit and has never eaten this before. Write a paragraph of directions.
2. Choose some simple, everyday activity such as making a peanut-
   butter sandwich or brushing your teeth and write a short essay
   describing the *process* (steps, necessary equipment) involved.
   Imagine that your reader has never handled jars, sliced bread, and
   toothbrush and toothpaste.

The Cook

Barbara Lewis (student)

Barbara Lewis takes us through the process of preparing dinner at a busy restaurant. She juggles meat, potatoes, and a seemingly endless stream of sauces and other delectables in a two-hour race with the dinner bell. And she does all this after a day of classes at Cuyahoga Community College in Cleveland, Ohio.

Words to Know

au jus   natural, unthickened juices or gravy
escargots   snails
requisition   a formal written order
sauté   to fry food quickly in a little fat
scampi   shrimp

Getting Started

At what times in your life have you felt like the busiest, most pressured person in the world? What factors contributed to your state of mind?

Preparing food for the sauté line at the restaurant where I work is a hectic two-hour job. I come to work at 3:00 P.M. knowing that everything must be done by 5:00 P.M. The first thing I do is to check the requisition for the day and order my food. Then I have to clean and season five or six prime rib roasts and place them in the slow-cooking oven. After this, I clean and season five trays of white potatoes for baking and put them in the fast oven. Now I have two things cooking, prime ribs and potatoes, at different times and temperatures, and they both have to be watched very closely. In the meantime, I must put three trays of bacon in the oven. The bacon needs very close watching, too, because it burns very easily. Now I have prime ribs, potatoes, and bacon all cooking at the same time—and all needing constant watching. Next, I make popovers, which are unseasoned rolls. These also go into an oven for baking. Now I have prime ribs, baking potatoes, bacon, and popovers cooking at the same time and all of them needing to be closely watched. With my work area set up, I must make clarified butter and garlic butter. The clarified butter is for cooking liver, veal, and fish. The garlic butter is for stuffing escargots. I have to make ground meat stuffing also. Half of the ground meat will be mixed with wild rice and will be used to stuff breast of chicken. The other half of the ground meat mixture will be used to stuff mushrooms. I have to prepare veal, cut and season scampi, and clean and sauté mushrooms and onions. In the meantime, I check the prime ribs and potatoes, take the bacon and the popovers out of the oven, and put the veal and chicken into the oven. Now I make au jus, which is served over the prime ribs, make the soup for the day, and cook the vegetables and rice. Then I heat the bordelaise sauce, make the special for the day, and last of all, cook food for the employees. This and sometimes more has to be done by five o'clock. Is it any wonder that I say preparing food for the sauté line at the restaurant where I work is a very hectic two-hour job!

Questions About the Reading

1. Run through the cook's list again. For about how many people do you think she is preparing food?
2. Classify the food the cook is responsible for.
3. Do you think the cook likes her job? Explain your answer.

Questions About the Writer's Strategies

1. Where is the topic sentence of the paragraph? Does the writer restate the topic sentence anywhere in the paragraph? If so, where? Does the sentence then serve a second purpose? What is that purpose?
2. Do you think *hectic* is an effective word for describing this job?
3. The cook states at the beginning that she has two things to watch carefully. The list of things she watches continues to grow during the paragraph. Identify the sentences where she reemphasizes this point. Does this help support her statement that the job is hectic?
4. What order does the writer use to organize her information in the paragraph?

Writing Assignments

1. We all have moments when we feel under pressure. Write a process paragraph illustrating one of your busy days.
2. Imagine that the restaurant has decided to hire a helper for the cook and that you are to be that helper. Write a process paragraph explaining the steps you would take to assist the cook and how you would blend your activities with hers.

Here's How to
Revive a Computer

Bill Husted

If your computer "conks out" or "freezes" on you, here's a process you can follow to revive it.

Words to Know

equivalent   like, same as
quivery   shaky, nervous

Getting Started

What process would you follow if your car, lawnmower, or washing machine went "dead" on you? What process would you follow if your lights went out?

My stepson is a computer wizard. An evil wizard. Computers do 1 things for him that aren't ordinary. And none of these things is good.

So I wasn't surprised when he managed to wreck his computer again. 2 This time he really did it. It was dead, and, unlike most times a computer freezes up, it offered no signs of returning to life when I tried to restart it.

It's worth your time today to suffer through my attempts to get the 3 computer going.

There are only two kinds of computer users: those who have already 4 experienced a dead machine and those who will. I am not talking about a balky machine. These are machines that just flat don't work.

I'll tell you what I did to return his machine to life. I started off—as 5 you should—with the easiest ways of restarting the machine. Even though the easy ways didn't work with his PC, you may be luckier. So pay attention. Just as is true when fixing a car, it's always smart to start with the obvious. Before you tear the engine apart, check to see if it's out of gas.

That's why my first effort involved turning the PC off and then on 6 again. Sometimes a PC has the equivalent of a human hiccup. It freezes because of a one-time problem that needs no fixing at all. If you try this and the computer runs fine when it restarts, don't do anything else. More machines get messed up from unneeded "fixing" than by computer viruses or lightning.

Next I tried to start the machine in Safe Mode. When Windows starts   7
up that way, it loads only the bare necessities. Even a seemingly dead
machine will sometimes start in Safe Mode.

Once there, you can attempt to undo the causes of the PC's problems.   8
In my case, Ryan had connected his digital video camera just before the
machine died. Sometimes loading a program or adding hardware can be
the cause.

You can also run fix-it programs like Norton SystemWorks or   9
Windows' own defragmentation and ScanDisk utilities. Let me tell you
a Safe Mode secret. Sometimes just starting the machine in Safe Mode
and then shutting it down will fix things. I have no idea why. But a man
should not question the gods.

To get to Safe Mode, tap on the F8 key as Windows tries to start. That   10
will take you to a menu that includes Safe Mode. I never got that far. All
that happened with me was the appearance of a screen that was a rather
nice shade of blue. So my day wasn't over yet.

Ryan's PC has Windows XP. With that version of Windows, as well as   11
Windows ME, there's a really handy feature called a Restore Point.
Remember that menu that included the option for Safe Mode? It also has
an option called Last Known Good Configuration. If you select that,
Windows will reset itself to the last time it was working correctly.

That seemed like a good notion to me. So I tried it. Again, I saw that   12
same blue screen.

I was getting a little quivery by now. I wasn't completely sure what to   13
do to fix things since—to repair the problem—I needed access to a semi-
working computer, not a blue screen. It was getting late.

Luckily, there was more that could be done. I used the Windows XP   14
CD to start the computer. On our machine, you can force it to boot up
from the CD by pressing the F12 key as it starts. The method may be different for your PC, so check the manual that came with it, or watch for
on-screen messages as the computer starts up. Often you will find directions there.

Starting the machine from the CD makes it think that you are   15
installing Windows for the first time. But don't panic. You probably
don't need to do that (although it's always a last-ditch possibility). Just
sit back and watch as the CD prepares to install Windows. You will finally
arrive at a screen where you can tell it to go ahead and start the installa-
tion or select an option called Recovery Console, which will try to fix
things up.

Once I got to Recovery Console, I was given the option of running a   16
utility that goes all the way back to the DOS days. It's called Chkdsk and
it attempts to fix errors on the hard disk. When a computer refuses to
start, that's often where the problems are.

Working with the Recovery Console, you won't have a Windows 17
screen. So you have to work the old-fashioned way: by typing. So I typed
"chkdsk/r" to tell Windows to check things out and fix them, too.

After more than an hour, chkdsk finished running.   18

I restarted the machine, and good ol' Windows greeted me. By now, 19
Ryan had lost interest in the process. So I left him a note saying that the
computer was running again. The world was again safe from evil wizards.

Questions About the Reading

1. What are the two kinds of computer users?
2. What is the first step to follow in trying to restart a computer?
3. What is the second step to follow and what are the options or steps
   to follow if the second step doesn't work?
4. What does the writer call his stepson?

Questions About the Writer's Strategies

1. What is the tone of the essay?
2. What is the point of view of the essay? Is it consistent? If it changes,
   is there a reason?
3. What is the writer's purpose?
4. Does the writer use any modes of development in addition to
   process? If so, what are they?

Writing Assignments

1. *Working Together* Join with some of your classmates and write an
   essay explaining the process you would follow if there was a hurri-
   cane warning for your school area.
2. Write an essay explaining the process you would follow if your car
   broke down on the highway.

The Beekeeper

Sue Hubbell

Preparing for a job as a beekeeper is a painstaking process that actually requires, as Sue Hubbell shows us, taking pain.

Words to Know

anaphylactic   severe reaction with possible collapse or death

supers   wooden boxes that contain the bees' honey

Getting Started

Do you follow a process in getting ready to do your homework?

The time to harvest honey is summer's end, when it is hot. The temper of the bees requires that we wear protective clothing: a full set of overalls, a zippered bee veil and leather gloves. Even a very strong young man works up a sweat wrapped in a bee suit in the heat, hustling 60-pound supers while being harassed by angry bees. It is a hard job, harder even than haying, but jobs are scarce here and I've always been able to hire help. 1

This year David, the son of a friend of mine, is working for me. He is big and strong and used to labor, but he was nervous about bees. After we had made the job arrangement I set about desensitizing him to bee stings. I put a piece of ice on his arm to numb it and then, holding a bee carefully by its head, I put it on the numbed spot and let it sting him. A bee stinger is barbed and stays in the flesh, pulling loose from the body of the bee as it struggles to free itself. The bulbous poison sac at the top of the stinger continues to pulsate after the bee has left, pumping the venom and forcing the stinger deeper into the flesh. 2

That first day I wanted David to have only a partial dose of venom, so after a minute I scraped the stinger out. A few people are seriously sensitive to bee venom; each sting they receive can cause a more severe reaction than the one before—reactions ranging from hives, breathing difficulties, accelerated heart beat and choking to anaphylactic shock and death. I didn't think David would be allergic in that way, but I wanted to make sure. 3

We sat down and had a cup of coffee and I watched him. The spot where the stinger went in grew red and began to swell. That was a normal reaction, and so was the itching that he felt later on. 4

The next day I coaxed a bee into stinging him again, repeating the pro- 5
cedure, but I left the stinger in place for 10 minutes, until the venom sac
was empty. Again the spot was red, swollen and itchy but had disappeared in 24 hours. By that time David was ready to catch a bee himself
and administer his own sting. He also decided that the ice cube was a
bother and gave it up. I told him to keep to one sting a day until he had
no redness or swelling and then to increase to two stings. He was ready
for them the next day. The greater amount of venom caused redness and
swelling for a few days, but soon his body could tolerate it without reaction and he increased the number of stings once again.

Today he told me he was up to six stings. His arms look as though 6
they have track marks on them, but the fresh stings are having little
effect. I'll keep him at it until he can tolerate 10 a day with no reaction
and then I'll not worry about taking him out to the bee yard.

Questions About the Reading

1. When is the honey harvested? Why is the honey harvested then?
2. How much do the supers that hold the honey weigh?
3. Why is the beekeeper able to hire help in harvesting the honey?
4. How many stings per day does the beekeeper want her helper to tolerate before taking him to the bee yard?

Questions About the Writer's Strategies

1. Identify the steps in the desensitizing process.
2. Could the selection as a whole or the sentences within it be classified
   by any other modes of development? If so, which modes and which
   sentences?
3. What is the thesis of the selection? Is it stated? If so, identify it; if not,
   state the thesis in your own words.

Writing Assignments

1. Write an essay in which you explain the process you follow in getting
   ready for work, doing your laundry, or repairing your car or some
   household item.
2. Write an essay in which you explain the process you follow in preparing to buy groceries and then in buying them.

The Wine Experience

Leo Buscaglia

In contemporary life we often are too far removed from the actual process of growing and making things. We buy all our food and clothes in stores without any knowledge of their original sources. This essay describes the joyful step-by-step procedure of wine making in a traditional Italian-American home.

Words to Know

connoisseur   someone with shrewd, clever discrimination concerning matters of taste; an expert

cylindrical   circular and tubelike

dissertation   a speech, lecture, or long essay on a specific subject

oenophile   someone who loves the study of wine

precariously   without stability, without balance

prelude   an introduction

Getting Started

Why is it so satisfying to make something from scratch?

––––––––––––––––––

Like all good Italians, Papa loved his wine, although I never knew him   1
to drink to excess. A glass or two of wine to accompany his dinner was his limit. He never touched hard liquor.

Papa's love of wine went far beyond the simple enjoyment of drinking   2
it. He was truly an oenophile, a connoisseur. He always made his own wine, from ripened grapes to dated label. His cool, dark cellar was full of dusty bottles and cylindrical, wooden barrels of varying sizes, all carefully marked to indicate the type of grape and the year of the harvest.

When I was growing up, we had many festivities in our home. None,   3
except Christmas and Easter, topped the one night each year that we made the new wine. The anticipation and preparation began in July and August, long before the eventful September evening when the truckload of grapes was delivered. By then Papa had made several visits to his friends—grape growers in Cucamonga, about forty miles from our home—to observe the progress of his grapes. He had spent hours scouring the barrels in which the wine would be made and stored, and applying antirust varnish on

every visible metal part of the wine-making equipment. The fermenting vat had been filled with water to swell the wood.

On the appointed evening, the truck would arrive after nightfall, brim- 4 ming with small, tough-skinned, sweet-smelling Cabernet grapes. The boxes of grapes were hand-carried about two hundred feet to the garage, where a giant empty vat awaited. A hand-powered crusher was positioned precariously on top of the vat, ready to grind noisily into the night, as thousands of grapes were poured into it. It was an all-male operation that included Papa, his relatives, and friends. Dressed in their undershirts, bodies glistening with perspiration, they took turns cranking the crusher handle. My job was to stack the empty crates neatly out of the way as a prelude to what for me was the most exciting part of the evening.

After all the grapes had been mashed and the empty boxes stacked, it 5 was time for us to remove our shoes, socks, and pants and slip into the cool, dark moisture for the traditional grape stomping. This was done, of course, to break up the skins, but I couldn't have cared less why it was necessary. For me it was a sensual experience unlike any other, feeling the grape residue gushing between my toes and watching as the new wine turned my legs the rich, deep color of Cabernet Sauvignon.

While this "man's work" was being accomplished, the "woman's 6 work" was progressing in the kitchen. The heady fragrance of the crushed grapes, mingled with the savory aromas of dinner wafting from the house, caused our feet to move in step with our growing appetites. The traditional main course for our wine-making dinner was gnocchi, a small, dumplinglike pasta that would be cooked to perfection and topped with a wonderful sauce that had been simmering for hours.

Like Christmas Eve, this particular night was unique in many ways. 7 Throughout the rest of the year, we routinely sat down to dinner by 5:30 each evening. But for this occasion dinner was never served until the wine making was finished, sometimes as late as 10 P.M. By then, we were all purple from grape juice, exhausted, and famished.

No matter how tired and hungry we were, however, Papa always 8 prefaced the dinner with a dissertation on "the wine experience." This ceremony called for his finest wines, which had been aging in his modest but efficient wine cellar. Drinking wine, he would remind us, was a highly respected activity, not to be taken lightly. The nectar of the grape had brought joy to human beings long before recorded history.

"Wine is a delight and a challenge and is never meant to be drunk 9 quickly. It's to be savored and sipped slowly," he'd tell us. "All the senses are awakened when you drink wine. You drink with your eyes, your tongue, your throat, your nose. Notice the colors the wine makes in the glass—all the way from dark purple, like a bishop's robe, to the golden amber of an aspen leaf."

He would hold up the glass to the light as if we were about to share a 10
sacrament, then swirl the wine around in his glass, guiding us through
the whole ritual, from the first sip to the final, all-important swallow.
    "Alla salute!"   11

Questions About the Reading

1. How do you think the writer feels about his father? What leads you
   to this conclusion?
2. How often did the Buscaglia family make wine?
3. What happened to the grapes after they were crushed?
4. What did wine making and Christmas have in common to the writer
   as a child?

Questions About the Writer's Strategies

1. What is the writer's thesis? Can you identify the thesis statement, or
   is the thesis implied?
2. What is the point of view in the essay? Could another point of view
   be used?
3. In what ways is this paragraph subjective? In what ways is it
   objective?
4. Is the writer's purpose to instruct a beginner in how to make wine?
   If so, what are the main steps? If not, what else would you need to
   know?

Writing Assignments

1. Write a first-person essay about a family tradition in your home that
   involves a holiday or a special event. Write it as a process so that your
   readers could try to duplicate the celebration at home.
2. Choose a skill you have learned from one of your parents and write
   a second-person process essay describing it.
3. *Working Together*   Join with some classmates and think of an item
   that all of you have eaten, worn, or used recently. Write an essay in
   which you explain the process involved in producing the item (for
   example, a spiral-bound notebook, a pair of tennis shoes, or a blackboard).

How Dictionaries Are Made

S. I. Hayakawa

When we look at familiar, everyday objects, we rarely think, "Someone made this." How often have you looked up a word in your dictionary this year? Did you ever wonder, "Who wrote this definition? What makes it correct?" S. I. Hayakawa, who has been a teacher, a university president, the author of several books on language, and a United States senator, here tells us how the definitions that appear in a dictionary are determined.

Words to Know

context   statements that occur before or after a word and that determine its meaning

decreed   ruled

disseminate   distribute

docility   passiveness

grammarian   person who is an expert in grammar

prophecy   ability to see into the future

Getting Started

What process do you follow in doing your homework?

It is an almost universal belief that every word has a "correct meaning," 1 that we learn these meanings principally from teachers and grammarians (except that most of the time we don't bother to, so that we ordinarily speak "sloppy English"), and that dictionaries and grammars are the "supreme authority" in matters of meaning and usage. Few people ask by what authority the writers of dictionaries and grammars say what they say. The docility with which most people bow down to the dictionary is amazing, and the person who says, "Well, the dictionary is wrong!" is looked upon with smiles of pity and amusement which say plainly, "Poor fellow! He's really quite sane otherwise."

Let us see how dictionaries are made and how the editors arrive at def- 2 initions. What follows applies, incidentally, only to those dictionary offices where first-hand, original research goes on—not those in which editors simply copy existing dictionaries. The task of writing a dictionary begins with the reading of vast amounts of the literature of the period or subject that it is intended to cover. As the editors read, they copy on cards

197

every interesting or rare word, every unusual or peculiar occurrence of a common word, a large number of common words in their ordinary uses, and also the sentences in which each of these words appears, thus:

> pail
> The dairy *pails* bring home increase of milk
> Keats, *Endymion*
> I, 44–45

That is to say, the context of each word is collected, along with the word itself. For a really big job of dictionary writing, such as the *Oxford English Dictionary* (usually bound in about twenty-five volumes), millions of such cards are collected, and the task of editing occupies decades. As the cards are collected, they are alphabetized and sorted. When the sorting is completed, there will be for each word anywhere from two or three to several hundred illustrative quotations, each on its card.

To define a word, then, the dictionary editor places before him the stack of cards illustrating that word; each of the cards represents an actual use of the word by a writer of some literary or historical importance. He reads the cards carefully, discards some, re-reads the rest, and divides up the stack according to what he thinks are the several senses of the word. Finally, he writes his definitions, following the hard-and-fast rule that each definition must be based on what the quotations in front of him reveal about the meaning of the word. The editor cannot be influenced by what he thinks a given word ought to mean. He must work according to the cards, or not at all.

The writing of a dictionary, therefore, is not a task of setting up authoritative statements about the "true meanings" of words, but a task of recording, to the best of one's ability, what various words have meant to authors in the distant or immediate past. The writer of a dictionary is a historian, not a law-giver. If, for example, we had been writing a dictionary in 1890, or even as late as 1919, we could have said that the word "broadcast" means "to scatter," seed and so on; but we could not have decreed that from 1921 on, the commonest meaning of the word should become "to disseminate audible messages, etc., by wireless telephony." To regard the dictionary as an "authority," therefore, is to credit the dictionary writer with gifts of prophecy which neither he nor anyone else possesses. In choosing our words when we speak or write, we can be guided by the historical record afforded us by the dictionary, but we cannot be bound by it, because new situations, new experiences, new inventions, new feelings, are always compelling us to give new uses to old words. Looking under a "hood," we should ordinarily have found, five hundred years ago, a monk; today, we find a motorcar engine.

Questions About the Reading

1. Describe the process used to write a dictionary.
2. Do meanings of words change over time?
3. How does the editor of a dictionary decide what meaning a word should have?
4. Do you think a dictionary from the 1880s would be useful for writing college papers now? Why or why not?

Questions About the Writer's Strategies

1. Which sentences in the essay state how to make a dictionary? Are they arranged in chronological order?
2. What is the tone of this essay? Is this a good model for college writing? Why or why not?
3. Divide this essay into introductory, development, and concluding paragraphs. (See chapter 1.) Does the author restate his thesis in the concluding paragraph?

Writing Assignments

1. There are some similarities between organizing a dictionary and organizing a term paper. What are the steps you would recommend for writing a term paper?
2. *Working Together* With some classmates imagine you are planning to write a short biography of Abraham Lincoln or another president you all admire. Write an essay in which you describe possible ways of finding information, making sure to include several methods.

The Art of Making Fimo Beads

Julie Gifford (student)

Julie Gifford, a student at Pennsylvania State University, tells us how to make fimo beads.

Words to Know

cylindrical   round
fimo   a synthetic, claylike material
perimeter   outer boundary or edges
prisms   solid, equal-sided figures

Getting Started

What is the process you would follow in planting a garden, fixing a car or bicycle, or sorting your week's laundry?

———————————————

The "Generation X" population of today's society has made the wear-   1
ing of beaded necklaces containing fimo beads quite a fashion statement. These necklaces contain small, round, colored plastic beads and other intricate beads made out of different colored fimo. Fimo is a synthetic material similar to modeling clay and can be used to make thousands of types of beads. These beads can then be incorporated into necklaces. However, to accurately describe the process of making this style of bead, a simple pattern will be used as an example. Specifically, the fimo example described will have a pattern with a small, yellow, circular center surrounded by three small green triangles and three small red triangles. The following process will allow anyone without artistic ability to create a simple, inexpensive fimo bead that can later be used in stylish necklaces.

The first step in the process involves taking a trip to a local craft store,   2
like A. C. Moore, or a department store such as Wal★Mart, to buy the necessary supplies. For the example fimo bead, red, yellow, and green fimo must be purchased. To make a complete necklace, other colored plastic beads would have to be bought along with a spool of beading thread and a silver clasp. Also, a sharp flat-edged cutting tool (for example, a razor blade) and a thick, large pin will also be necessary tools in the final stages of the bead making process.

Once the supplies are gathered, the bead making process is ready to   3
begin. The fimo color that will make up the center circle in the bead (in
this case, yellow) is the color that is first readied. A piece of fimo with the
diameter of a quarter and the width of a pencil is pinched off from the
larger slab of fimo. It is then rubbed between both hands in a circular
motion until it is warm and no longer cracks when folded in half. Then,
from that small, primed piece of fimo, a smaller, nickel-sized piece is
pinched and rolled on a flat surface. The fimo is rolled into a cylindrical
log that is approximately three inches long. It is important to ensure that
the log is not too thin, meaning it does not easily pull apart. Once the log
is rolled to the desired thickness (slightly thinner than that of a pencil)
place it aside for later use. The same process is followed for the green
and red fimo colors, also, except for those colors three logs must be prepared instead of only one.

After the three logs each of green and red fimo are formed they must   4
be shaped into three-dimensional triangular prisms. This is easily accomplished by placing them on a flat surface (one at a time) and pinching the
pointer finger and thumb together (to form a small triangle). The pinched
fingers are then pressed down gently on the top and sides of the fimo logs
so the logs become prisms. Once this is finished, the prisms are ready to
be placed around the circular, yellow center. First place the base of the
green prisms around the yellow log, leaving equal amounts of space
between all three prisms. When doing this make sure to press hard
enough so the green prisms are firmly attached to the yellow center. Then
position the base of each of the red prisms between the spaces left
between the green prisms. By this point the spaces around the yellow
center should be evenly filled. The addition of the red and green prisms
form the perimeter of the new log that contains the desired bead pattern.

Next comes one of the final stages in the fimo bead making process.   5
The new log that has been formed from placing the red and green triangles around the yellow center must be rolled using the palm of the hand.
This is done until the outside of the log is smooth and only one color. The
purpose of this is to lengthen the log and to decrease the size of the
beads. The beads can then be cut from the log so that they are approximately one-quarter inch thick. The beads are cut by using a razor blade
(or other sharp cutting tool) and positioning it along the top of the log at
the desired thickness of bead. Then the log is gently rolled back and
forth while slight pressure is applied to the razor blade until it cuts completely through the log. The reason the log is cut in such a manner is to
avoid distorting the design that is on the face of the bead. The small
piece that is cut from the original log is the fimo bead. The rest of the log
is cut in the same way until no more beads can be obtained. Depending

on the exact thickness of each bead and the starting length of the log, there should be a net yield of approximately ten to twenty beads.

Finally, rounding out the bead making process, a thick pin must be [6] used to put a hole on each side and throughout the fimo bead. This is done so the bead can later be strung along beading thread with other plastic beads to make a necklace. To make a hole in the bead, place the bead with its two faces positioned between the pointer and thumb. Then you poke the pin through the middle of one of the sides and gently twist the pin as it goes in the bead and eventually comes out the other side. This procedure is completed for the rest of the beads, as well. Lastly, all the beads must be placed on a baking pan and baked until they are hard, approximately ten to fifteen minutes at 250 degrees. The finished products can then be used in many creative ways, in combination with small, round plastic beads to make beautiful, fashionable necklaces.

The art of making fimo beads is really a study in the art of creativity [7] and patience. It is a relaxing hobby that allows an individual's creativity to take control. Although many people think that the process requires special artistic talent, that is really only a myth. Anyone who follows the procedure described above or similar procedures in craft books would be able to make the simplest of fimo styles. After the simple styles are mastered, they can easily be combined to form more intricate designs. Once this occurs, a real sense of accomplishment can be felt, and you can proudly say, "I created that all by myself!"

Questions About the Reading

1. What are the supplies you need to make fimo beads?
2. After the material is readied, what are the steps in the process of making a fimo bead?
3. How many logs of yellow should be prepared for the example fimo bead? How many red and how many green?
4. What is the purpose of rolling the log?
5. How is the hole in the bead made?
6. What is the final step in the process of making a fimo bead?

Questions About the Writer's Strategies

1. What is the point of view of the essay? Is it consistent? If it changes, is there a reason?
2. Does the writer use any modes of development in addition to process? If so, what are they?

3. What is the tone of the essay?
4. Why does the writer paragraph the essay as she does? How does the paragraphing relate to the steps in the process?

Writing Assignments

1. Write an essay in which you explain the process you would follow in planting a garden.
2. Write an essay in which you explain the process you follow in sorting your week's laundry.
3. Write an essay in which you explain the process you follow in repairing some appliance in your house.

8

Cause and Effect

IN YOUR LOCAL newspaper you notice a story about a car accident that took place late on a Saturday night. The driver missed a curve, slammed into a tree, and was badly injured. Police investigators reported that the young victim had been drinking heavily with friends and lost control of the car on the way home. This news article is a relatively clear example of a **cause,** heavy consumption of alcohol, and an **effect,** a serious accident.

Sometimes you can recognize immediately that cause and effect is part of a writer's **mode of development** because the writer uses words that signal a cause-and-effect relationship—transitional words like *because, therefore, as a result,* and *consequently.* However, writers will not necessarily indicate cause and effect so directly. Sometimes a cause-and-effect relationship will be clear only from the arrangement of ideas or the narrative sequence of events. Usually, though, the **topic sentence** or **thesis statement** will indicate that the writer is describing a cause-and-effect situation.

A cause-and-effect explanation tells *why* something turns out the way it does. In some cases, a single cause may contribute to one or more effects. In the following paragraph, the writer says that a single cause— the early release of prisoners—led to an increase in crimes.

Cause	To save money in the early 1980s, Illinois released 21,000 prisoners an average of three months early. James Austin of the National Council on Crime and Delinquency calculates
Effects	that the early releases produced 23 homicides, 32 rapes, 262 arsons, 681 robberies, 2,472 burglaries, 2,571 assaults and more than 8,000 other crimes. According to Harvard

Effect

> researchers David P. Cavanaugh and Mark A. R. Kleiman,
> the $60 million the state saved cost Illinois crime victims
> $304 million, directly or indirectly.

Eugene H. Methvin,
"Pay Now—Or Pay Later"

A writer may also say that several causes contributed to or resulted in a particular effect.

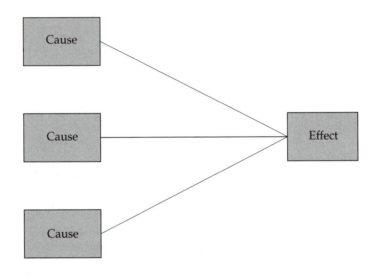

For example, in the following essay, the writer suggests three causes for the disappearance of moonshining—the secret manufacturing of whiskey—as a fine art.

The manufacture of illicit whiskey in the mountains is not   1
dead. Far from it. As long as the operation of a still remains
so financially rewarding, it will never die. There will always
be men ready to take their chances against the law for such
an attractive profit, and willing to take their punishment
when they are caught.

Effect

> Moonshining as a fine art, however, effectively disap-   2
> peared some time ago. There were several reasons. One was

Cause 1: decline
in use of home
remedies contain-
ing corn whiskey
Cause 2: young
people finding
easier ways to
make money

> the age of aspirin and modern medicine. As home doctoring
> lost its stature, the demand for pure corn whiskey as an
> essential ingredient of many home remedies vanished along
> with those remedies. Increasing affluence was another rea-
> son. Young people, rather than follow in their parents' foot-
> steps, decided that there were easier ways to make money,
> and they were right.

Cause 3: greed
causing producers
to care more for
quantity than
quality

Third, and perhaps most influential of all, was the arrival,   3
even in moonshining, of that peculiarly human disease
known to most of us as greed. One fateful night, some force
whispered in an unsuspecting moonshiner's ear, "Look.
Add this gadget to your still and you'll double your production. Double your production, and you can double your
profits."

Soon the small operators were being forced out of busi-   4
ness, and moonshining, like most other manufacturing
enterprises, was quickly taken over by a breed of men bent
on making money—and lots of it. Loss of pride in the product, and loss of time taken with the product increased in
direct proportion to the desire for production; and thus
moonshining as a fine art was buried in a quiet little ceremony attended only by those mourners who had once been
the proud artists, known far and wide across the hills for the
excellence of their product. Too old to continue making it
themselves, and with no one following behind them, they
were reduced to reminiscing about "the good old days when
the whiskey that was made was *really* whiskey, and no questions asked."

Suddenly moonshining fell into the same category as   5
faith healing, planting by the signs, and all the other vanish-
ing customs that were a part of a rugged, self-sufficient culture that is now disappearing.

Eliot Wigginton,
"Moonshining as a Fine Art"

In still other cases, one cause may have several effects.

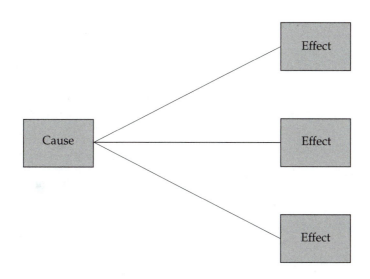

In the following paragraph, the writer explains that the explosion of a nuclear bomb (the cause) has five primary effects. Notice as you read that the writer combines **process** with the cause-and-effect explanation.

Topic

Cause

Effect 1: initial
nuclear radiation

Effect 2:
electromagnetic
pulse

Effect 3: thermal
pulse

Effect 4: blast
wave

Effect 5: radioactive
fallout

Whereas most conventional bombs produce only one destructive effect—the shock wave—nuclear weapons produce many destructive effects. At the moment of the explosion, when the temperature of the weapon material, instantly gasified, is at the superstellar level, the pressure is millions of times the normal atmospheric pressure. Immediately, radiation, consisting mainly of gamma rays, which are a very high-energy form of electromagnetic radiation, begins to stream outward into the environment. This is called the "initial nuclear radiation," and is the first of the destructive effects of a nuclear explosion. In an air burst of a one-megaton bomb—a bomb with the explosive yield of a million tons of TNT, which is a medium-sized weapon in present-day nuclear arsenals—the initial nuclear radiation can kill unprotected human beings in an area of some six square miles. Virtually simultaneously with the initial nuclear radiation, in a second destructive effect of the explosion, an electromagnetic pulse is generated by the intense gamma radiation acting on the air. In a high-altitude detonation, the pulse can knock out electrical equipment over a wide area by inducing a powerful surge of voltage through various conductors, such as antennas, overhead power lines, pipes, and railroad tracks. . . . When the fusion and fission reactions have blown themselves out, a fireball takes shape. As it expands, energy is absorbed in the form of X rays by the surrounding air, and then the air re-radiates a portion of that energy into the environment in the form of the thermal pulse—a wave of blinding light and intense heat—which is the third of the destructive effects of a nuclear explosion. . . . The thermal pulse of a one-megaton bomb lasts for about ten seconds and can cause second-degree burns in exposed human beings at a distance of nine and a half miles, or in an area of more than two hundred and eighty square miles. . . . As the fireball expands, it also sends out a blast wave in all directions, and this is the fourth destructive effect of the explosion. The blast wave of an air-burst one-megaton bomb can flatten or severely damage all but the strongest buildings within a radius of four and a half miles. . . . As the fireball burns, it rises, condensing water from the surrounding atmosphere to form the characteristic mushroom cloud. If the bomb has been set off on the ground or close enough to it so that the fireball touches the surface, a so-called ground burst, a crater will be formed, and tons of dust and debris will be fused with the intensely radioactive fission products and sucked up into the mushroom cloud. This mixture will return to earth as radioactive fallout, most of it in the form

└ of fine ash, in the fifth destructive effect of the explosion. Depending upon the composition of the surface, from 40 to 70 percent of this fallout—often called the "early" or "local" fallout—descends to earth within about a day of the explosion, in the vicinity of the blast and downwind from it, exposing human beings to radiation disease, an illness that is fatal when exposure is intense.

Jonathan Schell,
The Fate of the Earth

You should notice still another characteristic in this sample paragraph: the writer describes both main causes and subordinate causes, and main effects and subordinate effects. One main cause, the explosion of the bomb, causes a series of five initial (main) effects. However, these effects become the causes for still other effects. The initial nuclear radiation (effect 1), for example, is also a cause that results in the death of unprotected human beings in a six-square-mile area (a subordinate effect). The electromagnetic pulse (effect 2) that is generated by the explosion is the cause, in turn, of the knocking out of electrical equipment (a subordinate effect). The thermal pulse (effect 3) causes second-degree burns (a subordinate effect) in exposed humans in a 280-square-mile area. The blast wave (effect 4) causes the destruction of buildings (a subordinate effect), and the radioactive fallout (effect 5) causes radiation disease (a subordinate effect) in humans. As the following chart shows, cause-and-effect relationships can be complicated.

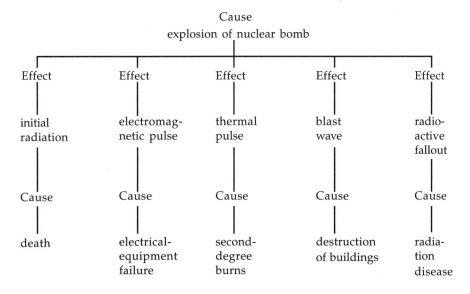

You should keep two factors in mind when you are writing and **revising** a cause-and-effect essay. First, be sure that you have actually thought through the causes and effects very carefully. You should not be satisfied with considering only obvious or simple causes. For example, we tend to oversimplify and cite one cause as the reason for a war—the attack on Pearl Harbor for the United States entering World War II, the firing on Fort Sumter for the start of the Civil War, and so on. For the most part, these tend to be the last of many contributing causes that have led to the war. A thoughtful discussion of such a topic in your writing would include an explanation of some of the contributing, less obvious but perhaps more important, causes.

Second, you should be careful that you do not mistake an event as a cause simply because it preceded a particular effect. For instance, if a child swallows a coin and then comes down with measles, it would be inaccurate and faulty reasoning, a *fallacy*—in this case, a *post hoc* (meaning "after this, therefore because of this") *fallacy*—to assume that swallowing the coin was a cause of the measles. Other common fallacies you should guard against in both your reading and your writing include the following.

- The *hasty generalization*, which is reasoning based on too few examples or insufficient evidence. "The cause of World War II was the Japanese bombing of Pearl Harbor."
- The *non sequitur*, which is claiming an effect that does not necessarily follow from the stated cause. "He believes in the supernatural because he has read the Harry Potter books."

Even though you need to guard against fallacies, you should also be aware that writers do not always state a cause-and-effect relationship directly. Sometimes they **imply** the relationship and leave it to the reader to infer the relationship. That is, the writer does not state the relationship, but arranges certain information in such a way that the reader will be able to conclude that the relationship exists, as in the following sentences.

> On the ground next to the parked Jeep, the compass glinted in the moonlight. Deep in the woods, shielded from the moon, the hungry teenager circled in the dark with little idea where he had been or how to get where he wanted to go.

Although the writer does not directly state what happened, it is not hard to infer that the teenager dropped his compass without realizing it, with the effect that he is now lost.

You will need to make inferences when you read cause-and-effect writing as well as other **modes of development.** When you make an inference, be sure that you can pinpoint the information and trace the logic on which your inference is based. When you are writing about cause and effect, be sure to give enough information, directly or indirectly, so that your reader can determine the cause-and-effect relationship.

You use cause-and-effect reasoning every day in solving problems and making decisions. Legislators create laws to address the causes of certain problems. In a similar way, scientists find cures for diseases when they are able to isolate the causes of those diseases. Understanding the relation between causes and effects is extremely important in both day-to-day living and long-range planning. Communicating your understanding in writing is significant evidence of your ability to reason clearly and accurately.

An Eyewitness Account

Jack London

Jack London (1876–1916) is best known for such adventure novels as The Call of the Wild. *In this paragraph from an essay published in May, 1906, in* Collier's Weekly, *he describes the effects of the devastating San Francisco earthquake of April 16, 1906.*

Words to Know

conflagration   destructive fire
imperial   magnificent, majestic
nabobs   rich men
wrought   caused

Getting Started

Have you ever seen a fire, flood, or other natural disaster?

The earthquake shook down in San Francisco hundreds of thousands of dollars' worth of walls and chimneys. But the conflagration that followed burned up hundreds of millions of dollars' worth of property. There is no estimating within hundreds of millions the actual damage wrought. Not in history has a modern imperial city been so completely destroyed. San Francisco is gone! Nothing remains of it but memories and a fringe of dwelling houses on its outskirts. Its industrial section is wiped out. Its social and residential section is wiped out. The factories and warehouses, the great stores and newspaper buildings, the hotels and the palaces of the nabobs, are all gone. Remains only the fringe of dwelling houses on the outskirts of what was once San Francisco.

Questions About the Reading

1. According to the writer, how many dollars' worth of property were destroyed by the earthquake?
2. If the earthquake shook down walls and chimneys, what do you think caused the devastating fire that followed?
3. What happened to the San Francisco industrial section?
4. What were the only things that remained of San Francisco after the earthquake?

Questions About the Writer's Strategies

1. What is the tone of the paragraph?
2. Is the paragraph objective, subjective, or both?
3. Identify the cause-and-effect elements in the paragraph.
4. What modes of development does the writer use in addition to cause and effect?

Writing Assignments

1. Watch your local news report and write a paragraph in which you suggest the cause and effects of a reported fire, flood, robbery, or accident.
2. Write a paragraph in which you identify some of the effects of the closing of a business that employs many people in your city or town.
3. Write a paragraph in which you explain the possible effects on a business of its product being determined harmful.

The Power of Place

Winifred Gallagher

There are many ways in which the physical environment in which we live and work affects our well-being. In this paragraph about the effect of computer screens on computer operators, journalist Winifred Gallagher explains why you can't always blame your boss for a bad day at the office.

Words to Know

clarity   clearness

irritants   things that cause annoyance or physical discomfort

microanalysis   analysis of quantities weighing one milligram or less

noxious   harmful to health

occupational   pertaining to jobs and work

overtly   openly, not hidden

stressor   something that causes stress

VDTs   video display terminals or computer screens

Getting Started

What are the factors that cause you the most physical stress in your daily life?

Few places are as overly stimulating as the rush-hour subway, yet some of the less overtly jittery spots where we spend far more time exact their tolls as well. As we move further into the postmodern age of information, the workplace is changing fast, causing occupational safety specialists to focus on problems that would have seemed light-weight to their predecessors. Not long ago, for example, "industrial fatigue" meant the hard-hat exhaustion of steelworkers and coal miners. Now it is just as likely to refer to the weariness, eyestrain, and aches and pains of computer operators who spend long periods with poorly designed VDTs, desks, and chairs. Environmental psychologists have shown that the proper adjustment of a single element at a computer station calls for painstaking microanalysis. To evaluate the screen, for example, one must consider its height, tilt, and distance from the operator, the size and clarity of its characters, and its brightness, glare, and flickering. Because its effects are often subtle, combined with other irritants, and bother us after exposure ceases, trying to pinpoint an environmental stressor is difficult for the layman. As a result, we often end up blaming its noxious influence on something else—the project, the boss, or "stress" in general—thus perpetuating the dilemma.

———————————

Questions About the Reading

1. What are the most common complaints of computer operators?
2. What are the variations in screen design and use that environmental psychologists evaluate?
3. What do you think the writer means by "hard-hat exhaustion"? What would be a good name for the more modern industrial fatigue the writer describes?
4. In what ways does the author show that circumstances are rapidly changing in the field of occupational safety? Give examples.

Questions About the Writer's Strategies

1. Identify the cause-and-effect elements in this paragraph.
2. Besides cause and effect, what other mode of development does the writer use in this paragraph?
3. According to the writer, why is it difficult for the average worker to pinpoint environmental stressors?
4. Is this paragraph written subjectively or objectively? Use words and phrases from the paragraph to support your answer.

Writing Assignments

1. Do you think the government should spend more money researching the effects of VDTs on workers' stress levels? Using cause-and-effect elements, write a paragraph discussing why it is important to keep office environments safe.
2. Write a paragraph in which you identify some of the effects on your body of your own work and study environments.
3. Do some experimenting with the lighting, chair position, and screen position in your own computer environment. Then write a paragraph about the effects of these changes on your stress level while you work at the computer.

A Momentous Arrest

Martin Luther King, Jr.

Martin Luther King, Jr., was catapulted into international fame when, working for the Southern Christian Leadership Conference, he organized blacks in Montgomery, Alabama, to boycott that city's segregated buses in 1955 and 1956. King, preaching nonviolent resistance to segregation, became the most important leader in the civil rights movement that changed American life so radically over the next decade. Here, in a simple matter-of-fact tone, King tells of the incident that sparked the Montgomery bus boycott.

Words to Know

accommodate   to make space for, oblige
complied   carried out willingly

Getting Started

Have you ever disobeyed a rule because you thought it was unfair?

On December 1, 1955, an attractive Negro seamstress, Mrs. Rosa Parks, boarded the Cleveland Avenue Bus in downtown Montgomery. She was returning home after her regular day's work in the Montgomery Fair—a leading department store. Tired from long hours on her feet, Mrs. Parks sat down in the first seat behind the section reserved for whites. Not long after she took her seat, the bus operator ordered her, along with three other Negro passengers, to move back in order to accommodate boarding white passengers. By this time every seat in the bus was taken. This meant that if Mrs. Parks followed the driver's command she would have to stand while a white male passenger, who had just boarded the bus, would sit. The other three Negro passengers immediately complied with the driver's request. But Mrs. Parks quietly refused. The result was her arrest.

Questions About the Reading

1. Was Mrs. Parks breaking any law or custom in sitting where she did?
2. Why didn't Mrs. Parks move when the bus driver asked her to? Do you think she would have moved if the white passenger had been a woman instead of a man?
3. Was Mrs. Parks thinking about the civil rights movement when she refused to move? Explain your answer.
4. What is it about Mrs. Park's action that seems so symbolic of the early civil rights movement?

Questions About the Writer's Strategies

1. Which sentence states the cause in this paragraph? Which one states the effect?
2. Do you think the writer presents the incident objectively or subjectively? Use words and phrases from the paragraph to support your answer.
3. Other than cause and effect, what mode of development dominates in this paragraph?
4. What is the order in which the incidents in the paragraph are arranged?
5. Do you sympathize with Mrs. Parks? Explain your answer, citing examples from the essay that influence your feelings.

Writing Assignments

1. Think of a situation that made you angry enough to defy authority and risk discipline or even arrest. Perhaps you protested an unfair grade, a school rule, an unjust traffic ticket, or something of more consequence, like contamination of your city's water supply. Using cause and effect as your mode of development, describe in a paragraph what happened. Try to write objectively.
2. The civil rights movement of the 1950s and 1960s brought about many positive changes in our country's attitude toward minorities. There are, however, still steps that can be taken. In a paragraph, suggest one possible change the country can make, and speculate on the effects it could have on the lives of minority citizens.

On Being Unemployed

Nelliejean Smith (student)

In the paragraph that follows, we learn of the many effects that unemployment can have on a person's life. The writer makes us see—and feel with her—that unemployment is a traumatic experience. Nelliejean Smith has proven, however, that she can cope with it, for she wrote this paragraph as a student at Cuyahoga Community College.

Words to Know

bureaucracy   an administrative section of government that is often impersonal and inflexible; red tape

evoke   to summon or call forth; to elicit

Getting Started

In what ways do the effects of unemployment reach deeper than an empty bank account?

$\mathbf{B}$eing unemployed creates many problems for my family and me. First of all, there are financial problems. We have cut back on the quality of groceries we purchase. We now buy two pounds of hamburger in place of two pounds of sirloin. This hamburger is also divided into quantities sufficient for three meals: one may be creole beef, one chili, and the other spaghetti. There is also less money for clothing. Dresses must be altered and made into blouses; pants make nice skirts after some alteration. I have two more very sticky problems. I've fallen behind in the rental payments for our apartment, and now I am experiencing difficulties trying to pay the back rent. The other sticky problem is my son's tuition payments. There does not seem to be any way that I can send a complete payment to his college. These are not the only problems I face. I also have psychological problems as a result of unemployment. Often I wonder why this has happened to me. Then depression and confusion take over, and I feel drained of all my abilities. The one question that fills my mind most often is the following: Why can't I get employment? This question evokes in me a lack of self-confidence and self-worth. I am haunted by an overall feeling of uselessness. My other problems center on trying to cope with the bureaucracy of the Employment Bureau. Once I get to the Employment Bureau, I stand in line to sign up. I then wait in another line to which I must report. Once I go through all of this, I am

sent out for job interviews, only to find that the employer wants someone with more experience. To top everything off, I had to wait almost six
months to receive my first unemployment check. As you can see, there is
often a frustratingly long delay in receiving benefits. My family and I
have suffered through many problems because of my unemployment.

Questions About the Reading

1. What do you think makes the inability to pay rent and her son's
   tuition particularly "sticky" problems for the writer?
2. What makes the writer feel "drained" of her abilities?
3. What psychological effects do you think the writer's unsuccessful job
   interviews have on her?

Questions About the Writer's Strategies

1. What is the main idea of this paragraph? Where is this idea first introduced? Where is it repeated?
2. Transitional words and phrases provide a bridge between points in
   this paragraph. Identify the writer's transitions.
3. The writer uses many examples to illustrate the effects of her unemployment. Identify two effects and two examples for each of these
   effects.
4. What order does the writer use in discussing the problems?

Writing Assignments

1. Is the employment bureau the writer describes doing a good job? In
   a paragraph, describe the effects of the bureau's procedures.
2. *Working Together*   Discuss with some classmates the effects unemployment has on the American people as a whole. Do you think it has
   changed our image of ourselves as a nation? Then collaborate to write
   a cause-and-effect paragraph or essay in which you describe some of
   the social effects of unemployment. You may want to read some articles on this topic in the library before you write.
3. Although being employed has more positive than negative effects,
   work does have effects that may not always be pleasant. Write a paragraph on how a particular job or certain types of jobs can have negative effects.

The Pleasures of Age

Robert MacKenzie

The writer convinces us that getting older has pleasures that may differ from those of youth but are just as pleasurable.

Words to Know

foibles   weaknesses, frailties
gyrate   revolve, whirl

Getting Started

What career do you expect to follow? Do you know an older person who works or worked in that field?

The pleasures of age are not less than the pleasures of youth, according to Somerset Maugham, who noted this when he had a lot of rings on his own tree. The novelist and playwright did allow, though, that the pleasures of age are different from those of youth.   1

Assembling my own list of the pleasures one experiences with accrued mileage, I include the following: 2

1. You get to learn how everyone turns out. If life is something like a slow-motion movie, it's only by living a while that you see the plot play itself out. You watch the virtues, flaws and foibles of your friends, relatives and enemies lead to their consequences, good and bad. You find out whether it's true that nice guys finish last and how many cooks it takes to spoil the broth. And, of course, you are witness to your own unfolding drama . . . or comedy. With any luck, by the time the fat lady sings, you have seen quite a show.   3

2. You stop doing things you don't enjoy, to please people you don't like. If standing around at cocktail parties listening to strangers and distant acquaintances talk about the properties they could have bought for a song is no longer your idea of fun, one day you simply stop doing it. If squeezing onto a jammed dance floor to gyrate to viciously overamplified music is something you stopped enjoying sometime in your youth but kept doing because you thought you were supposed to . . . well, sometime in maturity you wake up to the blessed revelation that you never have to do that again. Drop that invitation gently into the circular file, step out onto your porch and enjoy the sunset. Ah, silence.   4

3. You learn you don't have to win the arguments. Hildy, a friend in her 5
   late 60s, says it this way: "I still have passionate opinions, but I'm no
   longer interested in arguing with all the people who aren't smart
   enough to see it my way. Let them rant. When they're bellowing
   away at some totally wrongheaded notion as though their entire ego
   structure depends on being right, I just smile and say, 'Hmmm.' It
   drives them crazy, and it saves my breath."

4. You start choosing comfort over style. After a lifetime of aching feet, 6
   there comes a moment in a woman's life when she packs her high-
   heeled shoes into a cardboard box and happily sends them off to the
   Salvation Army—keeping a pair or two for the occasional party. My
   mother, who used to say "You might as well be dead as out of style,"
   arrived at greater wisdom late in life—she kept only a few chic out-
   fits in the closet, mainly for morale purposes, and opted for an old
   sweater and a pair of sneakers. Finally, you reach the highest fashion
   plateau of all, that realm of serene enlightenment in which you know
   comfort *is* style.

5. You start getting a lot of help. Theaters, thrift shops and bus lines 7
   begin offering you senior discounts long before you feel decrepit. The
   children who were so much work to raise actually start *doing* some
   work. For their parents. Sometimes. And even strangers pitch in. "All
   I have to do is look a little helpless," says Hildy, "a bit stooped and
   confused, you know, and there are people wanting to carry my bags,
   drive me to the store and do my laundry. It's wonderful."

6. You learn about love—the long-haul kind that gets deeper and richer 8
   as the years pile up. It can be a friendship that outlasts the strains and
   the changes. "A friend is someone who knows all about you and still
   likes you," as the saying goes. And, for the luckiest of us, it can be an
   enduring relationship with someone of the opposite sex. We all know
   widows and widowers who aren't interested in marrying again
   because they got and gave enough love in their marriages to last a
   lifetime.

7. You get the irreplaceable satisfaction of having been there, of having 9
   fought the fights and bitten the bullets and learned the lessons. Even
   if we only get partway up the mountain, we can look back and see the
   valley, smog and all. I'm thinking of the 97-year-old grandfather of a
   good friend. He is confined to a nursing home these days but is sharp
   as a razor and a delight to visit. He is pleased to have done what he
   did and been where he has been. But ask him how the rest of us can
   get to 97, and he just grins. "Stay out of traffic," he says.

Questions About the Reading

1. What are the pleasures of age, according to the writer?
2. What does the ninety-seven-year-old grandfather mean by "Stay out of the traffic"?
3. What is meant by "by the time the fat lady sings"?
4. Which of the pleasures do you think is most important?

Questions About the Writer's Strategies

1. What is the main idea of the essay? Is it stated or implied? If stated, identify the sentences. If implied, state it in your own words.
2. What is the cause or causes and what are the effects in the essay?
3. What is the metaphor in the first paragraph?
4. What modes of development does the writer use in addition to cause and effect?

Writing Assignments

1. Interview an older person who is retired from the career field you hope to enter and write an essay explaining the effect the person feels the choice of career had on his or her life.
2. Think of a choice you have made that turned out to be a mistake. Write an essay in which you explain what made you make the mistake and the effect or effects the mistake has had on your life.

The Bounty of the Sea

Jacques Cousteau

Jacques Cousteau, the famous French oceanographer, brought the world of the oceans to us through his books and television documentaries. His love for the oceans extended to a lifelong concern for protecting and conserving the marine environment. In the following essay, written in the mid-1960s, he vividly describes the sickening of the ocean and the effects that the death of the oceans would have on humankind.

Words to Know

buffer   something that protects

cheek by jowl   very close together

effluents   outflows of waste, sewage

insupportable   unbearable

plankton algae   microscopic plant life that grows in water

remorseless   without regret or pity

stench   stink, bad smell

teemed   swarmed

trawlers   fishing boats that drag large nets along the bottom of the ocean

Getting Started

How can the world community understand—and undo—the effects of pollution before it's too late?

During the past thirty years, I have observed and studied the oceans 1
closely, and with my own two eyes I have seen them sicken. Certain reefs that teemed with fish only ten years ago are now almost lifeless. The ocean bottom has been raped by trawlers. Priceless wetlands have been destroyed by landfill. And everywhere are sticky globs of oil, plastic refuse, and unseen clouds of poisonous effluents. Often, when I describe the symptoms of the oceans' sickness, I hear remarks like "they're only fish" or "they're only whales" or "they're only birds." But I assure you that our destinies are linked with theirs in the most profound and fundamental manner. For if the oceans should die—by which I mean that all life in the sea would finally cease—this would signal the end not only for marine life but for all other animals and plants of this earth, including man.

With life departed, the ocean would become, in effect, one enormous 2
cesspool. Billions of decaying bodies, large and small, would create such
an insupportable stench that man would be forced to leave all the coastal
regions. But far worse would follow.

The ocean acts as the earth's buffer. It maintains a fine balance 3
between the many salts and gases which make life possible. But dead
seas would have no buffering effect. The carbon dioxide content of the
atmosphere would start on a steady and remorseless climb, and when it
reached a certain level a "greenhouse effect" would be created. The heat
that normally radiates outward from the earth to space would be
blocked by the CO_2, and sea level temperatures would dramatically
increase.

One catastrophic effect of this heat would be melting of the icecaps at 4
both the North and South Poles. As a result, the ocean would rise by 100
feet or more, enough to flood almost all the world's major cities. These
rising waters would drive one-third of the earth's billions inland, creating famine, fighting, chaos, and disease on a scale almost impossible to
imagine.

Meanwhile, the surface of the ocean would have scummed over with 5
a thick film of decayed matter, and would no longer be able to give
water freely to the skies through evaporation. Rain would become a rar-
ity, creating global drought and even more famine.

But the final act is yet to come. The wretched remnant of the human 6
race would now be packed cheek by jowl on the remaining highlands,
bewildered, starving, struggling to survive from hour to hour. Then
would be visited upon them the final plague, anoxia (lack of oxygen).
This would be caused by the extinction of plankton algae and the reduc-
tion of land vegetation, the two sources that supply the oxygen you are
now breathing.

And so man would finally die, slowly gasping out his life on some 7
barren hill. He would have survived the oceans by perhaps thirty years.
And his heirs would be bacteria and a few scavenger insects.

Questions About the Reading

1. How does Cousteau know that the oceans are sick? What evidence
   does he give?
2. What is the "greenhouse effect" (paragraph 3)?
3. What is CO_2?

Questions About the Writer's Strategies

1. What is the thesis of this essay? Is it directly stated or implied? If it is directly stated, where in the essay is it stated?
2. Identify the cause-and-effect elements of this essay.
3. Apart from cause and effect, does the writer use any other modes of development?
4. How are you affected by the use of such words as "scummed over," "thick film of decayed matter," and "cesspool" to describe the ocean?

Writing Assignments

1. Use the Internet to research the causes and effects of air pollution, and then write an essay based on your findings. Include a list of the web-site addresses you use. To find helpful sites, use a search engine such as Google (**http://www.google.com/**), or Yahoo! (**http://www.yahoo.com/**) and type in keywords such as "air pollution."
2. What personal steps can you take to stop pollution? Write an essay that describes what you as an individual can do and what effects you think your actions would have.
3. Why do people pollute? Write an essay identifying some of the things that cause people to harm the environment and the types of pollution that result.

It Took This Night to
Make Us Know

Bob Greene

Eleven Israeli athletes were murdered by Palestinian terrorists at the 1972 summer Olympics in Munich, in what was then West Germany. The news shocked and horrified the world. It also made at least one man—Chicago newspaper columnist Bob Greene—look deep inside himself and think, for perhaps the first time, about where he came from, who he was, and what it means to be born Jewish in today's world.

Words to Know

abstraction a remote, unreal idea

patronized treated in an offensive, condescending manner

Getting Started

In what ways can prejudice and violence be seen as integral parts of the human experience?

Washington—It is not supposed to be very strong in us, for we can- 1
not remember. We are the young Jews, born after Hitler, and we have never considered the fact that we are Jewish to be a large part of our identity. A lot of us have not been near a temple in ten years, and we laugh along with the Jewish jokes to show that we are very cool about the whole thing. We are Americans, we have told ourselves, we do not go around calling ourselves Jews: that is for the elderly men with the tortured faces, the old Jews we feel a little embarrassed to be around. Let them recall the centuries of hurt, we think; it is over now, so let them recall those years while we live our good todays.

It is not supposed to be very strong in us, and yet I am sitting at a 2
typewriter in a hotel room hundreds of miles from home trying to write a story about a presidential campaign, and I cannot do it. For the television has just got done telling the story, the story of how once again people who hate the Jews have knocked on a door in the middle of the night and done their killing, and I can think of nothing else. Now the lesson is being taught all over again; it is not up to us to decide how to treat our Jewishness. That was decided for us centuries ago.

It is not supposed to be very strong in us, because all the barriers are 3
down now, and a hotel will not turn us away or a restaurant will not deny

us a table if our name does not sound right. And yet when the killings began, they thought to get a young man named Mark Spitz out of Germany, because he may be the best swimmer in the world, but first of all he is a Jew, and no one wanted to think what might happen to him. Many of the people who thrilled as he won his gold medals were very surprised to find out now that Spitz is a Jew. Later they will say that of course it doesn't matter what his religion is. But Spitz knew that it mattered; we all knew that it mattered, and that it would be smarter for him to go.

It is not supposed to be very strong in us, and we have heard the term "six million Jews are dead" so often that it is just an abstraction to us. And yet if the Dachau concentration camp, just a few miles from the Olympic site, was not enough to remind us, the killers in the Munich darkness made sure that we remembered. There is a hate for us that goes back centuries, and every time it seems to have weakened with the years there is another band of men ready to show us that the hate is still strong enough to make them kill in the night. 4

When the news was certain, when there was no question but that the young Jewish men were dead, I called some friends and we talked about it. They were thinking the same way I was. For all these years we have acted bored with the Jewish traditions, smirked at the ancient, detailed ceremonies, patronized the old ones who insisted on showing their link with the past. 5

And for us, it took this one night to make us know that maybe it will never go away. We are all Jews who were born into a world where money and education and parents who speak with no accent were part of the package, and that can fool you. But this is the oldest hate the world has ever seen, and 25 years of Jewish prosperity in the United States are hardly enough to erase it from the earth. 6

It is nothing that we young ones have ever talked much about, and there are not many words to tell it now. Words cannot tell it as well as the look we have seen for years in the faces of the oldest Jews, the look of deepest sorrow that has been there for as many centuries as the hate. 7

This time the look is there because of a group of Arab terrorists. But it goes so far beyond Middle Eastern politics; the look was there in this same Germany 30 years ago, it was there in Egypt centuries ago, it has been there in every place there have ever been Jews who were not wanted because they were Jews. And because there have been so many of these places, the look has been reborn and reborn and reborn. 8

There are young men who are dead this week who should be alive, and it would be a horrible thing no matter who they were. But of course they were Jews; the reason that they are dead is because they were Jews, and that is why on this night there are so many of us starting to realize for the first time what that means. 9

It is not supposed to be very strong in us, for we cannot remember. We 10
grew up laughing at the solemn old Jewish phrases that sounded so
mournful and outmoded and out of date in the second half of the twen-
tieth century. Ancient, outmoded phrases from the temples, phrases like
"Let my people go." Phrases that we chose to let mean nothing, because
it is not supposed to be very strong in us.

Questions About the Reading

1. Why, according to the writer, are young Jews embarrassed to be
   around old Jews with "tortured faces" (paragraph 1)?
2. Why is the writer having difficulty writing a story about a presidential campaign?
3. What effect does the killing of several Jewish men at the Olympics
   have on the young Jewish people living in the United States?
4. What "is not supposed to be very strong" in young American Jews?
5. Consider the title of the essay. What is it that the writer and his con-
   temporaries now know?

Questions About the Writer's Strategies

1. In your own words, express the main idea or thesis of the essay. Does
   the writer ever state this idea explicitly in a single sentence, or must
   the reader infer it?
2. What is the writer's tone in the essay? What attitude does he have
   toward the event described—and toward himself and his friends as a
   result of the event?
3. Identify the cause-and-effect elements in the essay.
4. How does the writer use repetition in the essay? What is its effect?

Writing Assignments

1. *Working Together*   Join with some classmates to write an essay in
   which you discuss what you perceive to be the causes of racial violence and their effects on society.
2. Do the Olympic Games decrease tensions among people of different
   nations, cultures, and races? Write a cause-and-effect essay on this topic.
3. Recall an incident in which you were ridiculed, harassed, or mis-
   treated for no apparent reason other than groundless hostility. If you
   have never experienced anything like this, maybe someone among
   your friends could describe such an incident for you. Using the incident as the cause, write an essay about its effects on you or your
   friend.

The Thirsty Animal

Brian Manning

*In this personal essay, Brian Manning recounts how he developed into a
problem drinker and describes his life now as an alcoholic who has quit
drinking. Straightforwardly, he tells of his bittersweet memories of drinking and of his struggle, successful so far, to keep the thirsty "animal living inside" locked in its cage.*

Words to Know

accouterments   the items and sensations accompanying a certain activity
Bordeaux   a type of French wine, usually red
lolling   lounging, relaxing

Getting Started

Can you describe some of the negative effects of alcohol on you or
someone you know?

I was very young, but I still vividly remember how my father fasci-   1
nated my brothers and me at the dinner table by running his finger
around the rim of his wineglass. He sent a wonderful, crystal tone wafting through the room, and we loved it. When we laughed too raucously,
he would stop, swirl the red liquid in his glass and take a sip.

There was a wine cellar in the basement of the house we moved into   2
when I was eleven. My father put a few cases of Bordeaux down there in
the dark. We played there with other boys in the neighborhood, hid
there, made a secret place. It was musty and cool and private. We wrote
things and stuck them in among the bottles and imagined someone way
in the future baffled by our messages from the past.

Many years later, the very first time I drank, I had far too much. But I   3
found I was suddenly able to tell a girl at my high school that I was mad
about her.

When I drank in college with the men in my class, I was trying to   4
define a self-image I could feel comfortable with. I wanted to be "an
Irishman," I decided, a man who could drink a lot of liquor and hold it.
My favorite play was Eugene O'Neill's *Long Day's Journey into Night*, my
model the drunken Jamie Tyrone.

I got out of college, into the real world, and the drunk on weekends   5
started to slip into the weekdays. Often I didn't know when one drunk

ended and another began. The years were measured in hangovers. It took a long time to accept, and then to let the idea sink in, that I was an alcoholic.

It took even longer to do anything about it. I didn't want to believe it, 6 and I didn't want to deny myself the exciting, brotherly feeling I had whenever I went boozing with my friends. For a long time, in my relationships with women, I could only feel comfortable with a woman who drank as much as I did. So I didn't meet many women and spent my time with men in dark barrooms, trying to be like them and hoping I'd be accepted.

It is now two years since I quit drinking, and that, as all alcoholics 7 know who have come to grips with their problem, is not long ago at all. The urge to have "just one" includes a genuine longing for all the accouterments of drink: the popping of a cork, the color of Scotch through a glass, the warmth creeping over my shoulders with the third glass of stout. Those were joys. Ever since I gave them up I remember them as delicious.

I go to parties now and start off fine, but I have difficulty dealing with 8 the changing rhythms as the night wears on. Everyone around me seems to be having a better time the more they drink, and I, not they, become awkward. I feel like a kid with a broken chain when everyone else has bicycled around the corner out of sight. I fight against feeling sorry for myself.

What were the things I was looking for and needed when I drank? I 9 often find that what I am looking for when I want a drink is not really the alcohol, but the memories and laughter that seemed possible only with a glass in my hand. In a restaurant, I see the bottle of vintage port on the shelf, and imagine lolling in my chair, swirling the liquid around in the glass, inhaling those marvelous fumes. I think of my neighbor, Eileen, the funniest woman I ever got smashed with, and I want to get up on a bar stool next to her to hear again the wonderful stories she told. She could drink any man under the table, she claimed, and I wanted to be one of those men who tried. She always won, but it made me feel I belonged when I staggered out of the bar, her delighted laughter following me.

I had found a world to cling to, a way of belonging, and it still attracts 10 me. I pass by the gin mills and pubs now and glance in at the men lined up inside, and I don't see them as suckers or fools. I remember how I felt sitting there after work, or watching a Sunday afternoon ball game, and I long for the smell of the barroom and that ease—toasts and songs, jokes and equality. I have to keep reminding myself of the wasting hangovers, the lost money, the days down the drain.

I imagine my problem as an animal living inside me, demanding a 11 drink before it dies of thirst. That's what it says, but it will never die of thirst. The fact an alcoholic faces is that this animal breathes and waits. It is incapable of death and will spring back to lustful, consuming life with even one drop of sustenance.

When I was eighteen and my drinking began in earnest, I didn't play 12 in the wine cellar at home anymore; I stole there. I sneaked bottles to my room, sat in the window and drank alone while my parents were away. I hated the taste of it, but I kept drinking it, without the kids from the neighborhood, without any thought that I was feeding the animal. And one day, I found one of those old notes we had hidden down there years before. It fell to the ground when I pulled a bottle from its cubbyhole. I read it with bleary eyes, then put the paper back into the rack. "Beware," it said, above a childish skull and crossbones, "all ye who enter here." A child, wiser than I was that day, had written that note.

I did a lot of stupid, disastrous, sometimes mean things in the years 13 that followed, and remembering them is enough to snap me out of the memories and back to the reality that I quit just in time. I've done something I had to do, something difficult and necessary, and that gives me satisfaction and the strength to stay on the wagon. I'm very lucky so far. I don't get mad that I can't drink anymore; I can handle the self-pity that overwhelmed me in my early days of sobriety. From time to time, I daydream about summer afternoons and cold beer. I know such dreams will never go away. The thirsty animal is there, getting a little fainter every day. It will never die. A lot of my life now is all about keeping it in a very lonely cage.

Questions About the Reading

1. What went along with drinking for the writer? Why did he need alcohol to get those effects?
2. Why are parties difficult for the writer?
3. Why did the writer stop drinking?
4. When you finished reading the essay, what opinions had you formed of the writer's personality and character? Cite specific details from the essay to support your opinions.

Questions About the Writer's Strategies

1. What is the main idea of this essay? In which sentences is it most clearly stated?

2. What are the causes in this essay? What are the effects? Do they overlap at all?
3. Other than cause and effect, what modes of development does the
   writer use? Cite paragraphs in which he uses other modes.
4. The "animal" introduced in paragraph 11 is a metaphor. What does it
   stand for? Interpret it in your own words.
5. Identify the simile in paragraph 8. Is it effective in helping you understand how the writer feels?

Writing Assignments

1. Describe in an essay the effects that alcohol has on you. If you do not
   drink, describe the effects that you have seen it have on others.
2. Do you know anyone who abuses alcohol or other substances? If not,
   you have surely come across the lure of drugs in the media or in
   school awareness programs. On the basis of what you know and
   what you have learned from reading this essay, write an essay
   describing the causes and effects of substance abuse.

Racial Stereotypes Go Underground

Cynthia Merriwether-deVries

We can't dispel our racial misconceptions and stereotypes, according to the writer, unless we are willing to admit we have them and are willing to talk about them.

Words to Know

articulating   talking or speaking about
deterrent   discouragement, prevention
ingrained   established, fixed
intimidated   made fearful or timid

Getting Started

Do you have friends who are of a race this is different from yours?

Quick: What comes to mind first when you think of an African- 1
American? Can't come up with anything? Or too uncomfortable to admit
what you're thinking?

Everyone is aware of the racial and ethnic preconceptions, miscon- 2
ceptions and stereotypes that exist in American society. Yet many college
students, believe it or not, claim they can't think of a single stereotype
about blacks, Asians, Hispanics and Arabs.

As part of a research project, I interviewed more than 80 students at 3
my predominantly white, middle-class campus about their perceptions
of race and gender. Most had no problem articulating popular stereotypes about men and women: "macho," "aggressive" and "competitive"
for men; "self-conscious" and "sensitive" for women.

But asked to turn their attention to racial stereotypes, many fell silent. 4
More than half claimed they could think of no stereotypes associated
with Asians or Hispanics. A third said they had no preconceptions of
Arabs. About a quarter claimed ignorance of any stereotypes associated
with African-Americans.

What is happening in our country—specifically, on our college 5
campuses—is the result of years of speech codes and "political correctness" that have covered over racial stereotypes and misconceptions but
done little to eliminate them. So instead of honest discourse, we get the
Bambi approach: If you can't say anything nice, don't say anything at all.

But I know racial and ethnic stereotypes still exist: I am an African- 6
American woman from a working-class background at a small, private
liberal arts school, where the most well-meaning students unmask their
ingrained stereotypes only when they let their guard down. Some of my
students, for example, are surprised to find out I was raised in a two-
parent household (married parents, at that).

From an educator's point of view, it's tragic to see college students 7
intimidated into thinking it's taboo to speak certain words or ideas associated with racial and ethnic groups. The thoughts and words are there,
but students aren't comfortable expressing them.

As a sociologist and an academic, it's my job to combat misconcep- 8
tions by putting them on the table where we can talk about their origins,
why they're invalid and how to dispel them. The current climate on campus is a deterrent to that goal. So we're left with a social and political climate that suppresses only the expressions—but not the sentiments.

Questions About the Reading

1. What are the stereotypes that the college students had about men and
   women?
2. How did the students respond when asked about racial stereotypes?
   Why?
3. What percent of the students claimed they had no stereotypes of
   Asians or Hispanics?
4. What percent claimed they had no preconceptions of Arabs? What
   percent claimed they did not know of any stereotypes associated
   with African-Americans?

Questions About the Writer's Strategies

1. What is the thesis of the essay? Is it stated or implied? If stated, identify the sentences. If implied, state the thesis in your own words.
2. What are the cause and the effect in the essay?
3. Besides cause and effect, what other modes of development does the
   writer use?
4. Is the essay objective or subjective or both? Support your answer
   with examples from the essay.

Writing Assignments

1. Write a cause-and-effect essay about the pros and cons of political
   correctness.
2. *Working Together* Join with some classmates and write a cause-
   and-effect essay about stereotypes.

9

Definition

WHEN WRITERS USE words that they think may be unfamiliar to their readers, they usually will define the words. A **definition** is an explanation of the meaning of a word or term.

In its shortest form, the definition may be simply a **synonym**—a familiar word or phrase that has the same meaning as the unfamiliar word. For example, in "she shows more *empathy* for, or true understanding of, older people than her sister," the word *understanding* is a synonym for *empathy*. Or the writer may choose to use an **antonym**—a word or phrase that has the opposite meaning of the unfamiliar word—as in "she is a compassionate rather than an *inconsiderate* person." Here the word *inconsiderate* gives the reader the opposite meaning of *compassionate*.

The writer may also choose to use the kind of precise definition found in dictionaries, called a **formal definition.** In a formal definition, the writer first uses a form of **classification,** assigning the word to the **class** of items to which it belongs, and then describing the characteristics that distinguish it from other items of that class. Here is an example of a formal definition.

Word defined: tiger; class: cat family	⌐ A <u>tiger</u>, a member of the <u>cat family</u>, is native to Asia,
Description of characteristics	⌐ usually weighs over 350 pounds, and has tawny and black- ⌐ striped fur.

Connotation, which refers to the impressions or qualities we associate with a word, and **denotation,** the dictionary definition of a word, are important in writing a definition. Think of the word *pig,* for instance.

The dictionary may tell you that a pig is simply a domestic animal with hooves, short legs, bristly hair, and a blunt snout; and a farmer may tell you that a pig is relatively smarter and cleaner than other farm animals. However, the negative connotations of this word are so strong that you are likely to have trouble thinking of a pig without thinking of filth, fat, and greed.

In writing definitions, it is particularly important to choose your words in such a way that their connotations as well as their denotations will give your readers the correct impression of what you are defining. As you are writing and **revising,** remember to search for the single best word for conveying your ideas.

When you search for connotative words and expressions to use in your writing, beware of **clichés.** Clichés are words or phrases—such as "rosy red," "silly goose," "bull in a china shop," "weird," or "outrageous"— which have become so overused that they indicate a lack of imagination and thought on the part of the writer who uses them. Symbols, too, can be clichés. If you are defining *courage,* for example, using Superman as a symbol to enhance your definition is unlikely to impress your readers. You should also be aware that many clichés take the form of **similes:** "as filthy as a pig," for example. Try to make sure your similes are always of your own creation, not ones you have heard before.

Many complex words and abstract ideas—such as *truth* and *justice*— require longer and more detailed explanations, which are called **extended definitions.** In an extended definition, the writer may use one or more of the methods of development—description, examples, classification, and so forth—that you have learned about in the earlier chapters of this book. For example, the writer might use **process, description,** or **narration**—or all three—as the method of development in an extended definition.

Topic sentence: formal definition	A glacier is an accumulation of snow and ice that continually flows from a mountain ice field toward sea level.
Process	Glaciers are formed when successive snowfalls pile up, creating pressure on the bottom layers. Gradually, the pressure causes the snow on the bottom to undergo a structural change into an extremely dense form of ice called glacier ice, a process that may take several years. Once the ice begins to
Extended definition: descriptive narration	accumulate, gravity causes the mass to move downhill. Glaciers usually take the path of least resistance, following stream beds or other natural channels down the mountainside. As they move, they scrape along the surface of the earth, picking up rocks and other sediment on the way. The ice and the debris carve a deep U-shaped valley as they proceed down the mountain. If they advance far enough, they will eventually reach the sea and become tidewater glaciers that break off, or calve, directly into salt water. Southeast

> Alaska is one of only three places in the world where tide-water glaciers exist. (They also are found in Scandinavia and Chile.) Other glaciers, called hanging glaciers, spill out of icy basins high up on valley walls and tumble toward the valley floor.
>
> Sarah Eppenbach,
> *Alaska's Southeast*

In the example that follows, the writer combines a formal definition with **classification, examples, comparison** and **contrast.**

Formal definition: map Classification: conventional picture Characteristics: area of land, sea, or sky	A map is a <u>conventional picture</u> of an <u>area of land, sea, or sky.</u> Perhaps the maps most widely used are the <u>road maps</u> given away by the oil companies. They show the cultural features such as states, towns, parks, and roads, especially paved roads. They show also natural features, such as rivers and lakes, and sometimes mountains. As <u>simple maps</u>, most automobile drivers have on various occasions used sketches drawn by service station men, or by friends, to show the best automobile route from one town to another.

1

Example: road maps

Example: simple maps

Contrast: chart represents water; map represents land	The distinction usually made between "maps" and "charts" is that a chart is a representation of an area consisting chiefly of water; a map represents an area that is predominantly land. It is easy to see how this distinction arose

2

Contrast: chart for navigation — in the days when there was no navigation over land, but a truer distinction is that charts are specially designed for use in navigation, whether at sea or in the air.

Example: use of maps	Maps have been used since the earliest civilizations, and explorers find that they are used in rather simple civilizations at the present time by people who are accustomed to traveling. For example, Arctic explorers have obtained considerable help from maps of the coast lines showing settlements, drawn by Eskimo people. Occasionally maps show not only the roads, but pictures of other features. One of the earliest such maps dates from about 1400 B.C. It shows not only roads, but also lakes with fish, and a canal with crocodiles and a bridge over the canal. This is somewhat similar to the modern maps of a state which show for each large town some feature of interest or the chief products of that town.

3

Example: features of some maps

Comparison: features of early maps with ones of modern maps

> C. C. Wylie,
> *Astronomy, Maps, and Weather*

As you can see, you may use any method of development that is appropriate when you need to extend the definition of a word or term.

Whether you are writing an extended definition or relying primarily on some other mode of development, always remember to define any words or terms you use that may be unfamiliar to your readers—particularly any words they must know to understand your meaning. You should also define words with any special or technical meaning.

Nostalgia

Richard Shelton

*What is the crepuscular? Richard Shelton misses it, along with the bu-
colic and idyllic. Although he does not define the word, a careful reading
tells us what it means.*

Words to Know

bucolic   pastoral, rural, rustic
carnage   slaughter, bloodshed
gentility   politeness, refinement
idyllic   pleasing, simple, picturesque
mayhem   mutilation

Getting Started

Is there something that you remember from your childhood and
now miss?

Whatever happened to the crepuscular? It's never mentioned anymore. Years since I heard any reference to the crepuscular. I wonder if
anybody notices it now as we once did, creeping in and out with silent
majesty, leaving some of us with lumps in our throats. It would be a
relief from the carnage and mayhem. I remember sometimes at that time
of day in the autumn when there was a chill in the air and somebody was
burning leaves somewhere, I could nearly die of happiness. But I am
older now and it's illegal to burn leaves. So I guess nobody notices the
crepuscular anymore. Or the bucolic. Nobody ever says, "Let's go spend
a bucolic weekend in the country." And nobody calls anything idyllic.
Whatever became of idyllic afternoons beside the river? And grand passions? Passions don't seem to be grand anymore, just sort of everyday
affairs. I guess it's hard to have a grand passion without idyllic afternoons and crepuscular evenings, and we are just too busy to take the
time for such things. And nightingales? I never heard one myself, but I
certainly read about them, and they seemed to be almost everywhere at
one time. Perhaps they were no longer needed and they died out or somebody shot them. Might be a few left in a zoo somewhere, I wouldn't know
about that. But surely gentility has survived. You mean gentility is

gone too? Lord! But whatever happened to peace and quiet? Somewhere there still must be some peace and quiet. And whatever happened to kindness . . .?

Questions About the Reading

1. According to the writer, how did people feel when they noticed the crepuscular?
2. How did the writer feel when somebody was burning leaves somewhere?
3. What would a bucolic weekend in the country be like?
4. What would an idyllic afternoon be like?

Questions About the Writer's Strategies

1. What is the main idea of the paragraph? Is it stated or implied?
2. What does *crepuscular* mean? How did you figure out the meaning?
3. What modes of development does the writer use?
4. What is the tone of the paragraph?

Writing Assignments

1. Write a paragraph in which you define one of the following terms: *democracy, religion, ethics*. Include a formal definition from an online dictionary such as yourDictionary.com (**http://www.yourdictionary .com/**), and use at least two other modes of development. Make a copy of the web page on which you find your definition and attach it to your paragraph.
2. Write a paragraph in which you define one of the following sports: baseball, football, basketball, soccer.
3. Write a paragraph about some holiday celebration that you remember and now miss.

Walking

Henry David Thoreau

Henry David Thoreau, in Walden and Other Writings, *defines "the art of walking" as to be a saunterer and then tells us what being a "saunterer" means to him.*

Words to Know

derived   taken from
Sainte Terre   Holy Land
sedulously   steadily, diligently
vagabonds   wanderers
vagrant   wanderer, roamer

Getting Started

Do you have a walking, running, or other regular exercise program? How would you define it?

I have met with but one or two persons in the course of my life who understood the art of Walking, that is, of taking walks—who had a genius, so to speak, for SAUNTERING, which word is beautifully derived "from idle people who roved about the country, in the Middle Ages, and asked charity, under pretense of going a la Sainte Terre," to the Holy Land, till the children exclaimed, "There goes a Sainte-Terrer," a Saunterer, a Holy-Lander. They who never go to the Holy Land in their walks, as they pretend, are indeed mere idlers and vagabonds; but they who do go there are saunterers in the good sense, such as I mean. Some, however, would derive the word from sans terre without land or a home, which, therefore, in the good sense, will mean, having no particular home, but equally at home everywhere. For this is the secret of successful sauntering. He who sits still in a house all the time may be the greatest vagrant of all; but the saunterer, in the good sense, is no more vagrant than the meandering river, which is all the while sedulously seeking the shortest course to the sea. But I prefer the first, which, indeed, is the most probable derivation. For every walk is a sort of crusade, preached by some Peter the Hermit in us, to go forth and reconquer this Holy Land from the hands of the Infidels.

Questions About the Reading

1. What does Thoreau say is "the art of walking"?
2. What does Thoreau say is the derivation of "sauntering"? Does he give more than one derivation source? If so, what is it?
3. What is the "secret of successful walking"?
4. What is the relation of the last sentence of the paragraph to "sauntering"?
5. Why is the saunterer, "in the good sense," not like the meandering river?

Questions About the Writer's Strategies

1. What is the main idea of the paragraph? Is it stated or implied? If stated, identify the sentence or sentences. If implied, state it in your own words.
2. What modes of development does the writer use to define "sauntering"?
3. What are the metaphors in the paragraph?

Writing Assignments

1. Write a paragraph in which you define your exercise program, its purpose, and your feelings about it. Identify the modes of development you use.
2. Write a paragraph in which you define one of the following terms: faith, hope, liberty, freedom, or poetry. Identify the modes of development you use.

3. Use the Internet to gather information about Thoreau's life, and then write a paragraph in relation to when and where he lived and his most important writings based on your findings.

What Does It Mean to Be Creative?

S. I. Hayakawa

S. I. Hayakawa was a United States senator, the president of San Francisco State College, and an authority on semantics—the study of the development, structure, and changes of language. In this paragraph, he defines the creative person.

Word to Know

examining   investigating, looking at

Getting Started

What do you think it means to be creative?

A creative person, first, is not limited in his thinking to "what everyone knows." "Everyone knows" that trees are green. The creative artist is able to see that in certain lights some trees look blue or purple or yellow. The creative person looks at the world with his or her own eyes, not with the eyes of others. The creative individual also knows his or her own feelings better than the average person. Most people don't know the answer to the question, "How are you? How do you feel?" The reason they don't know is that they are so busy feeling what they are supposed to feel, thinking what they are supposed to think, that they never get down to examining their own deepest feelings.

Questions About the Reading

1. According to the writer, how does the creative person look at the world?
2. What distinguishes the creative individual from the average person?
3. Why do most people not know the answer to "How are you? How do you feel?"

Questions About the Writer's Strategies

1. What is the writer's definition of a creative person?
2. What are two transitional words the writer uses? Would the definition be clearer by changing one of the transitional words? What transitional words would you use in the definition?

Writing Assignments

1. Write a paragraph in which you define and give examples of a creative person.
2. Write a paragraph in which you explain how someone in a certain sport might be creative.

Grandparents

Nancy Merrell (student)

*In the paragraph that follows, Nancy Merrell provides us with an ex-
tended definition of the word* grandparents *by telling us what they do
and how we feel about them at different times in our lives and theirs. By
making us understand her feelings about grandparents, she makes us
aware of our own attitudes and feelings.*

Words to Know

accomplishments achievements
appreciated valued

Getting Started

How would you define an excellent teacher?

Of all family members, grandparents are probably the least appreciated. They are just people who are always around. They make a fuss
over the children in the family, brag to their friends about the accomplishments of this child or that child, and show countless pictures of new
babies. Grandfathers can fix anything, and grandmothers always have
homemade cookies around. When you are small, it's fun to stay with
your grandparents because they always let you do things you can't do at
home, and of course they buy you things. They are always available to
babysit because they don't go out much and actually prefer to see their
grandchildren. They are usually good for a small loan now and then that
doesn't need to be paid back because they turn it into a gift. You respect-
fully listen to their advice but don't follow it because they are old and
don't understand how things are in this day and age. You thank them
politely for what they do for you, and then don't call or visit them until
you need something else. And of course you never tell them how dear
they are to you because they know how you feel about them anyway.
Then all of a sudden, they are no longer there to do the things that only
grandparents do, and you find yourself wishing that you had told them
what they meant to you as people and not just as grandparents.

Questions About the Reading

1. What inferences can you draw about the writer's grandparents from the paragraph? Support your answer with statements from the paragraph.
2. What is the function of the last sentence of the paragraph?
3. What are some of the examples that the writer uses to define grandparents? What are some of the examples she uses to explain how we treat grandparents?

Questions About the Writer's Strategies

1. What is the main mode of development that the writer uses to define grandparents?
2. Does the writer use more than one mode? If so, which one(s)?
3. What is the point of view in the paragraph? Does it change? If so, could the writer have maintained the same point of view throughout the paragraph? If so, explain how this could be done.

Writing Assignments

1. Write a paragraph in which you define a true friend by giving examples of the person's behavior.
2. Write a paragraph in which you define a person or place by using descriptive details.
3. Write a paragraph in which you define what the word *parent* means to you. Use several modes of development—such as examples, description or narration. You might want to consider process; in particular, how to be a good parent.

Total Eclipse of the Son

Tiffany Kay

In Japan, a society long known for valuing and respecting parents and elders, young people are withdrawing from them in a phenomenon known as hikikomori. *(Tiffany Kay, "Total Eclipse of the Son,"* PSYCHOLOGY TODAY, *Jan/Feb 2003. Reprinted with permission from* PSYCHOLOGY TODAY *Magazine, Copyright © (2003) Sussex Publishers, Inc.)*

Words to Know

agoraphobia   fear of being in the open or in public places
bastion   protector
controversial   debatable, arguable
ramifications   consequences
syndrome   illness, disease

Getting Started

How would you define good parenting and bad parenting?

A syndrome known as *hikikomori*, in which the outside world is   1
shunned, is wreaking havoc on young people in Japan, a country known
for its communal values. And an older generation—the very bastion of
those old-fashioned values—may be to blame, according to a controversial new theory.

Hikikomori (the term refers to the behavior itself and to those who suf-   2
fer from it) was first recognized in the early 1990s. One million Japanese,
or almost 1 percent of the population, are estimated to suffer from *hikikomori*, defined as a withdrawal from friends and family for months or
even years. Some 40 percent of *hikikomori* are below the age of 21, according to a 2001 government report.

Western psychologists compare *hikikomori* with social anxiety and   3
agoraphobia, a fear of open places. The affliction has also been likened
to Asperger's syndrome, a mild variant of autism. But these theories
carry little weight in Japan, where the disorder is considered culturally
unique and is linked to violence.

Yuichi Hattori, M.A., a psychologist currently treating 18 patients   4
with the disorder, believes that *hikikomori* is caused by emotionally neg-
lectful parenting. Hattori argues that none of his patients had been sexually or physically abused, yet they all show signs of posttraumatic
stress disorder.

As the cultural gap between Japan's youth and elders widens, some 5
young Japanese may view their parents as too stony-faced and reserved.
Hattori speaks of Japanese society's deep-rooted division between *hone*
and *tatemae*—one's true feelings and one's actions—to illustrate the frustration his patients express toward aloof parents.

"Patients tell me their mothers have no emotions," says Hattori. "Six 6
patients have called their parents zombies."

Hattori's findings, presented in November to the International 7
society for the Study of Dissociation, are reminiscent of the now-
discredited theory of the "refrigerator mother," which attributed autism
to a detached style of parenting.

"*Hikikomori* looks more to me like an extreme case of social anxiety," 8
says David Kupfer, Ph.D., a psychologist with a private practice in
Virginia. Emotionally unresponsive parents are only one of the factors
involved in the development of this disorder, says Kupfer, who points
out that "in Japan, the pressure to succeed is a unique cultural source of
trauma."

For now, Eastern and Western psychologists agree only that *hikikomori* 9
is unique to Japan and has serious ramifications for both generations.

Questions About the Reading

1. What is *hikikomori*?
2. What percent of the Japanese population suffer from *hikikomori*?
3. What is the age of 40 percent of the persons who suffer from *hikikomori*?
4. What is the cause of *hikikomori,* according to the psychologist Yuichi
   Hattori?

Questions About the Writer's Strategies

1. What is the definition of *hikikomori*?
2. What other modes of development does the writer use? Identify them.
3. Could the essay be classified under any other modes of development? If so, what are they?
4. What is the tone of the essay?

Writing Assignments

1. Write an essay in which you define good parenting and bad parenting. Identify the modes of development you use.
2. Write an essay in which you define good teaching. Identify the modes
   of development you use.

Earning Their Pinstripes

Rick Reilly

It may look like an easy job and lots of fun, but Rick Reilly shows us that being a batboy for a major league baseball team is a tough, demanding, and low-paying job. (Rick Reilly, "Earning Their Pinstripes," SPORTS ILLUSTRATED, Sept. 23, 2002, p. 92. Reprinted by permission of Sports Illustrated.)

Word to Know

volcanic   violent, explosive

Getting Started

What job would you like to have? Do you know what the requirements of the job are and what it pays?

So, kid, you want to be a New York Yankees batboy? Hang out with 1 Derek Jeter? Ride in the parades? Great. But, first, maybe you'd better take a look at a batboy's typical day.

2 P.M.—Pete Shalhoub, 17, shows up for a 7:15 game and starts setting 2 up the dugout. Sure, most of the players won't be arriving for at least two hours, but so what? Pete'll be here two hours after the players have left, too.

You think batboys still only run out and get Johnny Blanchard's bat? 3 Get real. Pete and the six other Yankees batboys—clubhouse boys are valets, cabbies, maids, deliverymen, shrinks and short-order cooks. And they're not 12 years old anymore. They're all 16 and older because the average sixth-grader doesn't do well when he's also working 75-hour weeks.

Some nights Pete has to show up at 3 in the morning to help unload 4 the road-trip truck, do laundry and set up players' lockers. That takes four hours. Then he goes straight to high school in Jersey City, and then right back to the Stadium, where he'll work until about 1 A.M., go to bed at 2 and get up again at 6 the next morning to go to class.

"It's like I tell him," says Joe Lee, another member of the crew. "In this 5 job you've got to sleep twice as fast."

3:45 P.M.—One of Pete's 1,000 jobs is mixing Gatorade for the dugout. 6 That can be dangerous. A few years ago former visiting team batboy Joe Rocchio made green, not knowing volcanic Cleveland Indians star

Albert Belle drank only red. Belle spit it out, knocked the jug over in the dugout, and Joe had to clean it up. Glamorous job, no?

4 P.M.—When players arrive, batboys start hopping. They're each 7 player's little Jeeves. "Anything they ask for, they pretty much get," says Pete. That includes everything from, "Go get my wife a birthday present" to "Go get my brother-in-law at the airport." From going to a player's home to pack his bags to making dinner reservations. One player asked Lee to go to the ballpark every day during a 12-day road trip and idle his car for a half hour. "Keeps the engine clean," the player said.

Of course, there *are* rewards. When Jason Giambi was with Oakland, 8 he sent an A's batboy to McDonald's. Giambi got three hits that day, so he kept sending the kid for the rest of the season. When Giambi won the MVP, he tipped him $5,000.

4:30 P.M.—A new kid shows up, the winner of a contest to be a batboy 9 for a day. He's lucky he doesn't get the initiation Craig Postolowski got. To start, Jeter sent him off to look for the key to the batter's box. Then Joe Torre told him to go get the knuckleballs ready. Then Don Zimmer needed the lefthanded fungo bat. Finally, when Bernie Williams asked him to get a bucket of steam from the shower to clean home plate, he realized he'd been had.

5:45 P.M.—It's Pete's day to shag flies in the outfield and run the balls 10 back to the batting practice pitcher. This is a gas. There's other cool stuff too. Some nights the clubhouse is lousy with celebs. You get to be in the team photo. And players have been known to lend batboys their sweet sleds for the prom. Of course, two years ago Manny Alexander of the Boston Red Sox lent his car to a batboy. Problem is, the kid got pulled over and police found steroids in it. Oops. Always check the glove compartment, Kid.

7:05 P.M.—Tonight Pete works balls for the home plate umpire. 11 Another guy works the rightfield line, snagging foul balls, and another works bats in the dugout. (The rest are stuck in the clubhouse.) Problem is, sometimes a kid will be so tired from lack of sleep that he'll be out there nodding off in front of 50,000 people. "I've done it," says Lee. "I'm just glad a line drive didn't wake me up."

10:30 P.M.—Game's over. The real, nasty work starts. "Everybody 12 thinks this is when we go home," says Pete. "But we've still got two hours of work to do." They pick up dirty uniforms, vacuum, straighten lockers, make food runs, empty trash, clean and polish 40 pairs of shoes. And they've got to do it all while dodging flying jocks, socks and towels thrown at their heads by millionaires. *Fwomp!*

12:30 a.m.—O.K., everything's done. Pete's spent, but he'll be in bed 13 before 2 A.M. for once. At least he saw some baseball. The boys who worked the clubhouse have to watch the highlights later.

So there it is, Kid. And remember, don't ask for tickets, autographs or 14
a raise. With the Yankees, you get the minimum, $5.15 an hour, even if
you've been on the job 10 years. Hey, don't forget your boss is George
Steinbrenner!

So, you want the job? Kid? *Kid?*   15

Questions About the Reading

1. How many batboys do the Yankees have?
2. How old must a batboy be?
3. What are the responsibilities of the batboys?
4. Are their any "rewards" to being a batboy? What are the examples
   the writer provides?

Questions About the Writer's Strategies

1. What is the point of view of the essay?
2. Is the essay objective or subjective or both? Support your answer
   with examples from the essay.
3. What is the order of the essay?
4. What does the last sentence of the essay imply?

Writing Assignments

1. Write an essay in which you define the requirements of a job you
   would like to have.
2. *Working Together* Join with some classmates and select a term or
   terms related to government and write an essay in which you define
   the terms. Identify the modes of development you use.

What Is Intelligence, Anyway?

Isaac Asimov

Many of us think that intelligence is something one is simply born with, or that it has to do with doing well in school or getting high scores on IQ tests. But did you ever stop to think about what IQ tests really measure? In the essay that follows, Isaac Asimov asks us to rethink our definition of intelligence.

Words to Know

aptitude   ability, talent

arbiter   someone who has the power to judge

complacent   self-satisfied

intricate   elaborate

KP   kitchen patrol

oracles   wise expressions or answers

raucously   loudly

Getting Started

Do you think that tests can ever really measure intelligence?

What is intelligence, anyway? When I was in the army I received a   1
kind of aptitude test that all soldiers took and, against a normal of 100, scored 160. No one at the base had ever seen a figure like that, and for two hours they made a big fuss over me. (It didn't mean anything. The next day I was still a buck private with KP as my highest duty.)

All my life I've been registering scores like that, so that I have the   2
complacent feeling that I'm highly intelligent, and I expect other people to think so, too. Actually, though, don't such scores simply mean that I am very good at answering the type of academic questions that are considered worthy of answers by the people who make up the intelligence tests—people with intellectual bents similar to mine?

For instance, I had an auto-repair man once, who, on these intelli-   3
gence tests, could not possibly have scored more than 80, by my estimate. I always took it for granted that I was far more intelligent than he was. Yet, when anything went wrong with my car I hastened to him with it, watched him anxiously as he explored its vitals, and listened to his pronouncements as though they were divine oracles—and he always fixed my car.

Well, then, suppose my auto-repair man devised questions for an   4
intelligence test. Or suppose a carpenter did, or a farmer, or, indeed,
almost anyone but an academician. By every one of those tests, I'd prove
myself a moron. And I'd *be* a moron, too. In a world where I could not
use my academic training and my verbal talents but had to do something
intricate or hard, working with my hands, I would do poorly. My intelligence, then, is not absolute but is a function of the society I live in and
of the fact that a small subsection of that society has managed to foist
itself on the rest as an arbiter of such matters.

Consider my auto-repair man, again. He had a habit of telling me jokes   5
whenever he saw me. One time he raised his head from under the automobile hood to say: "Doc, a deaf-and-dumb guy went into a hardware
store to ask for some nails. He put two fingers together on the counter
and made hammering motions with the other hand. The clerk brought
him a hammer. He shook his head and pointed to the two fingers he was
hammering. The clerk brought him nails. He picked out the sizes he
wanted, and left. Well, Doc, the next guy who came in was a blind man.
He wanted scissors. How do you suppose he asked for them?"

Indulgently, I lifted my right hand and made scissoring motions with   6
my first two fingers. Whereupon my auto-repair man laughed raucously and said, "Why, you dumb jerk, he used his *voice* and asked for
them." Then he said, smugly, "I've been trying that on all my customers
today." "Did you catch many?" I asked. "Quite a few," he said, "but I
knew for sure I'd catch *you*." "Why is that?" I asked. "Because you're so
goddamned educated, Doc, I *knew* you couldn't be very smart."

And I have an uneasy feeling he had something there.   7

Questions About the Reading

1. What does the writer mean when he says, "My intelligence, then, is not
   absolute but is a function of the society I live in. . . ." (paragraph 4)?
2. What distinction does the writer make between being educated and
   being smart?
3. Do you think the repairman is smarter than the writer? Why or why
   not?

Questions About the Writer's Strategies

1. What mode of development does the writer use in paragraphs 5 and
   6? What is the purpose of these paragraphs?

2. Does the writer actually define *intelligence*? If so, state his definition in your own words. If not, explain why you think he didn't.
3. In paragraph 6, the writer says he made the scissoring motions "indulgently." What does this tell you about his attitude toward the joke? Why is his attitude ironic?
4. Does the essay contain a thesis statement? If so, where is it located? If not, state it in your own words.
5. Is the repairman a symbol? If so, what does he represent?

Writing Assignments

1. Imagine a society in which intelligence is measured by how well people can work with their hands and fix machinery. Write a definition of intelligence for that society.
2. Write an essay defining the term *joke*. Use examples to illustrate your definition.
3. Pick one of the following terms and define it in an essay: *beauty, truth, wisdom,* or *quality.*

Rhythm Four Strings

Mark Holston

The guitar may or may not be the first musical instrument introduced in America, but versions of it are the "instrument of choice" in the Latin American countries.

Words to Know

enigmatic baffling, perplexing
indigenous native

Getting Started

What is your favorite musical instrument or favorite kind of music?

Ask any Puerto Rican to name the typical instrument most identified 1
with the island, and the answer will be immediate: the small guitar
known as the *cuatro*. But press the same person to provide any details
about the instrument's origin, and the response is likely to be silence.
Only in recent years have musicologists begun to probe the history of the
enigmatic string instrument, but the studies so far have proven little
more than what all Puerto Ricans take for granted. The *cuatro* and the
Caribbean island's folkloric music are so intertwined they are all but one
and the same.

Some may envision a homesick sailor aboard one of Christopher 2
Columbus' ships on the 1492 voyage, strumming a small Spanish *guitarra*.
The romantic notion that some form of guitar was among the first objects
of European culture to be introduced to the New World may or may not
be historically accurate; but there is no doubt that within a few years of
the Spaniards' arrival, the guitar was a part of everyday life in such
growing settlements as Havana, Santo Domingo and San Juan.

Most certainly, those first guitars were not what we associate today 3
with the classical Spanish guitar tradition. The Spanish guitar of the fif-
teenth century was a much smaller instrument, endowed with just four
(cuatro) strings. It matters little that the shape has changed over the centuries or that the *cuatro* may now have as many as ten strings. The personality of the instrument and the role it plays in Puerto Rican life
remains much the same today as it has been for almost five centuries.

While Puerto Ricans defend the *cuatro* as exclusively their own, 4
Venezuela claims its particular version, as well as a strikingly similar
instrument called the *tiple*. Indeed, throughout Latin America, and the
world, cousins of the *cuatro* have evolved, each finding its own form and
distinctive high pitched voice.

The *cavaquinho* is as revered by Brazilians as the *ukulele* is by 5
Hawaiians. In the interior of Panama, *campesinos* strum the *mejorana*.
High in the Andes of Peru and Bolivia, native craftsmen use the shell of
the armadillo as the sound chamber for their distinctive *charango*.
Mexicans call their version of the armadillo-based string instrument a
mandola de concha. In the outback of Brazil's northeast, the *vaqueiros*, or
cowboys, favor a small guitar with a short neck called the *viola sertaneja*.
Even Cuba's *tres* and the banjo of the rural U.S. South owe their lineage
to the same family of small string instruments dubbed by some as "the
poor man's guitar."

In this day of assembly lines, the *cuatro* and its kin remain major 6
exceptions to the standards of mass production. The best *cuatros* are still
crafted in much the same manner as they were hundreds of years ago.
In small villages throughout Puerto Rico, local artisans who learned
their skills from their fathers, work with materials as old as the mountains of *El Yunque* to fashion instruments as individual as the towns from
which they come. From trees with names as magical as the titles of folk
ballads come special ingredients, each suited to a particular part of the
cuatro's body. *Guaraguao, jiquey, majú, laurel, tulipán* and *yagrumo* woods
all come together in rich harmony to craft the *cuatro*'s finished form.

"The *cuatro* is my blood," says Puerto Rico's internationally known 7
guitarist, Yomo Toro. The rotund musician, now a resident of New York,
has expanded the use of the humble folk instrument far beyond the cus-
tomary role it plays in Puerto Rico's *jíbaro* (country) music. Toro, who
has spent years in the service of such legends of tropical music as Celia
Cruz, Willie Colón, Tito Puente and Rubén Blades, has also performed
with mainstream pop artists like Paul Simon and Linda Ronstadt. When
the music calls for that perfect touch of typical Puerto Rican flavor, Toro
is usually the first to be called.

When Toro started using the *cuatro* in tropical music groups, he sur- 8
prised a lot of traditionalists, but he proved that the instrument adapts
easily to many styles. "You can use it to play *salsa*, or classical music, or
anything you want. It sounds beautiful," he says. Toro recalls the day a
cuatro was first placed in his hands. Like many Puerto Rican children
with a knack for making music, his small hands could make sense of the
miniature fret and closely spaced strings. By the time he reached adult-
hood, with hands so large they enveloped the instrument, Toro's fingers
had been trained to negotiate the *cuatro*'s delicate neck with all the skill

and confidence associated with the world's great classical guitarists. His experience is not unique. In fact, such early exposure is almost a require- ment if one is to achieve any degree of expertise on the instrument. "You must start very young," Toro states. "Even an accomplished guitarist will know he has met his match if he picks up a *cuatro* for the first time as an adult."

Making the instrument all the more difficult to play is the fact that, in   9 reality, the *cuatro* has become a *cinco*. Not that anyone calls it that, but most modern *cuatros* have five strings, or actually, 10 strings, five sets of two with each pair tuned to the same note.

Where Yomo Toro has found popularity adapting the traditional *cua-* 10 *tro* style to the world of tropical music, others have expanded the instru- ment's potential into very nontraditional styles. Edwin Colón Zayas, a young Puerto Rican who has impressed even the veteran Toro, has set out to prove the *cuatro* has no limitations. He has brought the finesse of a classically trained guitarist to *cuatro* interpretations of compositions by Chopin and Rimsky-Korsakov (the demanding *Flight of the Bumble Bee*), the seldom heard Argentine *zambra* rhythm, and even the very Polish *Beer Barrel Polka*.

Taking perhaps even more liberties, a Puerto Rican group called 11 "Jibaro Jazz" has proven the *cuatro* is as adept at pure improvisation as is the most modern electric guitar. At the other end of the stylistic spec- trum, a group called "Mapeyé" is a self appointed keeper of the flame. "Mapeyé is respect to tradition and history," writes Puerto Rican critic Gloria Paniagua. "Mapeyé is indigenous, the evocation of the black earth and reddishness of our mountain land—a lesson of nationhood, of resistance, of love to those who deserve to be loved." Such is the range of emotion the music in its purest form evokes.

Across the Caribbean, Venezuelan Mauricio Reyna has devoted him- 12 self to broadening the base of interest in his country's version of the instrument, the *cuatro Venezolano*. Son of famous *cuatro* soloist Freddy Reyna, Mauricio has been kept busy by the Venezuelan Institute of Culture and Cooperation spreading the message of *cuatro* to islands throughout the Caribbean with a series of workshops. He has also intro- duced the sound of the *cuatro* to motion picture audiences through his score for the Venezuelan film *Un Domingo Feliz*, a screenplay by Colombian writer Gabriel García Marquez.

Reyna's passion for the instrument is not unlike that of his Puerto 13 Rican neighbors. "It is the purest," he notes, making reference to the *cua- tro*'s similarity to the original Spanish guitar.

But even as master artists like Toro and Colón Zayas continue to seek 14 new ways to challenge the capabilities of the *cuatro*, the instrument will continue to find comfort in its traditional role around the plazas of small

Puerto Rican towns. That is where the men who cut and craft the native woods into the finished *cuatro* live next door to those whose talents will always ensure a ready audience. In those unpretentious moments, under an open sky, when the simple folk tunes of many generations are enjoyed once more, the *cuatro* renews its true soul.

Questions About the Reading

1. What is the meaning of *cuatro*? Why is the term relevant to the kind of guitar identified with Puerto Rico?
2. When should a person start learning to play a *cuatro*? Why?
3. What do craftsmen in the Andes use as the sound chamber for their version of the *cuatro*?
4. What are the woods used by Puerto Rican craftsmen for particular parts of the *cuatro* body?
5. What changes have been made to the traditional *cuatro*?

Questions About the Writer's Strategies

1. What is the thesis of the essay? Is it stated or implied? If stated, identify the sentences. If implied, state the thesis in your own words.
2. Is the essay objective or subjective? Support your answer with examples from the essay.
3. What is the point of view of the essay? Is it consistent? If not, are the changes justified?
4. What modes of development does the writer use? Identify them with examples from the essay.

Writing Assignments

1. Use the Internet to learn the origin of your favorite instrument and to identify at least three persons who are famous for playing it. Write a definition essay about your favorite musical instrument, using information obtained through the Internet. Identify the modes of development used in your essay and the keywords you used in your Internet research.
2. *Working Together*   Join with some classmates and write a definition essay about the instruments that make up a symphony orchestra or that are associated with a particular ethnic group.

The Handicap of Definition

William Raspberry

An African-American Pulitzer Prize columnist for the Washington Post, *William Raspberry's columns also appear in over 200 other newspapers. Here he tells us that the "handicap" of the definitions of* black *and* white *is the negative and positive connotations associated with the terms.* (© **1982 Washington Post Writers Group. Reprinted with permission.**)

Words to Know

assumption expectation
elocution speech
inculcated expected or believed
innate inborn
quintessentially perfectly, purely

Getting Started

What were your expectations of your first year of college and of college "life"?

I know all about bad schools, mean politicians, economic deprivation 1 and racism. Still, it occurs to me that one of the heaviest burdens black Americans—and black children in particular—have to bear is the handicap of definition: the question of what it means to be black.

Let me explain quickly what I mean. If a basketball fan says that the 2 Boston Celtics' Larry Bird plays "black," the fan intends it—and Bird probably accepts it—as a compliment. Tell pop singer Tom Jones he moves "black" and he might grin in appreciation. Say to Teena Marie or The Average White Band that they sound "black" and they'll thank you.

But name one pursuit, aside from athletics, entertainment or sexual 3 performance in which a white practitioner will feel complimented to be told he does it "black." Tell a white broadcaster he talks "black," and he'll sign up for diction lessons. Tell a white reporter he writes "black" and he'll take a writing course. Tell a white lawyer he reasons "black" and he might sue you for slander.

What we have here is a tragically limited definition of blackness, and 4 it isn't only white people who buy it.

Think of all the ways black children can put one another down with 5 charges of "whiteness." For many of these children, hard study and hard work are "white." Trying to please a teacher might be criticized as acting "white." Speaking correct English is "white." Scrimping today in the interest of tomorrow's goals is "white." Educational toys and games are "white."

An incredible array of habits and attitudes that are conducive to suc- 6 cess in business, in academia, in the nonentertainment professions are likely to be thought of as somehow "white." Even economic success, unless it involves such "black" undertakings as numbers banking, is defined as "white."

And the results are devastating. I wouldn't deny that blacks often are 7 better entertainers and athletes. My point is the harm that comes from too narrow a definition of what is black.

One reason black youngsters tend to do better at basketball, for 8 instance, is that they assume they can learn to do it well, and so they practice constantly to prove themselves right.

Wouldn't it be wonderful if we could infect black children with the 9 notion that excellence in math is "black" rather than white, or possibly Chinese? Wouldn't it be of enormous value if we could create the myth that morality, strong families, determination, courage and love of learning are traits brought by slaves from Mother Africa and therefore quintessentially black?

There is no doubt in my mind that most black youngsters could 10 develop their mathematical reasoning, their elocution and their attitudes the way they develop their jump shots and their dance steps: by the combination of sustained, enthusiastic practice and the unquestioned belief that they can do it.

In one sense, what I am talking about is the importance of developing 11 positive ethnic traditions. Maybe Jews have an innate talent for communication; maybe the Chinese are born with a gift for mathematical reasoning; maybe blacks are naturally blessed with athletic grace. I doubt it. What is at work, I suspect, is assumption, inculcated early in their lives, that this is a thing our people do well.

Unfortunately, many of the things about which blacks make this 12 assumption are things that do not contribute to their career success— except for that handful of the truly gifted who can make it as entertainers and athletes. And many of the things we concede to whites are the things that are essential to economic security.

So it is with a number of assumptions black youngsters make about 13 what it is to be a "man": physical aggressiveness, sexual prowess, the refusal to submit to authority. The prisons are full of people who, by this perverted definition, are unmistakably men.

But the real problem is not so much that the things defined as "black" 14 are negative. The problem is that the definition is much too narrow.

Somehow, we have to make our children understand that they are 15 intelligent, competent people, capable of doing whatever they put their minds to and making it in the American mainstream, not just in a black subculture.

What we seem to be doing, instead, is raising up yet another genera- 16 tion of young blacks who will be failures—by definition.

———————————

Questions About the Reading

1. What is the "heaviest burden" African-American adults and children "have to bear"?
2. How would Larry Bird, Tom Jones, Teena Marie, or The Average White Band react to being told their performance was "black"?
3. How would a white broadcaster, reporter, or lawyer react to being told he does his job "black"?
4. What is the association made by "whites" with something being labeled "black" and by "blacks" with something being labeled "white"?
5. What does William Raspberry say must be done to change the associations with the words *black* and *white*?

Questions About the Writer's Strategies

1. What is the thesis of the essay? Is it stated or implied? State the thesis in your own words.
2. The writer begins some paragraphs with the conjunction "and" or "but." Although not generally "acceptable," it serves a legitimate purpose. What is that purpose?
3. What is the point of view of the essay? Is it consistent? If not, identify the changes and discuss whether they are justified.
4. Is the essay objective or subjective? Support your answer with examples from the essay.

Writing Assignments

1. Write an essay in which you define *prejudice* and *tolerance.*
2. Write an essay in which you define *ethnic* and *racial.*

10

Argumentation and Persuasion

ALL EFFECTIVE WRITING involves, to some extent, argumentation or persuasion. As you have learned from the preceding chapters, writers use various kinds of information to develop a **topic** or **thesis.** Such information can be said to "argue" or "persuade" in the sense that it convinces the reader that the writer's idea is true or believable. However, as **modes of development,** argumentation and persuasion have some particular characteristics that you should know about and be able to use in your own writing.

Let's look first at **persuasion** in its most obvious form—the advertisement. You should not use sentence fragments in your writing assignments, as the advertisement below does; and of course you should continue to structure your writing according to a main (general) idea and to support it according to the various modes of development. But you will want to appeal to the emotions, qualities, or values that a reader is likely to share or find desirable, as advertisers do. One way to appeal to a reader is to use words for their **connotations**—explained in the preceding chapter as the feelings or qualities a reader may associate with a word—rather than for their **denotations,** or dictionary definitions.

In the following example, the advertiser uses the words *clean, smooth, fresh,* and *pure innocence.* We associate such words with highly desirable qualities, and the advertiser intends to persuade us that a particular soap will give our skin these qualities. The word *new* implies that the product has been improved and, therefore, is better or more desirable than its predecessor or a competing product. Notice, too, that the ad appeals to our senses when it describes the soap's lather as *silky* and *soft.*

Connotation   Now. Clean skin with the touch of <u>innocence</u>. The joy of it.

Connotation   Of having skin <u>so clean</u>, <u>so smooth</u>, <u>so fresh</u>, it has the touch
of <u>pure innocence</u>. Today, you can capture that feeling, sim-

Connotation   ply by cleansing with the extraordinary <u>new</u> Olay Beauty

Connotation   Bar. Its special Olay lather, <u>silky and soft</u>, creams up to clean

Connotation   when you work it in. The tinier bubbles work in <u>natural
harmony</u> with your skin. They lift out impurities, then rinse

Connotation   <u>cleanly</u> away, leaving <u>better skin</u> even before you raise your
eyes to the mirror—<u>fresher</u> skin each time, <u>smoother</u> skin at
every touch. Again and again, new Olay Beauty Bar cleanses

Connotation   <u>innocence</u> into your skin.

The purpose of persuasion is to make the reader accept the writer's idea. That idea may be an opinion or judgment that the reader might not ordinarily share or have knowledge of. The idea may be controversial—as we shall see later, the idea of an argument must be—but it does not have to be. The idea may even be humorous. Whatever the idea, the writer will use words and information to appeal to the reader's emotions. Such information may be biased in favor of the writer's idea, but it should be honest and accurate. Notice the emotional strength of the writer's examples in the letter that follows.

R. J. Reynolds Tobacco Co.
4th and Main Street
Winston-Salem, N.C. 27102

Dear Sirs:

When my wife died of lung cancer in 1976, I wanted to write you about her love affair with Camel cigarettes. I concluded, however, that it would be an exercise in futility.

I take up the challenge now, because you have publicly announced an advertising campaign to cast doubt on medical reports that cigarettes are a public-health hazard. You call for an open debate. Okay, let's debate.

Example 1: wife   My wife died a painful death. She was just 56 and had smoked at least a pack of Camels a day for 40 years. Coincidentally, just 30 days before her demise her 47-year-

Example 2:
brother-in-law   old brother died of the same illness. Both experienced unbearable pain. He, too, was a heavy smoker.

Example 3:
father   But there is more to this horror story. In 1958, my father died suddenly of a cardiovascular ailment. He'd been a two-pack-a-day man for years, and would "walk a mile for a Camel" when younger. Later in life, he could hardly walk at all. But he still puffed away, day and night, before breakfast and with his meals. He endured continual nasal and respiratory problems, and never enjoyed a day free of a hacking cough.

A popular pharmacist, he had many doctor friends who urged him to stop smoking. But he was firmly hooked and had been since 1909. Ill with lung disease (emphysema and chronic bronchitis), he had long suffered intensely painful attacks of near-suffocation. In 1955 he was forced to retire and spend his "golden years" either lying on our sofa or propped up in a lounge chair.

In late summer of 1957, I took him to a specialist at the University of Maryland Hospital in Baltimore. There he was told there was no cure for his condition. But he could help himself. "How?" he asked. "Stop smoking," was the reply.

That is a tall order for anyone who has smoked for almost 50 years. But my father did not want to live the life of an invalid, so he determined to try. That he succeeded—cold turkey—is nothing short of a miracle. But he really had no other choice, except to suffer.

Within weeks he was breathing easier, and it was not long before he was walking about and driving his car. He got to enjoy life a bit. I'm convinced that giving up smoking added that near-year to his life.

Example 4: daughter

Today, I have a daughter—a working mother of two—who has been addicted to cigarettes since peer pressure in high school encouraged her to smoke. She wants desperately to quit. In fact, she has done so several times, only to be lured back by the smoking of others in her workplace.

Having presented four powerful extended examples, this writer goes on to a thorough persuasive conclusion. You will see next that he uses rhetorical questions to introduce and structure his conclusion. A **rhetorical question** is a question to which no real answer is expected because only one obvious reply can be made—and that reply will either support or restate the writer's point. Rhetorical questions are fairly common in persuasive writing and in argumentation because they offer a way for writers to emphasize the correctness of their viewpoints.

Okay, R. J. Reynolds, that's my story. What's yours? Are you prepared to tell us that the National Institutes of Health, the Surgeon General and the various voluntary health agencies are all wrong? Are the many scientific studies indicting smoking just so much hogwash?

For the sake of debate, let's assume smoking's critics are wrong. Can you deny that cigarette smoking is addictive? Isn't that fact precisely the reason why you sell so many cigarettes? Is it moral to manufacture and sell any product that causes addiction—even if it might otherwise be harmless? As bad as alcohol abuse is, alcohol is addictive to only a relatively small number of consumers. You can't say that about cigarettes. Smoking hooks nearly every consumer. And once hooked it is difficult to stop; for some, it seems impossible.

In a free society, people can't be forbidden to smoke. But government does have the obligation to warn the public of the dangers involved. It has the responsibility to hold R. J. Reynolds Tobacco Co. and others accountable for luring impressionable people to smoke, while suggesting that medical findings establishing a relationship between smoking and cancer, cardiovascular diseases and respiratory ailments are inconclusive.

It's hard to fight the rich tobacco industry, but just maybe, through education, we non-smokers will eventually win. As a witness to so much tragedy caused by smoking, I feel compelled to hope so.

Sincerely,
Gil Crandall

In summary, then, a persuasive paragraph or essay, like the other modes of development, is based on a main (general) idea developed by one or more of the modes of development and is characterized by the use of words or information that appeals to the reader's emotions. The information or evidence used in persuasion may be one-sided, but it should be honest and accurate. The topic, or thesis, of persuasion may be controversial, but it does not have to be.

Argumentation, on the other hand, must be based on a controversial idea—an idea that people have conflicting views or opinions about. Although argumentation may include some persuasion, its appeal to the reader should be rational and logical, as opposed to emotional, and **objective,** rather than one-sided. A classic or formal argument includes five elements:

- **Statement of the problem**
- **Solution,** the writer's thesis or answer to the problem
- **Evidence,** the information the writer presents to support or prove the thesis
- **Refutation,** the writer's acknowledgment of and response to opposing views
- **Conclusion,** the writer's summation of the evidence and, generally, a restatement of the thesis

Although you may seldom need to write a paragraph-length argument, it is helpful to examine an example of one. Notice in the following example that the writer has explained the problem, stated a solution or answer to the problem—which is the topic of the paragraph—provided evidence in support of the solution, refuted the opposing view, and summarized the position taken on the topic.

During the late sixties and early seventies, political and social activism was rampant on college campuses. Student protests—which were sometimes peaceful and other times violent—addressed issues related to civil rights, the environment, war, nuclear arms, and consumer protection and

Statement of the problem

rights. In recent years, student protests have been much less frequent and, generally, peaceful, causing some writers and politicians to label present-day students as apathetic.

Solution

Nonsense! Today's students are not apathetic. They simply have different concerns from the ones of the sixties and sev-

Evidence

enties. They are more concerned about, for instance, employment and the quality of their own lives. They are assessing, confronting even, themselves—their hopes, plans, desires, ambitions, and values. They are fighting quietly for their causes—personal or otherwise—by pursuing training and retraining opportunities and by exercising their voting privileges. To say they are apathetic is to ignore the stead-

Refutation

fastness with which they are pursuing their goals. To say they are apathetic is to imply that a person is not concerned about an issue unless that person takes to the streets or possibly engages in violent acts on behalf of that issue. The fact is, the current college population is older—the average age of community college students nationwide is about twenty-eight—more experienced, and in some ways wiser. As a consequence, they have perhaps learned that confrontation may win a battle but lose the war, that in the long run, they must live and work with those persons who hold opposing views.

Conclusion

Thus, while they are indeed quieter than their predecessors, they continue to be concerned about such important issues as employment (their own and others), nuclear arms, the environment, civil rights, and war. We make a mistake if we write off today's college students as apathetic simply because we do not see overt evidence of their concern.

In a full-length essay, you can develop your argument more fully and convincingly than you can in a paragraph. The order in which you present the elements of an argument may differ from the classic organization represented by the preceding paragraph. For instance, you may want to state the refutation before presenting the evidence for your argument. And sometimes one of the elements of your argument may be **implied** rather than stated, just as the topic sentence of a paragraph or the main idea of an essay may be implied.

No matter what method is used to develop an argument, however, always remember that the evidence presented to support the solution and the conclusion must be valid—true, supported by facts, accurately expressed, and based on sound reasoning. This is something to watch for not only in your own writing but also when you are reading arguments composed by others. When you read or write an argument, analyze not only the main conclusion but also all the ideas that support it. A conclusion may seem quite sensible based on the evidence the writer supplies, but if the evidence itself is not true and not presented logically, the conclusion will be viewed as faulty.

In the essay below, the writer follows the classic model in presenting her argument and supports her opinion with facts that give the reader sound reasons to accept her conclusion. Notice that she uses several modes of development, such as **contrast** and **examples.**

Statement of the problem	Each year, from late spring to early fall, thousands of high school students and their parents spend a great deal of time and money driving around the country to visit expensive and prestigious colleges that the students think they might like to attend. Each year, thousands of students go through the ritual of applying to and being rejected by these colleges.	1
Solution	Instead, they should go to a community college and, after earning their associate degree, transfer to a four-year university to complete their education.	
Evidence	Most community colleges offer a wide choice of career or technical programs as well as a curriculum paralleling that offered by a university. If the student has already made a career choice, an associate degree prepares the student to enter the workforce or to continue his or her career study in a four-year university. If the student has not decided on a career, a community college is an excellent place to learn more about many different career possibilities and to complete the general education courses required by either a career or university-parallel program.	2
Evidence	Most community colleges also have a more diverse population than that of the student's high school. In a community college the student has the opportunity to meet persons of all ages, abilities, and ethnic and racial backgrounds and to improve his or her knowledge and understanding of others.	3
Evidence	A community college is also much less expensive than most colleges. In addition to the lower cost of tuition and fees, the student can usually live at home and commute to classes, which also saves the high cost of dorm or apartment fees.	4
Refutation	It is true, of course, that a community college does not offer the prestige of the more famous universities. But if prestige is significant, the student could complete a baccalaureate and graduate work at a better-known school. Also, whether the education the student receives at a community college is equal to that provided by a more prestigious university can be determined only on a case-by-case basis, since much of the success of any education depends on the individual student.	5

Conclusion

> The fact is, for most students a community college is a   6
> sound educational and economic choice. Instead of engag-
> ing in the expensive and time-consuming spring-to-fall
> ritual of college shopping, most students would be as well
> or better served by taking advantage of the educational
> opportunity offered by their local community college.

When you read an argument, remember too that a writer may present facts selectively. That is, the writer may not give you all the facts relating to an issue or problem. For this reason, it is advisable to read and consider arguments on both sides of the controversy and to carefully analyze the facts when you are trying to form an opinion about an important issue. It will then be up to you when writing an argumentation paper to interpret the facts and conclusions, to decide which ones are most valid, and to choose the ones you will use to support your own thesis.

Be alert, too, for fallacies in your reasoning. In addition to the fallacies identified in chapter 8 (p. 210), guard against the following:

- *False analogy.* A false analogy assumes that two things that are alike are alike in all respects. A Honda and a Cadillac are both cars, but they are not alike in all respects.
- *Circular argument.* A circular argument restates an idea in different words: "The airports are too crowded because too many people are traveling."
- *Argument to the man* (argument ad hominem). An argument to the man attacks the person rather than the issue: "He gets poor grades. After all, he's a computer nerd."
- *Bandwagon.* A bandwagon fallacy claims that something is true because the majority believe or act on it: "Everyone thinks she should be elected class president" or "We should go to the concert because everyone else is."
- *Either-or.* An either-or argument assumes that only two things are possible: "The submarine sank because of poor maintenance and personnel training."
- *Begging the question.* Begging the question presents as a fact an idea or premise that is not proven: "If we removed all chat rooms from the Internet, children would not be enticed to meet people who could do them harm."

In summary, although argumentation and persuasion have a common **purpose**—to convince the reader to accept the writer's opinion—they differ principally in the way the writer appeals to the reader. In argumentation, the writer supports the topic or thesis by presenting objective, logical evidence that appeals to the reader's reason. In persuasion, the writer does not necessarily abandon objectivity or logic, but uses words or other information that appeals to the reader's emotions. Also, although the thesis of persuasion *may* be controversial, the thesis of an argument *must* be. In both argumentation and persuasion, the writer makes use of whatever modes of development are effective and appropriate.

In school and beyond, there will be occasions when you will want to use argumentation or persuasion to make a point to your **audience.** Whether you are doing so orally or in writing, being familiar with techniques used in argumentation and persuasion will help you.

The Declaration of Independence

On July 4, 1776, the Second Continental Congress approved the Declaration of Independence. Written primarily by Thomas Jefferson, the document states the principles, voted on two days earlier, on which the thirteen colonies would declare their freedom and independence from England. Following this paragraph, the Declaration lists the many causes and justifications for declaring their freedom and independence from English rule.

Words to Know

constrains   causes
deriving   coming from, originating from
despotism   government controlled by an absolute ruler
transient   passing, fleeting
unalienable   cannot be taken away
usurpations   taken without right

Getting Started

Have you ever felt you were treated unjustly?

We hold these truths to be self-evident, that all men are created equal, that they are endowed by their Creator with certain unalienable Rights, that among these are Life, Liberty and the pursuit of Happiness. That to secure these rights, Governments are instituted among Men, deriving their just powers from the consent of the governed. That whenever any Form of government becomes destructive of these ends, it is the Right of the People to alter or to abolish it, and to institute new Government, laying its foundation on such principles and organizing its powers in such form, as to them shall seem most likely to effect their Safety and Happiness. Prudence, indeed, will dictate that Governments long established should not be changed for light and transient causes; and accordingly all experience hath shown, that mankind are more disposed to suffer, while evils are sufferable, than to right themselves by abolishing the forms to which they are accustomed. But when a long train of abuses and usurpations, pursuing invariably the same Object evinces a design to reduce them under absolute Despotism, it is their right, it is their duty, to throw off such Government, and to provide new Guards for their future security.—Such has been the patient sufferance of these Colonies; and such is now the necessity which constrains them to alter their former

Systems of Government. The history of the present King of Great Britain is a history of repeated injuries and usurpations, all having in direct object the establishment of an absolute Tyranny over these States. To prove this, let Facts be submitted to a candid world.

Questions About the Reading

1. What is the government or "rule" that "it is the Right of the People to alter or abolish"?
2. What are our "unalienable Rights"?
3. What are the foundations on which new governments should be formed?
4. What are the causes that justify the overthrow of a government?

Questions About the Writer's Strategies

1. Is the paragraph argumentative or persuasive?
2. If the paragraph is argumentative, identify the elements.
3. If the paragraph is persuasive, identify the persuasive words and words used for their connotations.
4. What modes of development does the writer use, in addition to argumentation/persuasion?

Writing Assignments

1. Write a paragraph justifying the actions to take to correct bullying in a school.
2. *Working Together*   Join with some classmates and write a paragraph in which you argue for or seek to persuade your school administration to make a change in one of the following at your school: bookstore, cafeteria, registration process, or parking.

The Measure of Our Success

Marian Wright Edelman

"Children—my own and other people's—became the passion of my personal and professional life. For it is they who are God's presence, promise, and hope for humankind." These are the words of Marian Wright Edelman, the African-American civil rights lawyer and founder of the Children's Defense League. In the following paragraph from her book, The Measure of Our Success: A Letter to My Children and Yours, *Edelman urges her readers to face the mounting crisis of our country's impoverished children and families by taking action themselves.*

Words to Know

empathy   understanding
mentoring   being a counselor or teacher
neonatal   having to do with children born prematurely

Getting Started

What are some things you can do to help build a stronger community for all our children and their children's children?

The place to begin is with ourselves. Care. As you read about or meet some of the children and families in this country who need your help, put yourself in their places as fellow Americans. Imagine you or your spouse being pregnant, and not being able to get enough to eat or see a doctor or know that you have a hospital for delivery. Imagine your child hungry or injured, and you cannot pay for food or find health care. Imagine losing your job and having no income, having your unemployment compensation run out, not being able to pay your note or rent, having no place to sleep with your children, having nothing. Imagine having to stand in a soup line at a church or Salvation Army station after you've worked all your life, or having to sleep in a shelter with strangers and get up and out early each morning, find some place to go with your children, and not know if you can sleep there again that night. If you take the time to imagine this, perhaps you can also take the time to do for them what you would want a fellow citizen to do for you. Volunteer in a homeless shelter or soup kitchen or an afterschool tutoring or mentoring program. Vote. Help to organize your community to speak out for the children who need you. Visit a hospital neonatal intensive care nursery or AIDS and boarder baby ward and spend time rocking and caring for an individual child. Adopt as a pen pal a lonely child who never gets a letter from anyone. Give a youth a summer job. Teach your child tolerance and empathy by your example.

Questions About the Reading

1. According to the writer, how can people begin to make a difference in this country? Do you agree or disagree with her argument? Why?
2. What different methods of action does Edelman describe? Pick out some of the examples she uses.
3. What do you think Edelman means by the last sentence? Do you agree or disagree with her statement? Why?
4. Think about all the different suggestions Edelman makes. Which have you tried? Which might you consider trying?

Questions About the Writer's Strategies

1. Is there a topic sentence in the paragraph? If so, where is it? If not, state the main idea in your own words.
2. Is this a paragraph of argumentation, persuasion, or both? Support your answer with details from the paragraph.
3. Besides persuasion, what other mode of development does the writer use? Support your answer with details from the text.
4. Edelman uses numerous powerful images to support her thesis that we all need to work together to rebuild this country. What are some of the images Edelman uses when she asks us to imagine trading places with our less fortunate fellow Americans? What impact do the images have on you?
5. What is the tone of the paragraph? Why does Edelman use this tone?

Writing Assignments

1. Do you agree or disagree with Edelman's argument that all responsible people need to be active in their communities and their nation? Write a persuasive paragraph on your answer.
2. Do you agree or disagree that children learn tolerance and empathy—or, for that matter, prejudice and hate—by the example of their parents? Write a paragraph in which you argue for or against that statement. Use examples and details to support your position.

Upholding the Right to Life

Jacob Sullum

It is "right," according to the writer, to impose the death penalty when a person has taken another person's life.

Words to Know

affirm confirm, declare to be true
barbaric primitive, brutal
macabre horrible, gruesome

Getting Started

When is it right to take a person's life?

It is fashionable in some circles to view capital punishment as a barbaric institution that is destined to fade away. Watching some of the macabre pro-death-penalty demonstrations attracted by pending executions, one is tempted to agree. But the true mark of civilization is the extent to which a society upholds the rights of its members, especially the right to life. There is only one appropriate penalty for the willful, unprovoked violation of that right. By imposing this penalty on those who dare to break the most basic rule of existence, we affirm the dignity of every other individual.

Questions About the Reading

1. What is the "true mark of civilization"?
2. What is the writer's rationale for the death penalty?
3. What is the writer's opinion of pro-death-penalty demonstrations?

Questions About the Writer's Strategies

1. What is the main idea of the paragraph? Is it stated or implied? If stated, identify the sentences. If implied, state it in your own words.
2. Is the paragraph argumentation or persuasion? Support your answer with examples from the paragraph.
3. Do you think the writer has provided adequate support for his opinion of the death penalty? Why or why not?

Writing Assignments

1. Write an argumentation or persuasion paragraph in support of the death penalty.
2. Write an argumentation or persuasion paragraph for or against abortion.

Flunking

Mary Sherry

Let's hope you never flunk a course, but if you do, you can try to look at that "F" the way the writer does: "an expression of confidence" that you "have the ability" to pass the course.

Word to Know

conspiracy   plot

Getting Started

Do you agree or disagree with your school's policy regarding "F" and "incomplete" grades?

Flunking as a regular policy has just as much merit today as it did two generations ago. We must review the threat of flunking and see it as it really is—a positive teaching tool. It is an expression of confidence by both teachers and parents that the students have the ability to learn the material presented to them. However, making it work again would take a dedicated, caring conspiracy between teachers and parents. It would mean facing the tough reality that passing kids who haven't learned the material—while it might save them grief for the short term—dooms them to long-term illiteracy. It would mean that teachers would have to follow through on their threats, and parents would have to stand behind them, knowing their children's best interests are indeed at stake. This means no more doing Scott's assignments for him because he might fail. No more passing Jodi because she's such a nice kid.

Questions About the Reading

1. What is the writer's opinion of the flunking grade?
2. What would it take to make the flunking grade be viewed as an "expression of confidence"?
3. What is the result of "passing kids who haven't learned the material"?
4. What would teachers and parents have to do to support the flunking grade?

Questions About the Writer's Strategies

1. What is the main idea of the paragraph? Is it stated or implied? If stated, identify the sentences. If implied, state it in your own words.
2. What is the point of view of the paragraph? Is it consistent? If not, is the change justified?
3. Is the paragraph objective or subjective? Support your answer with sentences and words from the paragraph.
4. What is the tone of the paragraph?

Writing Assignments

1. Write an argumentation or persuasion paragraph in which you agree or disagree with your school's policy on the "F" grade.
2. Write an argumentation or persuasion paragraph in which you agree or disagree with your school's policy related to grades as the criteria for sports eligibility.

Banning Smoking

John Ruckdeschel

Dr. John Ruckdeschel argues that a ban on smoking in indoor workplaces should be adopted across the country.

Words to Know

carcinogens   cancer-causing agents
emphysema   respiratory disease caused by swelling in the lungs

Getting Started

What is the smoking policy in your school?

Although lung cancer lacks the high public profile of breast or prostate 1
cancer, it's responsible for more deaths than these two cancers and colo-
rectal cancer combined. According to the American Cancer Society,
156,900 Americans died of lung cancer in 2000—28 percent of all cancer
deaths.

Unlike some other serious diseases, we know the main cause of lung 2
cancer: cigarette smoking. Eighty percent of lung cancers are caused
directly by smoking, which is also a major factor in heart disease,
emphysema and low-birth-weight babies. The American Lung
Association estimates that smoking results in $150 billion in annual
health care costs and lost productivity.

That's why Michigan should follow the lead of Florida, California, 3
New York and Massachusetts by restricting smoking in virtually all public places.

Voters in Florida recently approved Amendment 6 to prohibit smok- 4
ing in all indoor workplaces, restaurants and other public places. Stand-
alone bars, tobacco stores, designated hotel rooms and private resi-
dences (except those where health or day care is provided) are exempt
from the smoking ban.

This policy really should be the gold standard across the country. It 5
has been proved that banning smoking in public places such as restaurants is not as devastating to businesses as some would argue. People
will patronize these places despite a smoking ban.

Restricting the places where smoking is permitted would reduce 6
exposure to tobacco-related carcinogens for millions of people. The
Florida law is expected to cause a significant decline in tobacco sales,

and of course, nonsmokers will no longer inhale the secondhand smoke that permeates most buildings where smoking is permitted in designated areas. By 1999, almost 70 percent of workers in the U.S. worked at a site with a smoke-free policy. It's time to extend that privilege to everyone.

In addition, businesses should promote smoking-cessation programs for their employees. Smoking is addictive, and relapses after quitting are   7 common. However, today we have nicotine patches, gums, sprays, inhalers and pills, along with many forms of behavioral therapy and support groups to help people quit smoking. Unfortunately, smoking-cessation programs usually are not covered by health insurance.

Business leaders, provide these programs in the workplace or ensure   8 that they are part of your benefits. It's a good investment in better health for your employees and for your company's bottom line.

Questions About the Reading

1. What is the annual estimated cost in health care and productivity due to smoking?
2. What places are exempt from Florida's smoking ban?
3. What was the percent of workers, in 1999, who worked in smoke-free sites?
4. In addition to providing a smoke-free workplace, what else should businesses promote?

Questions About the Writer's Strategies

1. What is the thesis of the essay? Is it stated or implied? If stated, identify the sentences. If implied, state the thesis in your own words.
2. Is the essay argumentation or persuasion?
3. If this essay is an argument, identify the elements. If persuasion, identify the persuasive sentences and words.
4. What other modes of development does the writer use?

Writing Assignments

1. Determine your school's policy regarding smoking and write an argumentation or persuasion essay for or against the policy.
2. *Working Together* Join with some classmates and write a formal argument for or against one of your school's policies.

A Burning Issue

Mary Boltz Chapman

Mary Boltz Chapman narrows the smoking issue to whether it should or should not be banned in restaurants.

Words to Know

constituency   a group of supporters
instituted   started

Getting Started

What is the smoking policy in the restaurants in your town?

There's a controversy blazing in several cities including Chicago, Dallas and Denver: Should local government ban smoking in all city restaurants? Politicians, restaurateurs, associations, lobbyists, health organizations, smokers and nonsmokers have been lining up to give their opinions. I submit that only one of those parties is entitled to an opinion. Restaurant management.   1

Where There's Smoke

Many existing and proposed regulations are confusing. A restaurant operator may have to decipher different rules set by the state, city and county. In Pittsburgh, a ban on smoking in restaurants and bars failed because a Pennsylvania state law, which actually restricts smoking, prohibits such a local ban.   2

Others are unfair. In some localities, smoking is allowed in bars but not restaurants. However, the line is blurry as many bars serve some kind of food, ranging from a rack of chips to sophisticated tasting menus. In California, the smoking ban instituted five years ago includes bars. Strict but fair, right? Not necessarily fair to restaurants in the state's border towns.   3

Some feel that if politicians are going to legislate the issue, the only fair way to do it would be on a national basis, to level the playing field. In Massachusetts, the state restaurant association threw up its hands over a potential statewide smoking ban. There, the differing laws make it impossible to support their constituency one way or the other without hurting some of them.   4

Proponents call it a work-place issue; employees should not be sub- 5
jected to the health risks of secondhand smoke. But some servers are
happy to work the smoking section. They say smokers linger over another drink or dessert, upping checks and tips. Others say they would rather
the smoking customers not linger so they can turn the table. Often one section or another is busier, and servers vie for those tables. It depends on the
restaurant.

For some operators, sales decline thanks to nonsmoking ordinances. 6
For others, profits increase.

At the end of the day, there is a difference between a public place 7
where a person goes because he has to, such as a courthouse, and a public place where he pays for the privilege, such as a restaurant. Each person can choose which eatery to patronize and is free to use the eatery's
smoking policy as a barometer.

It should be left up to the restaurant management to decide that 8
policy based on their staff's and customers' needs.

Questions About the Reading

1. What are the difficulties, according to the writer, in banning smoking
   in restaurants?
2. How do restaurant employees feel about a nonsmoking policy?
3. How does nonsmoking affect the profits of a restaurant?
4. Does the writer think there should be a difference between smoking
   policies in public places and restaurants? Why?

Questions About the Writer's Strategies

1. What is the thesis of the essay? Is it stated or implied? If stated, identify the sentences. If implied, state the thesis in your own words.
2. Is the essay argumentation or persuasion? If it is an argument, identify the elements of the argument. If persuasion, identify the persuasive sentences and words.
3. What modes of development does the writer use?

4. Are the two essays—"Banning Smoking" by John Ruckdeschel and
   "A Burning Issue" by Mary Boltz Chapman—objective or subjective?
   Use the Internet to find information about the two writers to help you
   decide your answer.

Writing Assignments

1. Determine the laws in your town regarding smoking and write an argumentation or persuasion essay for or against the laws.
2. *Working Together*   Join with some classmates and write a formal argument for or against the law banning the sale of cigarettes or liquor before age twenty-one or a bicycle helmet law.

The Jury Room Is No Place for TV

George F. Will

As the title of the essay makes clear, George F. Will is opposed to permitting television cameras in a jury room. (© **2003, The Washington Post Writers Group. Reprinted with permission.**)

Words to Know

conscripted   drafted, forced
corollary   similarity
flamboyant   showy
insatiable   cannot be satisfied
non sequitur   does not follow
obvious   unaware
postulated   claimed

Getting Started

Would being on television affect your behavior?

Seventy-five years ago, physicist Werner Heisenberg postulated the 1
uncertainty, or indeterminacy, principle: It is impossible to measure
simultaneously the velocity and position of a subatomic particle,
because measuring the velocity moves the particle in unpredictable
ways. A social corollary of Heisenberg's principle is that observing the
behavior of people who know they are being observed changes their
behavior. Which is one reason why televising juries' deliberations is a
terrible idea.

But armies on the march are no match for a terrible idea whose time 2
has come. And a flamboyant Texas judge (he has sentenced convicts to
wear signs proclaiming their offenses, and ordered two wife-beaters to
apologize on a public street) has granted the request of public television's "Frontline" to televise jury deliberations in the trial of a 17-year-
old accused of killing a man during a carjacking. Capital punishment is
possible. The tape will be held by the judge until the trial ends. The
defendant has agreed to all this, but the prosecutor is appealing the
judge's ruling.

A few jury deliberations in criminal trials in Arizona and Wisconsin 3
have been televised, but never in a capital case. Some televised jurors

have said they quickly became oblivious to the cameras. However, it is highly implausible that this would be true of most jurors, or of any in trials that attract intense public interest.

In fact, the Texas case already proves that televising juries shrinks the 4 pool of potential jurors: Fourteen of the first 110 prospective jurors in the Texas case asked to be excused rather than be conscripted into high-stakes public theater. And televising juries' work will skew jury selection and performance in other ways. Televising proceedings may make some persons eager to be jurors—but what kind of deliberators will *they* be? And shy, reticent or inarticulate jurors might be paralyzed by cameras that turn a private civic duty, akin to voting, into a public performance.

After trials, jurors are free to talk about their deliberations. But tele- 5 vising the deliberations robs jurors of an important part of the right of free speech—the right not to speak publicly.

Juries are supposed to be independent of the government prosecut- 6 ing, of the defendant—and of the community, with its passions and prejudices. Juries, unlike legislatures, are not representative institutions. They do apply the community's settled values, as codified in law, but must not reflect a community aroused by particular instances of crime and punishment. Televising House and Senate floor activities (for the first seven years after the Constitution was ratified, the Senate met behind closed doors) is not comparable because it involves coverage of elected representatives, and of activities long observable from spectator and press galleries.

Because, as a wit said, imitation is the sincerest form of television, per- 7 haps the campaign for televising juries owes something to the rise of "reality" television. (Which is unreal. See above, the social corollary of Heisenberg's principle.) And because public television is not an agenda-free zone, perhaps "Frontline" hopes its jury tapes will be ammunition for opponents of capital punishment. In any case, "Frontline" will edit the jury tapes for its program, thereby greatly diminishing the tape's educative value. And the request by "Frontline" for exclusive rights to the tape undercuts the contention that jury deliberations should be open to all journalists as public events.

Journalism's insatiable appetite for access to government processes is 8 understandable, but an appetite is not its own justification. And the Texas judge's justification for televising the jury is a crashing non sequitur: He says America's judicial system is excellent and "we shouldn't be ashamed of how it works." As though shame is the only reason for privacy.

In the sweltering Philadelphia summer of 1787, the Constitutional 9 Convention closed the doors and even the windows of Independence Hall so that statesmanship and compromise could flourish without concern for an audience of factions. Televising the Federal Reserve Board's decision-making would cause the decision-makers to adopt a stifling reticence to prevent market gyrations. If Supreme Court conferences were televised, they would become meaningless: the justices would do their serious conferring and compromising in another room, just as most of Congress' serious business occurs where cameras are absent.

In a society saturated by entertainment values, "the public's right to 10 know" can be an excuse for voyeurism started up as a journalistic imperative. However, the public's fundamental right is to good government, and the function of juries is to produce justice, not entertaining journalism.

Questions About the Reading

1. Why is televising jury deliberations "a terrible idea"?
2. What is the Texas trial for which the judge has allowed taping of jury deliberations?
3. Why is this trial different from other trials that have allowed televising jury deliberations?
4. How has allowing televising jury deliberations affected the jury selection in the Texas case?
5. What, in summary, are the writer's reasons for objecting to televising jury deliberations?

Questions About the Writer's Strategies

1. Is the essay objective or subjective? Support your answer with examples from the essay.
2. Is the essay an argumentation or persuasion essay? If the essay is argumentation, identify the elements of the argument. If the essay is persuasion, identify the persuasive sentences and words.
3. What is the metaphor in the essay?
4. What modes of development does the writer use in the essay?
5. What is the fallacy in the essay, according to the writer?

Writing Assignments

1. Write an argumentation or persuasion essay for or against "reality" TV.
2. Write an essay in which you argue or persuade your reader that cameras in school halls and other school areas influence or do not influence student behavior.

Cameras Give an Inside Look

John M. Parras

Claiming we are "better served" if we know what goes on in a jury room, John M. Parras defends televising jury deliberations.

Words to Know

capricious unpredictable, erratic
discernible apparent, visible
sanctity purity, sacredness
scrupulous careful, correct

Getting Started

If you served on a jury, would you want the jury deliberations to be televised?

Critics of the court decision to allow "Frontline" to record jury delib- 1
erations in the Cedric Harrison case say they are concerned about the
sanctity of the jury room in a death penalty trial. They argue that allowing cameras inside the jury room will turn the most serious of decisions
into a form of reality television in which jurors will grandstand for the
cameras. Experience proves otherwise.

Judge Ted Poe's decision has been sensationalized and mischaracter- 2
ized and was not capricious. As a former prosecutor, he tried eight death
cases. He has presided over 15 capital cases. Poe understands and
respects the power of the state, the severity of the penalty and the
absolute requirement for the integrity of the process.

Neither is there any reason to believe that the defendant's rights are 3
being compromised. The defendant, his mother and defense counsel all
consented to the filming and agreed not to use it as a basis for any
appeal. The defense lawyer explained it this way: "If the state of Texas
wants to attempt to execute a 17-year-old, I think the whole world
should be watching."

Nevertheless, the district attorney appealed Poe's decision, arguing 4
that "the desire to appear on a 'Survivor'-style reality television series
should not be an added qualification for jury service." His alarmist tone
was soon echoed by the media nationwide, which argued that the filming had only "superficial appeal" and repeatedly compared the case to
reality television.

Reality television places people in contrived or trivial situations for 5
the entertainment of the public. At a time when the death penalty is
under nationwide review, nothing could be more important or less trivial than understanding how 12 people decide whether a fellow citizen
should live or die.

Editorials across the country have claimed that cameras have never 6
been allowed in a jury room. Not true. PBS, CBS and ABC have all filmed
jury deliberations in criminal trials, including murder trials. The
Colorado Supreme Court just agreed to allow ABC to film jury deliberations in coming criminal trials, saying: "We believe that we do have a
responsibility to educate the public about what really goes on in the
courts, and criminal trials specifically."

Critics also have suggested that having a camera in the jury room will 7
affect the decision the jurors reach, either making them more (or, others
argue, less) likely to convict: "Jurors, especially less educated and artic-
ulate ones, may be wary of speaking out if they know they are being
judged," one editorial claimed. But interviews with jurors who have
been filmed deliberating indicate that the filming had no discernible
effect on their deliberations or verdicts.

"Frontline" had filmed for three days before proceedings were halted 8
to decide the camera issue. Only 14 of 110 potential jurors expressed
reservations about being filmed and were excused without objection by
either side. The remaining 90 percent told the court that the cameras
would not affect their deliberations.

Our criminal justice system functions on the premise that jurors will 9
follow the law. We trust jurors when they tell us that they will be fair and
impartial and will ignore inadmissible evidence. Why are jurors discounted in this instance?

When asked by a juror why he was allowing the trial to be filmed, Poe 10
said: The "more the public can know about the truth, the way things
really are, the better we are as a people. And the system benefits from
this."

Poe's decision has forced us to weigh the tension between the 11
assumption that secret jury deliberations are necessary for a fair trial vs.
the idea that our democracy will be better served—especially in matters
of life and death—if we know, every so often and under scrupulous judicial supervision, what is happening behind closed doors, even in the jury
room.

Questions About the Reading

1. What is the comparison the writer makes between cameras in the jury room and other television?
2. What was the reason the Colorado Supreme Court approved having cameras in the jury room in criminal trials?
3. Why do critics disapprove of cameras in the jury room?
4. What was Judge Ted Poe's reason for approving cameras in the jury room in seventeen-year-old Cedric Harrison's trial for murder?

Questions About the Writer's Strategies

1. Is the essay argumentation or persuasion?
2. If the essay is argumentation, identify the elements of the argument. If persuasion, identify the persuasive sentences and words.
3. Is the essay objective or subjective?
4. What modes of development does the writer use in supporting his argument/persuasion essay?

Writing Assignments

1. Assume you are to serve on a jury in the trial of a young person on serious charges. Write an argumentation or persuasion essay for or against having cameras televise your jury deliberations.

2. *Working Together* Join with some classmates and, using the Internet, find at least four more articles related to the issue of cameras in jury rooms. Write two formal arguments: one in support of and the other against jury deliberations.

The Death Penalty Is a Step Back

Coretta Scott King

Coretta Scott King has strong opinions about the death penalty. Despite the loss of two family members, including her husband, the Reverend Martin Luther King, Jr., by assassination, she remains firmly convinced that the death penalty is morally wrong and unjustifiable. A long-time civil rights activist, she believes that the practice of nonviolence is the way to make our society a more just and humane place to live. In the essay that follows, she argues passionately for her convictions.

Words to Know

abhor   detest, hate strongly
deterrent   something that prevents
inequitable   unfair
irrevocable   not reversible
legitimizing   making lawful
miscarriage   a failure
proponents   advocates, supporters
retaliation   act of revenge
sanctioned   approved
specter   ghost
unequivocally   clearly, without question
unwarranted   not supported by facts

Getting Started

Do you think the death penalty is a deterrent to murder?

When Steven Judy was executed in Indiana [in 1981] America took 1
another step backwards towards legitimizing murder as a way of dealing with evil in our society.

Although Judy was convicted of four of the most horrible and brutal 2
murders imaginable, and his case is probably the worst in recent memory for opponents of the death penalty, we still have to face the real issue squarely: Can we expect a decent society if the state is allowed to kill its own people?

In recent years, an increase of violence in America, both individual 3
and political, has prompted a backlash of public opinion on capital punishment. But however much we abhor violence, legally sanctioned executions are no deterrent and are, in fact, immoral and unconstitutional.

Although I have suffered the loss of two family members by assassi- 4
nation, I remain firmly and unequivocally opposed to the death penalty
for those convicted of capital offenses.

An evil deed is not redeemed by an evil deed of retaliation. Justice is 5
never advanced in the taking of a human life.

Morality is never upheld by legalized murder. Morality apart, there 6
are a number of practical reasons which form a powerful argument
against capital punishment.

First, capital punishment makes irrevocable any possible miscarriage 7
of justice. Time and again we have witnessed the specter of mistakenly
convicted people being put to death in the name of American criminal
justice. To those who say that, after all, this doesn't occur too often, I can
only reply that if it happens just once, that is too often. And it has
occurred many times.

Second, the death penalty reflects an unwarranted assumption that 8
the wrongdoer is beyond rehabilitation. Perhaps some individuals cannot be rehabilitated; but who shall make that determination? Is any
amount of academic training sufficient to entitle one person to judge
another incapable of rehabilitation?

Third, the death penalty is inequitable. Approximately half of the 711 9
persons now on death row are black. From 1930 through 1968, 53.5% of
those executed were black Americans, all too many of whom were represented by court-appointed attorneys and convicted after hasty trials.

The argument that this may be an accurate reflection of guilt, and 10
homicide trends, instead of a racist application of laws lacks credibility
in light of a recent Florida survey which showed that persons convicted
of killing whites were four times more likely to receive a death sentence
than those convicted of killing blacks.

Proponents of capital punishment often cite a "deterrent effect" as the 11
main benefit of the death penalty. Not only is there no hard evidence that
murdering murderers will deter other potential killers, but even the
"logic" of this argument defies comprehension.

Numerous studies show that the majority of homicides committed in 12
this country are the acts of the victim's relatives, friends and acquaintances in the "heat of passion."

What this strongly suggests is that rational consideration of future 13
consequences is seldom a part of the killer's attitude at the time he commits a crime.

The only way to break the chain of violent reaction is to practice non- 14
violence as individuals and collectively through our laws and
institutions.

Questions About the Reading

1. What does the writer think we should do instead of enforcing the death penalty?
2. According to the writer, who commits the majority of homicides?
3. What three "practical reasons" does the writer give as an argument against capital punishment?

Questions About the Writer's Strategies

1. Is this essay an example of argument, persuasion, or both? Support your answer with examples.
2. Why does the writer state that she has lost two family members by assassination? How does this contribute to the effectiveness of her argument?
3. What modes of development does the writer use to develop her argument?
4. Where is the thesis most clearly stated?

Writing Assignments

1. Write an essay that argues either for or against the death penalty.
2. Some states have enacted laws that mandate jail sentences for people who are convicted of drunk driving. Do you agree with such laws? Write an essay in which you provide evidence for your position.

Death to the Killers

Mike Royko

In the following essay, Mike Royko (1932–1997), a syndicated columnist, takes the opposing view of the death penalty from that of Coretta Scott King. He tells the stories of the families of several murder victims and says, "Opponents of the death penalty should try explaining to these people just how cruel it is to kill someone."

Words to Know

decomposed rotting
delegate to give duties to another
deter to keep from acting
dispatching getting rid of (in this context, putting to death)
retribution punishment

Getting Started

Do you think the justice system ensures that innocent people will not be put to death for crimes they did not commit?

---

1   Some recent columns on the death penalty have brought some interesting responses from readers all over the country.

2   There were, of course, expressions of horror and disgust that I would favor the quick dispatching of convicted murderers.

3   I really don't like to make fun of people who oppose the death penalty because they are so sincere. But I wish they would come up with some new arguments to replace the worn-out ones.

4   For example, many said something like this: "Wouldn't it be better to keep the killers alive so psychiatrists can study them in order to find out what makes them the way they are?"

5   It takes the average psychiatrist about five years to figure why a guy wants to stop for two drinks after work and won't quit smoking. So how long do you think it will take him to determine why somebody with an IQ of 92 decided to rape and murder the little old lady who lives next door?

6   Besides, we have an abundance of killers in our prisons—more than enough to keep all the nation's shrinks busy for the next 20 years. But shrinks aren't stupid. Why would they want to spend all that time listening to Willie the Wolfman describe his ax murders when they can get

$75 an hour for listening to an executive's fantasies about the secretarial pool?

Another standard is: "The purpose of the law should be to protect 7 society, not to inflict cruel retribution, such as the death penalty."

In that case, we should tear down all the prisons and let all the crim- 8 inals go because most people would consider a long imprisonment to be cruel retribution—especially those who are locked up. Even 30 days in the Cook County Jail is no picnic.

And: "What gives society the right to take a life if an individual 9 can't?" The individuals who make up society give it that right. Societies perform many functions that individuals can't. We can't carry guns and shoot people, but we delegate that right to police.

Finally: "The death penalty doesn't deter crime." I heard from a num- 10 ber of people who have a less detached view of the death penalty than many of the sensitive souls who oppose it.

For instance, Doris Porch wrote me about a man on Death Row in 11 Tennessee. He hired men to murder his wife. One threw in a rape, free of charge.

Porch wrote: "My family had the misfortune of knowing this man (the 12 husband) intimately. The victim was my niece. After her decomposed body was found in the trunk of her car, I made the trip to homicide with my sister."

Sharon Rosenfeldt of Canada wrote: "We know exactly what you are 13 talking about because our son was brutally murdered and sexually abused by mass murderer Clifford Olson in Vancouver.

"Words can't explain the suffering the families of murder victims are 14 left to live with. After two years, we're still trying to piece our lives back together mentally and spiritually."

Eleanor Lulenski of Cleveland said: "I'm the mother of one of the 15 innocent victims. My son was a registered nurse on duty in an emergency room. A man walked in demanding a shot of penicillin. When he was told he would have to be evaluated by a physician, he stomped out, went to his car, came back with a shotgun and killed my son.

"He was sentenced to life, but after several years the sentence was 16 reversed on a technicality—it being that at the time of his trial it was mentioned that this was his second murder."

And Susie James of Greenville, Miss.: "My tax dollars are putting 17 bread into the mouth of at least one murderer from Mississippi who showed no mercy to his innocent victim.

"He caught a ride with her one cold February night. She was return- 18 ing to her home from her job in a nursing home. She was a widow. The murderer, whom she had befriended, struck her on the head with a can of oil. Ignoring her pleas, he forced her through a barbed wire fence into the woods at knifepoint. He stabbed her repeatedly, raped her and left her for dead.

"When the victim's son walked down the stairs to leave the court- 19 house after the guilty sentence had been uttered, he happened to look at the killer's mother.

"She said: 'You buzzard, watching me.'   20

"The murder victim was my mother."   21

There are many others. The mother of the boy who angered some 22 drunken street thugs. They shot him and then ran him over repeatedly with a car. The mother whose son and daughter were beaten to death. The brother who remembers how his little sister would laugh as they played—until she was butchered.

They have many things in common. They suffered a terrible loss, and 23 they live with terrible memories.

One other thing they share: The knowledge that the killers are alive 24 and will probably remain alive and cared for by society.

Opponents of the death penalty should try explaining to these people 25 just how cruel it is to kill someone.

Questions About the Reading

1. Why does Royko think that psychiatrists are not interested in finding out why people kill?
2. What do the families and friends of homicide victims have in common?
3. How does the writer refute the argument that the death penalty won't deter criminals?

Questions About the Writer's Strategies

1. What is the predominant mode of development used to develop the argument?
2. Locate the writer's statement of the problem.
3. Is this essay an example of argumentation, persuasion, or a mixture of the two? Explain your answer.
4. Why does Royko refer to opponents of the death penalty as "sensitive souls" in paragraph 10?
5. Locate the writer's conclusion. Is it effective? Do you think it could have been expanded? Why or why not?

Writing Assignments

1. Write an essay in which you argue for or against the death penalty. Support your argument with information from at least three web sites, and include a list of their addresses. To find helpful sites, use a search engine such as Google (**http://www.google.com/**) or Yahoo! (**http://www.yahoo.com/**) and type in keywords such as "death penalty" or "capital punishment."

2. Some people support mandatory sentencing: people who commit certain crimes are automatically given prison sentences of a certain length. What purpose do you think mandatory sentencing would serve? Write an essay in which you support or reject the concept.

Combining the Strategies

IN THIS CHAPTER, you will find some additional reading selections. Although some of the readings have one dominant **mode of development,** most of them illustrate combinations of the different modes.

As you read, keep in mind what we have stressed in earlier chapters. Determine the

- topic of each paragraph
- thesis of each essay
- structure of the reading (introduction, development, conclusion)
- supporting details
- modes of development
- point of view (person, time, tone)
- method of organization (time, space, order of importance)
- transitional words
- effective words and sentences

Then, make use of these same strategies to write paragraphs and essays that are as clear and effective as those you have read.

Divorce Is Hard for Adult Children, Too

Holly Hubbard Preston

We often hear and read about the effect of divorce on young children, but Holly Hubbard Preston tells us that adult children also suffer when their parents divorce.

Words to know

cataclysmic   violent, catastrophic
fathom   understand
foreboding   ominous, scary
infractions   violations
unwarranted   not justified

Getting Started

Have you ever experienced the loss of a good friend?

It started out as a typical sandbox fight between 4-year-olds. Two pre- 1
school girls battling over a red plastic sand strainer. Suddenly one of the
little girls gave up. With her hands clenched at her side, she began to
bawl. Her pint-size opponent looked to me, a lunchtime volunteer mom,
for help. "All this over a sand toy?" her eyes said.

"What's really bothering you?" I asked, putting an arm around the 2
sobbing bundle before me. "I want my daddy . . . I want to go to his
house now . . . I want my mommy to come," she said, tears and words
pouring out in equal measure. I started to feel my own throat ache. I
clutched her closer as I debated whether to let her see my own tears.

Sarah (not her real name) is struggling to come to terms with her par- 3
ents' failing marriage. The fact that her dad recently moved out would
be foreboding to any child, 4 or 40. I should know. Nearly three years
ago my father moved out of our family home. Now my parents are
divorced after 35 years of marriage. Their split was not a total surprise;
they had been growing apart for years. Still, I had always held out hope,
childish as it might have been, that somehow Mom and Dad would find
a way back to one another. The fact that they never will has been a hard
reality to swallow, even as a seasoned, married 34-year-old.

Contrary to popular belief, divorce isn't any easier or less painful 4
when you are an adult child. The only difference between Sarah and me
is that I can try and sort through what has happened to my family on an
intellectual as well as emotional level. Sarah is left holding a bag of emotions she's not quite sure what to do with. So she throws tantrums and
fights with her friends. I've been there.

During the past three years I've lashed out at my own husband and 5
kids over seemingly minor infractions, like an unwillingness to pick up
clothes or toys. I have even cried over spilled milk.

I often find myself at a loss to explain how empty my parents' 6
breakup has left me. This is coming from someone who writes for a living. I can only imagine the pent-up emotions a young child like Sarah
harbors inside.

The sad thing is that the two people I often want to turn to for com- 7
fort—my mother and my father—cannot be good listeners in this circum-
stance. My pain incites their frustration, guilt and anger over the situation.
Somehow the conversation comes back to them and their suffering.

Grandparents and other relatives, I have found, are not always objec- 8
tive listeners. And much as I'd like to pour my heart out to my little
sister, I won't. She needs a listener too.

My husband tries to be a sounding board, but he has no clue what it 9
is like to be the kid of divorced parents. He comes from an unusually
functional family. He can't fathom the sorrow and betrayal I feel when
looking at a portrait of my mom, my dad, my sister and I when we were
still young and hopeful about our future together. He can't understand
the awkwardness of being invited to a party by a long-time family friend
who has opted not to invite my mother but my father and his fiancée
instead. Nor can he grasp the unwarranted shame I feel when someone
asks me if my parents are still married.

No child wants to see his or her parents unhappy. I know I didn't. For 10
me, understanding the necessity of the divorce was never the problem;
it was learning how to deal with the consequences of it.

Even though good things do come out of divorce—often-happier par- 11
ents, fractured but more peaceful family gatherings—the loss of that
original family unit and the hope tied to it is often irreplaceable for a
child. I'm convinced that even after my parents' financial settlement is
final, I'll never manage to fill the void that's been created. It's like
mourning the death of someone I loved and now miss terribly. In its
place I have a series of separate, compartmentalized relationships.

My parents will be my parents forever, no matter what they think of 12
one another or whom they might marry. After all, I didn't divorce them.
With that in mind, I have no choice but to divide my time and emotions

between the two. I am hardly alone. More than a million kids go through this exercise each year.

Yet, routine as divorce may be, to a child of any age it is a unique 13 event of cataclysmic proportions. I don't know if there's any way to make divorce a less grueling process for a kid. I do know that a little understanding goes a long way. My parents came to see that what I was struggling with was not so much their living apart but what their living apart would mean for me. Now, finally, we're piecing together a new family picture that doesn't feel hopelessly fractured.

———————

U.S. Parents Help Create Teen Trouble

Andy Lin (student)

Andy Lin—a Taiwanese student at Dos Pueblos High School in Goleta, California—maintains that American teenagers are rude and rebellious because their parents do not teach them "good habits and family values."

Words to Know

beneficial   helpful
detrimental   bad for
dysfunctional   disordered
hypocritical   insincere, false
intrinsically   naturally
leniency   forgiveness, excessive freedom
prospective   future
synthesized   combined

Getting Started

What do you think causes teenage rebelliousness?

Coming from Taiwan, I have made some shocking observations about 1
American society. Because parents neither spend enough time with their children nor teach them good habits and family values, their children grow up to be unruly and rebel when their parents try to discipline them. Most Americans are so used to this, however, that they do not regard this situation as unusual. To reverse this trend, the government should offer prospective couples free parenting programs that advocate teaching methods synthesized from different cultures.

Teen-agers today show very little respect for others by frequently 2
speaking in slang and insults, which can include obscenities that involve mothers. I believe this trend is partly the result of a larger conflict with authority, which has been called the "teenage rebellion." Many, if not most, American parents come to dread the time when their cute children grow into uncontrollable teen-agers, who talk back and in general do exactly the opposite of what their parents say; for them, "teen-ager" means "troublemaker."

As part of this rebellion, teen-agers look forward to obtaining their 3
driver's license so that they have the freedom to go and do anything
they want without their parents' watchful eyes following them.
Ironically, by this time, many parents are more than happy to supply a
car for their children; they just wish to be left in peace.

Because many teen-agers have too much time on their hands, they 4
tend to loiter outside with their equally bored friends, which can cause
problems. Once when I was waiting in a car at a traffic light, a teen
strolled in front of us along the crosswalk, and pointedly continued his
slow walk even after the signal had turned green. Despite making us
wait in an attempt to aggravate us, I felt rather calm; I understood that
his behavior was not completely his fault, but also the fault of his parents. If they had taught him correctly, goofing around would have been
the last thought on his mind as he would be too busy with other matters.

Despite my observations, teen-agers are not intrinsically wild. The 5
most fundamental reason for their rowdy behavior is the way they were
raised. In Taiwan and other countries, for example, spanking is not
unusual as a means of punishment. Here, however, many Americans
feel that children should not be spanked when they make a mistake
because they frequently confuse spanking with physical abuse. When
my young cousin was slapped by her mother once when she would not
stop whining, a passerby immediately dialed 9-1-1.

The police came and questioned my cousin, asking if she had been 6
abused. Because my cousin did not speak English at the time, she
answered "yes" to every question. Consequently, because they were
unaware that many Americans disapprove of spanking, my aunt and
uncle went through much hassle and pain as they sought to straighten
out things. Had my cousin been in Taiwan, people would have understood the situation. Young children who are spanked would be more
obedient and less likely to grow into troublesome teen-agers.

This example supports my belief that many American parents treat 7
their children too tenderly. They seek to please them and shield them
from any difficult tasks; it is much easier to let children watch television
than to make them do homework. In the process, however, they foster
bad habits.

My tennis coach has a 3-year-old daughter, whom I often see drag- 8
ging a racquet on the court, not bothering to keep it off the ground to
prevent any wear. When I mentioned this to my coach, all he said was,
"Don't worry about it. she's too young to understand." He wanted her
to enjoy tennis and to be motivated to play, so he tried not to give her
"difficulty" and make her lose motivation. While it may be true that she
may not understand the concept of respecting property, why should that
keep us from teaching her the habit of doing so?

Such leniency encourages children to make increasing demands as 9
well; whenever they want something, all they have to do is whine and
their parents will give it to them. When they are young, their demands
are not extreme enough to warrant any alarm. The seeds of their future
rebellion are being sowed, however; when they grow up, these children
may very well continue their demands, which may then get extreme.
When the parents finally understand the situation, it is too late.

To complicate the situation further, parents do not spend enough time 10
with their children. Too often, they have to work outrageous hours and
spend little time at home. Their contact with their children is essential in
the early stages of childhood, however, because they need to guide their
children into creating good habits.

They should start teaching their children math because it will become 11
important later in life. By having a good mathematical foundation, children will not only have the motivation to do homework, but they will
also have an advantage over other classmates. They will not have to work
so hard in school and can use that energy to get ahead in other areas.

My father forced me to develop my math skills early; because of this, I 12
am the top student in my grade. I have no trouble in any of my math or
science classes. On the contrary, my American friend spent his early childhood playing most of the time while I prepared for my future. Recently, he
told me that he has been trying hard to catch up in math over the summer,
which is not easy to do given the amount of time that is available to him.
He has less time to play, and I believe he would rather have foregone fun
when he was younger so he could enjoy more things today.

After some initial guidance, however, parents should decrease their 13
involvement. Because they have planted a seed, all they have to do is
watch it grow. It is not necessarily beneficial for parents to sit next to
their children and help them with homework; in fact, the results may be
detrimental because their children need to develop the ability to learn on
their own. My father made me educate myself by making a math program and having me practice problems without his help. Though I may
not have fully understood his motives at the time, he forced me to do it
and I appreciate his efforts today because I have the ability to teach
myself without the help of others.

What should we do to solve this complex problem? Parents must take 14
a different attitude when it comes to raising children. Children are not
pets; they are humans and have their own unique challenges as well as
rewards. There is a Chinese saying, which can be roughly translated as,
"Enjoy first, suffer later." If we provide our children with only fun things
without letting them experience difficult tasks, the results can be disastrous in the end, and, as the saying goes, it can bring much suffering for
the whole family.

As of yet, I have not seen any publicized parenting programs that 15
teach young adults the responsibilities and burdens of parenthood.
However, the Department of Education did establish the Partnership for
Family Involvement in Education in 1994, whose goal was to "increase
opportunities for families to be more involved in their children's learning at school and at home." The Department of Education needs to take
a more pronounced role in educating prospective parents. Having information on a Web site is just not enough; programs on parenting should
be offered and strongly recommended.

Before we set out to provide these programs, however, we must first 16
decide what lessons they will teach. Family experts need to take into
account their own biases that result from their backgrounds. Just as writers have difficulty in spotting mistakes in their own writing and need
outside readers to help them, experts must also deal with any prejudices
or assumptions that are present but hidden in their society.

We may need to hire new specialists too; it would be hypocritical to 17
have so-called "experts" tell us how to manage our families, while they
themselves are divorced or have dysfunctional families at home. If we
have a diverse collection of these specialists from different social backgrounds, however, we would be able to synthesize effective methods
from each culture and produce a set of family education guidelines that
work.

Change cannot happen overnight. Although we cannot track each 18
family individually, we can educate the public and many people will
begin to change themselves. Thus, we may break the bad cycle we are in
right now and plant a foot firmly in the right direction. We may not
achieve our goal in this generation, or the next, but perhaps in the future,
people will no longer equate "teen-ager" with "troublemaker."

The Dare

Roger Hoffmann

*Roger Hoffmann recounts an episode from his adolescence when approval
from his peers was more important than his personal safety. No matter
our age or particular adolescent experience, we are able to relate to the
pressure Hoffmann felt as a child. The desire for acceptance by friends
and colleagues is something we never outgrow.*

Words to Know

ambiguous   not clear; having many interpretations

escalated   increased

guerrilla act   warfare carried out by an independent military
force

implicit   understood although not directly stated

provoke   to cause anger or resentment

silhouette   an outline of something that appears dark against a
light background; a shadow

Getting Started

Have you ever taken a risk because of a dare?

The secret to diving under a moving freight train and rolling out the   1
other side with all your parts attached lies in picking the right spot
between the tracks to hit with your back. Ideally, you want soft dirt or
pea gravel, clear of glass shards and railroad spikes that could cause you
instinctively, and fatally, to sit up. Today, at thirty-eight I couldn't be
threatened or baited enough to attempt that dive. But as a seventh
grader struggling to make the cut in a tough Atlanta grammar school, all
it took was a dare.

I coasted through my first years of school as a fussed-over smart kid,   2
the teacher's pet who finished his work first and then strutted around
the room tutoring other students. By the seventh grade, I had more A's
than friends. Even my old cronies, Dwayne and O.T., made it clear I'd
never be one of the guys in junior high if I didn't dirty up my act. They
challenged me to break the rules, and I did. The I-dare-you's escalated:
shoplifting, sugaring teachers' gas tanks, dropping lighted matches into
public mailboxes. Each guerrilla act won me the approval I never got for
just being smart.

Walking home by the railroad tracks after school, we started playing 3
chicken with oncoming trains. O.T., who was failing that year, always
won. One afternoon he charged a boxcar from the side, stopping just
short of throwing himself between the wheels. I was stunned. After the
train disappeared, we debated whether someone could dive under a
moving car, stay put for a 10-count, then scramble out the other side. I
thought it could be done and said so. O.T. immediately stepped in front
of me and smiled. Not by me, I added quickly, I certainly didn't mean
that I could do it. "A smart guy like you," he said, his smile evaporating,
"you could figure it out easy." And then, squeezing each word for effect,
"I . . . DARE . . . you." I'd just turned twelve. The monkey clawing my
back was Teacher's Pet. And I'd been dared.

As an adult, I've been on both ends of life's implicit business and 4
social I-dare-you's, although adults don't use those words. We provoke
with body language, tone of voice, ambiguous phrases. I dare you to:
argue with the boss, tell Fred what you think of him, send the wine back.
Only rarely are the risks physical. How we respond to dares when we
are young may have something to do with which of the truly hazardous
male inner dares—attacking mountains, tempting bulls at Pamplona—
we embrace or ignore as men.

For two weeks, I scouted trains and tracks. I studied moving boxcars 5
close up, memorizing how they squatted on their axles, never getting
used to the squeal or the way the air felt hot from the sides. I created an
imaginary, friendly train and ran next to it. I mastered a shallow, head-
first dive with a simple half-twist. I'd land on my back, count to ten,
imagine wheels and, locking both hands on the rail to my left, heave
myself over and out. Even under pure sky, though, I had to fight to keep
my eyes open and my shoulders between the rails.

The next Saturday, O.T., Dwayne and three eighth graders met me 6
below the hill that backed up to the lumberyard. The track followed a
slow bend there and opened to a straight, slightly uphill climb for a solid
third of a mile. My run started two hundred yards after the bend. The
train would have its tongue hanging out.

The other boys huddled off to one side, a circle on another planet, and 7
watched quietly as I double-knotted my shoelace. My hands trembled.
O.T. broke the circle and came over to me. He kept his hands hidden in
the pockets of his jacket. We looked at each other. BB's of sweat appeared
beneath his nose. I stuffed my wallet in one of his pockets, rubbing it
against his knuckles on the way in, and slid my house key, wired to a
red-and-white fishing bobber, into the other. We backed away from each
other, and he turned and ran to join the four already climbing up the hill.

I watched them all the way to the top. They clustered together as if I 8
were taking their picture. Their silhouette resembled a round shouldered

tombstone. They waved down to me, and I dropped them from my mind and sat down on the rail. Immediately, I jumped back. The steel was vibrating.

The train sounded like a cow going short of breath. I pulled my shirt- 9 tail out and looked down at my spot, then up the incline of track ahead of me. Suddenly the air went hot, and the engine was by me. I hadn't pictured it moving that fast. A man's bare head leaned out and stared at me. I waved to him with my left hand and turned into the train, burying my face into the incredible noise. When I looked up, the head was gone.

I started running alongside the boxcars. Quickly, I found their pace, 10 held it, and then eased off, concentrating on each thick wheel that cut past me. I slowed another notch. Over my shoulder, I picked my car as it came off the bend, locking in the image of the white mountain goat painted on its side. I waited, leaning forward like the anchor in a 440-relay, wishing the baton up the track behind me. Then the big goat fired by me, and I was flying and then tucking my shoulder as I dipped under the train.

A heavy blanket of red dust settled over me. I felt bolted to the earth. 11 Sheet-metal bellies thundered and shook above my face. Count to ten, a voice said, watch the axles and look to your left for daylight. But I couldn't count, and I couldn't find left if my life depended on it, which it did. The colors overhead went from brown to red to black to red again. Finally, I ripped my hands free, forced them to the rail, and, in one convulsive jerk, threw myself into the blue light.

I lay there face down until there was no more noise, and I could feel 12 the sun against the back of my neck. I sat up. The last ribbon of train was slipping away in the distance. Across the tracks, O.T. was leading a cavalry charge down the hill, five very small, galloping boys, their fists whirling above them. I pulled my knees to my chest. My corduroy pants puckered wet across my thighs. I didn't care.

Poetry

Kirsten Bauman (student)

That scary poetry assignment in an English class doesn't frighten Kirsten Bauman, a student at the University of Cincinnati Raymond Walters College in Blue Ash, Ohio. Here, she tells us about her good and bad poetry assignments.

Words to Know
boundaries   limits, confines
confused   lacking understanding
self-conscious   ill-at-ease

Getting Started
What is your favorite poem? Have you ever written a poem?

Poetry is a form of free-thought expressed on paper. No boundaries or 1
limitations are set on the poet.

Many people think a poem has to rhyme or have a pattern, but that is 2
not the case. Poetry sets a mood or a tone by being humorous, sad, or
serious. Poetry lets readers make their own inferences about the meaning of the poem. For that reason, a poem may be more meaningful or
special to one person than to another.

Many of my fellow students, as well as some adults, say they don't 3
like poetry. Maybe the reason I do is because of my early experiences
with poetry.

I can remember sitting on my bed with my Dad as he read aloud to 4
me from an old story book he had when he was a child. I remember that
it was a collection of children's poems that I loved, no matter how many
times my Dad read them to me. I liked the simple nature of the poems. I
liked the fact that I could memorize them so I could "read along" with
my Dad. I still remember what the book looked like. It was a tall, narrow
book with a wood cover. Because it looked different from all my other
books, I still remember it so clearly today.

I can also remember reading aloud from a wide, white poem book 5
called *A Light in the Attic* by Shel Silverstein. I remember liking the
poems because I could relate to them as a child, and they made me
laugh.

Some of my later experiences with poetry weren't as pleasant. In ninth 6
grade English class, we read Shakespeare's *Romeo and Juliet.* I remember
having to read aloud and being confused by Shakespeare's use of words.
I remember wondering why we were being tortured by reading something that everyone in the class clearly didn't understand.

In a later high school English class, we were divided into groups of 7
three. Our assignment was for each of us to write a poem that illustrated
a different element of poetry. Our group was to illustrate the simile.

I had difficulty getting started on my poem; but once I had a begin- 8
ning place, thoughts and ideas just came naturally to me. I actually liked
writing the poem. But we still had to present our poems in front of the
class, and I was self-conscious about sharing my ideas with other people.
It was hard to get in front of the class and read my poem aloud, but my
turn was soon over. The class seemed to like my poem, so I decided that
writing poetry was almost as pleasant as reading it.

A Very Basic Decision

Mary Mebane

Mary E. Mebane discovered that prejudice can exist within as well as between races when she attended a North Carolina college for blacks in the 1950s. The light-skinned, urban, middle-class blacks who made up the faculty and most of the student body could not believe that a dark-skinned black girl from a poor rural family could be a superior student. In "A Very Basic Decision," a passage from Mary: An Autobiography, *Mebane tells of two meetings she had with the wife of the English department's chairman, a light-skinned woman who was convinced that Mebane could not be as talented as her test scores and grades showed. But Mebane decided not to give up her quest for a college degree. She graduated at the top of her class and is now a college English professor.*

Words to Know

appalled   dismayed
bolstered   supported, propped up
criteria   standards
defer   submit, yield
indistinguishable   not able to be recognized or seen as different
noncommittal   to show no opinion or preference
nonplussed   confused, perplexed, baffled
pinnacle   peak, top
recourse   choice, option

Getting Started

What experiences have influenced your choice of a school program?

———————————

Northorth Carolina College at Durham (it used to carry the words "for Negroes" in its official title—it said so on the sign right on the lawn) is located in the southern part of the town. Its immaculately groomed lawns and neat, squarish, redbrick classroom buildings and dormitories mark it as an oasis of privilege and ease. Looking at the postcard scenes through the low-hanging branches of the surrounding trees, one would not have believed that this was six minutes away from some of the worst slums in the South. The college hadn't forgotten their existence; it simply never acknowledged that they were there. The black dispossessed murmured against the "big dogs," and bided their time. I often thought that if and when "the revolution" came and the black masses in America awakened

1

310

from their long sleep, their first target was going to be the black professional class and it would be a horrendous bloodbath. . . .

During my first week of classes as a freshman, I was stopped one day 2
in the hall by the chairman's wife, who was indistinguishable in color from a white woman. She wanted to see me, she said.

This woman had no official position on the faculty, except that she was 3
an instructor in English; nevertheless, her summons had to be obeyed. In the segregated world there were (and remain) gross abuses of authority because those at the pinnacle, and even their spouses, felt that the people "under" them had no recourse except to submit—and they were right, except that sometimes a black who got sick and tired of it would go to the whites and complain. This course of action was severely condemned by the blacks, but an interesting thing happened—such action always got positive results. Power was thought of in negative terms: I can deny someone something, I can strike at someone who can't strike back, I can ride someone down; that proves I am powerful. The concept of power as a force for good, for affirmative response to people or situations, was not in evidence.

When I went to her office, she greeted me with a big smile. "You 4
know," she said, "you made the highest mark on the verbal part of the examination." She was referring to the examination that the entire freshman class took upon entering the college. I looked at her but I didn't feel warmth, for in spite of her smile her eyes and tone of voice were saying, "How could this black-skinned girl score higher on the verbal than some of the students who've had more advantages than she? It must be some sort of fluke. Let me talk to her." I felt it, but I managed to smile my thanks and back off. For here at North Carolina College at Durham, as it had been since the beginning, social class and color were the primary criteria used in determining status on the campus.

First came the children of doctors, lawyers, and college teachers. Next 5
came the children of public-school teachers, businessmen, and anybody else who had access to more money than the poor black working class. After that came the bulk of the student population, the children of the working class, most of whom were the first in their families to go beyond high school. The attitude toward them was: You're here because we need the numbers, but in all other things defer to your betters.

The faculty assumed that light-skinned students were more intelli- 6
gent, and they were always a bit nonplussed when a dark-skinned student did well, especially if she was a girl. They had reason to be appalled when they discovered that I planned to do not only well but better than my light-skinned peers. . . .

When the grades for that first quarter came out, I had the highest 7
average in the freshman class. The chairman's wife called me into her

office again. We did a replay of the same scene we had played during the first week of the term. She complimented me on my grades, but her eyes and voice were telling me something different. She asked me to sit down; then she reached into a drawer and pulled out a copy of the freshman English final examination. She asked me to take the exam over again.

At first I couldn't believe what she was saying. I had taken the course 8 under another teacher, and it was so incredible to her that I should have made the highest score in the class that she was trying to test me again personally. For a few moments I knew rage so intense that I wanted to take my fists and start punching her. I have seldom hated anyone so deeply. I handed the examination back to her and walked out.

She had felt quite safe in doing that to me. After all, she was the chair- 9 man's wife, and so didn't that give her the right to treat the black farm girl as she chose? (Life is strange. When in the mid-1960s the department started hiring native-born whites, it was she who most bitterly resented their presence.)

It was that incident which caused me to make a very basic decision. I 10 was in the world alone; no one bolstered my ambitions, fed my dreams. I could not quit now, for if I did I would have no future. . . . If I was going to get through college, I would have to be bland, noncommittal. I would simply hang on. I needed a degree and I would stay until I got it.

Time to Look and Listen

Magdoline Asfahani (student)

Magdoline Asfahani, an Arab and a Muslim, gives us a sensitive and thoughtful account of the effect of discrimination on her life. Asfahani is a student at the University of Texas, El Paso.

Words to Know

alluding   referring, suggesting
incompatible   not in agreement
medley   mixture, assortment
monotheistic   having a belief in one God
nuances   subtleties, slight variations or differences

[handwritten: prejudice exists within race between races]

Getting Started

Do you feel that you discriminate against a group of people?

 I love my country as many who have been here for generations cannot.   1
Perhaps that's because I'm the child of immigrants, raised with a con-
scious respect for America that many people take for granted. My parents chose this country because it offered them a new life, freedom and
possibilities. But I learned at a young age that the country we loved so
much did not feel the same way about us.

Discrimination is not unique to America. It occurs in any country that   2
allows immigration. Anyone who is unlike the majority is looked at a little suspiciously, dealt with a little differently. The fact that I wasn't part
of the majority never occurred to me. I knew that I was an Arab and a
Muslim. This meant nothing to me. At school I stood up to say the
Pledge of Allegiance every day. These things did not seem incompatible
at all. Then everything changed for me, suddenly and permanently, in
1985. I was only in seventh grade, but that was the beginning of my
political education.

That year a TWA plane originating in Athens was diverted to Beirut.   3
Two years earlier the U.S. Marine barracks in Beirut had been bombed.
That seemed to start a chain of events that would forever link Arabs with
terrorism. After the hijacking, I faced classmates who taunted me with
cruel names, attacking my heritage and my religion. I became an outcast
and had to apologize for myself constantly.

After a while, I tried to forget my heritage. No matter what race, reli-   4
gion or ethnicity, a child who is attacked often retreats. I was the only
Arab I knew of in my class, so I had no one in my peer group as an ally.
No matter what my parents tried to tell me about my proud cultural history, I would ignore it. My classmates told me I came from an uncivi-
lized, brutal place, that Arabs were by nature anti-American, and I
believed them. They did not know the hours my parents spent studying,
working, trying to preserve part of their old lives while embracing, willingly, the new.

I tried to forget the Arabic I knew, because if I didn't I'd be forever   5
linked to murderers. I stopped inviting friends over for dinner, because
I thought the food we ate was "weird." I lied about where my parents
had come from. Their accents (although they spoke English perfectly)
humiliated me. Though Islam is a major monotheistic religion with
many similarities to Judaism and Christianity, there were no holidays
near Chanukah or Christmas, nothing to tie me to the "Judeo-Christian"
tradition. I felt more excluded. I slowly began to turn into someone without a past.

Civil war was raging in Lebanon, and all that Americans saw of that   6
country was destruction and violence. Every other movie seemed to feature Arab terrorists. The most common questions I was asked were if I
had ever ridden a camel or if my family lived in tents. I felt burdened
with responsibility. Why should an adolescent be asked questions like
"Is it true you hate Jews and you want Israel destroyed?" I didn't hate
anybody. My parents had never said anything even alluding to such sentiments. I was confused and hurt.

As I grew older and began to form my own opinions, my embarrass-   7
ment lessened and my anger grew. The turning point came in high
school. My grandmother had become very ill, and it was necessary for
me to leave school a few days before Christmas vacation. My chemistry
teacher was very sympathetic until I said I was going to the Middle East.
"Don't come back in a body bag," he said cheerfully. The class laughed.
Suddenly, those years of watching movies that mocked me and listening
to others who knew nothing about Arabs and Muslims except what they
saw on television seemed like a bad dream. I knew then that I would
never be silent again.

I've tried to reclaim those lost years. I realize now that I come from a   8
culture that has a rich history. The Arab world is a medley of people of
different religions; not every Arab is a Muslim, and vice versa. The Arabs
brought tremendous advances in the sciences and mathematics, as well
as creating a literary tradition that has never been surpassed. The language itself is flexible and beautiful, with nuances and shades of meaning unparalleled in any language. Though many find it hard to believe,

Islam has made progress in women's rights. There is a specific provision in the Koran that permits women to own property and ensures that their inheritance is protected—although recent events have shown that interpretation of these laws can vary.

My youngest brother, who is 12, is now at the crossroads I faced. 9 When initial reports of the Oklahoma City bombing pointed to "Arab-looking individuals" as the culprits, he came home from school crying. "Mom, why do Muslims kill people? Why are the Arabs so bad?" She was angry and brokenhearted, but tried to handle the situation in the best way possible: through education. She went to his class, armed with Arabic music, pictures, traditional dress and cookies. She brought a chapter of the social-studies book to life, and the children asked intelligent, thoughtful questions, even after the class was over. Some even asked if she was coming back. When my brother came home, he was excited and proud instead of ashamed.

I only recently told my mother about my past experience. Maybe if I 10 had told her then, I would have been better equipped to deal with the thoughtless teasing. But, fortunately, the world is changing. Although discrimination and stereotyping still exist, many people are trying to lessen and end it. Teachers, schools and the media are showing greater sensitivity to cultural issues. However, there is still much that needs to be done, not for the sake of any particular ethnic or cultural group but for the sake of our country.

The America that I love is one that values freedom and the differences 11 of its people. Education is the key to understanding. As Americans we need to take a little time to look and listen carefully to what is around us and not rush to judgment without knowing all the facts. And we must never be ashamed of our pasts. It is our collective differences that unite us and make us unique as a nation. It's what determines our present and our future.

Glossary

Various terms are used throughout this edition of Patterns Plus to explain the basic strategies of writing. These terms are boldfaced in the chapter introductions, and they are boldfaced and defined here in the following pages. Terms in bold type within the definitions are also defined in the Glossary.

Alternating Method   The alternating method of **comparison** and **contrast,** also called point-by-point method, compares and contrasts two subjects item by item. (See also **Block Method** and **Mixed Method.**)

Antonym   An antonym is a word that has a meaning *opposite* that of another word. For example, *pleasure* is an antonym of *pain.* Using an antonym is one method writers use to define an unfamiliar word.

Argumentation   Argumentation is a **mode of development** used to express a controversial idea. A classic or formal argument includes five elements: statement of the problem, solution, evidence, refutation, and conclusion. Argumentation may or may not include some persuasion, but should be rational, logical, and objective rather than emotional. (See also **Persuasion.**)

Audience   A reader or readers of a piece of writing. More specifically, an audience is that reader or group of readers toward which a particular piece of writing is aimed. (See also **Purpose** and **Occasion.**)

Block Method   In the block method of **comparison** and **contrast,** the writer first explains the characteristics of the first item in a block and then explains the characteristics of the second item in a block. (See also **Alternating Method** and **Mixed Method.**)

Body   The body is the development of the **thesis** in a group of related paragraphs in an **essay.** (See also **Introduction** and **Conclusion.**)

Brainstorming   A prewriting technique that many writers use to generate ideas for writing. In brainstorming, a writer jots down as many details and ideas on a subject as come to mind.

Cause   A cause is a reason why something happens or an explanation of why some effect occurs. Writers explain why an effect (or result) comes about by explaining its causes. See chapter 8, "Cause and Effect," for further discussion.

Chronological Order See **Order.**

Class   In **classification** and **division,** a writer can classify or divide items if they are of the same type—that is, if they belong to the same class.

Classification Classification is the process of sorting a group of items into categories on the basis of some characteristic or quality that the items have in common. As a **mode of development,** classification is used by writers to organize and develop information included in a **paragraph** or **essay.** Classification is sometimes combined with division to develop a **topic** or **thesis.** See chapter 5, "Classification and Division," for further discussion.

Cliché Clichés are words or phrases that have become so overused they have lost their expressive power. Examples of clichés are "rosy red," "silly goose," "bull in a china shop," and "works like a horse."

Coherence   Coherence refers to the logical flow of a piece of writing. Writing is coherent when the **main idea** is clearly stated and the connections between the supporting **details** and the main idea are obvious. (See also **Unified/Unity.**)

Collaboration/Collaborative Writing   Collaboration or collaborative writing is the working together of two or more persons in developing and producing a piece of writing.

Comparison/Compare   When making a comparison, the writer discusses the similarities of objects or ideas. Writers sometimes combine comparison with **contrast** in developing their **main idea.** See chapter 6, "Comparison and Contrast," for further discussion.

Conclusion   In writing, the term *conclusion* is used to refer to the sentence or **paragraph** that completes the composition. Within the conclusion, the writer may restate the **main idea** of the composition or sum up its important points.

In reading, the term *conclusion* refers to the idea the reader can draw from the information in the reading selection. Drawing a conclusion involves making an **inference**—that is, deriving an idea that is implied by the information stated within a composition.

Connotation   Connotation refers to the feelings or qualities a reader associates with a word. In **persuasion,** writers often use the connotations of words to appeal to their readers. (See also **Denotation.**)

Contrast   When making a contrast, the writer discusses the differences among objects or ideas. Writers sometimes combine contrast with **comparison** in developing an idea. See chapter 6, "Comparison and Contrast," for further discussion.

Deductive Order   In deductive order—also called general-to-specific order—the writer presents the argument or discussion by beginning with a general statement, such as the topic of a paragraph or thesis of an essay, and proceeding to the specific information that supports the statement.

Definition   A definition explains the meaning of a word or term. Writers frequently use a variety of methods for defining the words and terms they use. They may use a dictionary definition, a **synonym,** or an **antonym.** They may also use any combination of the **modes of development** explained in this text.
   An **extended definition** is one composed of several sentences or paragraphs. It is often used to define complex objects or concepts. See chapter 9, "Definition," for further discussion.

Denotation   Denotation refers to the exact definition, or dictionary definition, of a word. (See also **Connotation.**)

Description   In a description, the writer discusses the appearance of a person, place, or object. In descriptions, writers use words and details that appeal to the senses in order to create the **impression** they want the reader to have about what is being described.

Details   Details are specific pieces of information—examples, incidents, dates, and so forth—that explain and support the general ideas in a composition. Writers use details to make their general ideas clearer and more understandable to the reader.

Development   Development refers to the detailed explanation of the main—and usually more general—ideas in a composition. The **main idea** (or **topic**) of a paragraph is developed by providing specific information in the sentences within the paragraph. The main idea or **thesis** of an **essay** is explained or developed through **paragraphs.**

Dialogue   Dialogue is conversation, usually between two or more persons. It is used by writers to give the exact words spoken by people and is always set off by quotation marks. The writer usually uses a new paragraph to indicate a change of speaker. Dialogue is commonly found in **narration.**

Division   In division, the writer breaks down or sorts a single object or idea into its components or parts and then gives detailed information about each of the parts. Division is sometimes used in combination with **classification.** See chapter 5, "Classification and Division," for further discussion.

Draft   A draft is the first version of a piece of writing. Preparation of a draft follows prewriting in the writing process. A draft requires rewriting, revising, and editing. (See also **Edit, Prewriting, Revising,** and **Rewriting.**)

Edit Editing is the final step in the writing process and involves checking the piece of writing for accuracy of spelling, sentence structure, grammar, and punctuation. (See also **Draft, Prewriting, Revising,** and **Rewriting.**)

Effect An effect is the result of certain events or **causes.** An effect may be the result of one or more causes. Writers often combine cause and effect to explain why something happens. See chapter 8, "Cause and Effect," for further discussion.

Essay An essay is a written composition based on an idea, which is called its **thesis.** An essay usually consists of at least three **paragraphs.** In the paragraphs, writers usually introduce and state the **thesis,** develop or explain the thesis, and conclude the essay. See chapter 1, "The Basics of Writing: Process and Strategies," for further discussion.

Event An occurrence or happening that a writer wishes to portray, often as part of a **fictional** or **nonfictional narrative.**

Example An example is a specific illustration of a general idea or statement. Writers may use one or more examples and may extend a single example over an entire essay in order to illustrate and support their ideas.

Extended Definition See **Definition.**

Extended Example An extended example is described in several sentences or paragraphs. It is used as a way of providing additional support for a **topic sentence** or **thesis statement.** See chapter 4, "Examples," for further discussion.

Fact(s) Any thing or things known with certainty. Writers often present facts as a way of showing they are **objective** about a subject. (See also **Opinion.**)

Fallacy A fallacy is an error in the writer's reasoning or logic. Types of fallacies include the post hoc (meaning "after this, therefore because of this"), hasty generalization, non sequitur (claiming an effect that does not follow from the cause), false analogy, circular argument, argument to the man (argument ad hominem), bandwagon, either-or, and begging the question. See chapters 8, "Cause and Effect," and 10, "Argumentation and Persuasion," for further discussion.

Fiction/Fictional Narrative A **paragraph** or an **essay** that presents a story or event that did not occur or that differs significantly from a real or true event is called fiction. (By contrast, see **Nonfiction/Nonfictional Narrative.**)

Figure of Speech A word or phrase used to compare unlike things to create an image or **impression.** Examples are "He fought like a tiger" and "A little girl is sugar and spice." (See also **Metaphor** and **Simile.**)

First Person See **Person.**

Formal Definition A formal definition assigns the word or term being defined to the **class** or **classification** of items to which it belongs and then describes the characteristics that distinguish it from other items in that class.

Freewriting Freewriting is a prewriting exercise that involves writing without stopping for a set period of time, often five to ten minutes. Freewriting is an effective way to start writing and to generate ideas.

General Idea/General Statement A general idea or statement is broad and sweeping and therefore must usually be explained with more specific information. The **main idea** of a **paragraph** or an **essay** is a relatively general idea, involving only the main features of the thought. In a paragraph or an essay, the general ideas and statements must be supported by more specific information.

Imply/Implied To imply is to hint at or indicate indirectly. Writers sometimes only imply their ideas rather than state them directly. An implied idea requires the reader to draw **conclusions** or make **inferences** in order to determine the idea.

Impression The effect, feeling, or image that an author tries to create through **description.**

Incidents Incidents are the more specific, detailed happenings that make up a particular event. The **narration** of an event will include an account of the specific incidents that occurred as part of the event.

Inductive Order In inductive order—also called specific-to-general order—the writer presents the argument or discussion by beginning with specific supporting information and proceeding to the **general statement,** such as the **topic** of a **paragraph** or **thesis** of an **essay.**

Infer/Inference An inference is a conclusion drawn by the reader based on information known or **implied.** Writers sometimes imply their ideas rather than state them. Readers must make inferences and use the information that is known or stated to determine the writer's ideas.

Inform Inform means to relate or tell about something. Writers often use **process** as a **mode of development** to inform their readers, although any of the modes discussed in this text can be used to inform.

Instruct Instruct means to teach or educate. Writers often use **process** as a **mode of development** to instruct their readers.

Introduction The introduction of a **paragraph** or **essay** is at its beginning. The introduction of an essay is often where the writer places the **thesis statement.** (See also **Body** and **Conclusion.**)

Irony The use of a relationship that is contradictory or unexpected. Writers often use irony to amuse, sadden, instruct, or anger their readers.

Main Idea The main idea of a composition is the general concept, broad **opinion,** or argument on which the composition is based. The main idea of a **paragraph** is called the **topic.** The main idea of an **essay** is called the **thesis.**

Metaphor A metaphor is a **figure of speech** that compares unlike items by attributing the qualities or characteristics of one item to the other. A metaphor compares the items without the use of the words *like* or *as*. (See also **Simile**.)

Mixed Method The mixed method of **comparison** and **contrast** explains similarities and then differences, or differences first and then similarities. (See also **Alternating Method** and **Block Method**.)

Mode of Development The mode of development refers to the kind of information used to support and explain the **main idea** of a paragraph or essay. Writers commonly use, either singly or in combination, the modes discussed in this text: **narration, description, examples, classification** and **division, comparison** and **contrast, process, cause and effect, definition,** and **argumentation** and **persuasion.**

Narration/Narrative Writing Narration is a **mode of development** used by writers to tell a story or give an account of a historical or fictional event. See chapter 2, "Narration," for further discussion.

Nonfiction/Nonfictional Narrative A paragraph or essay that presents a story or event that actually happened. (By contrast, see **Fiction/Fictional Narrative**.)

Objective A paragraph or essay that presents the facts without including the writer's interpretation of those facts is said to be objective. (By contrast, see **Subjective**.)

Occasion An occasion is a set of circumstances under which a particular piece of writing occurs. The writing assignments in this text are occasions for writing **paragraphs** and **essays**.

Opinion An opinion is a belief or conclusion that may or may not be based on fact. Writers often use opinion as a way of presenting a subjective description of an event or object. (By contrast, see **Fact[s]**.)

Order Order refers to the sequence in which the information in a composition is organized or arranged. Information is commonly organized in chronological order, order of importance, or spatial order. In **chronological order,** the information is arranged according to time. In **order of importance,** the information may be arranged from the least to the most important—or from the most to the least important. In **spatial order,** the information is presented from a particular vantage point: the door to a room, front to back, floor to ceiling, and so forth.

Order of Importance See **Order.**

Paragraph A paragraph is usually a set of two or more sentences that help explain an idea. The major use of a paragraph is to mark a division of the information within a composition. Another use of the paragraph is to set off **dialogue**. In this text, a paragraph is considered as a unit. The first word of a paragraph is usually indented a few spaces from the left margin of the printed page.

Person Person is indicated by the personal pronouns used in a composition. Writers use the first person (*I, we*) to represent themselves as participants or firsthand observers of their subject. They use the second person (*you*) to address the reader directly. They use the third person (*he, she, it, one, they*) to provide the reader with a less limited and more objective view of the subject than may be possible by using first or second person. (See also **Point of View.**)

Persuasion Persuasion is a **mode of development** in which the writer appeals to the reader's emotions in an attempt to convince the reader to accept the writer's **opinion** or judgment. The writer's **thesis** may or may not be controversial. (See also **Argumentation.**)

Point-by-Point Method See **Alternating Method.**

Point of View Point of view refers to the way writers present their ideas. Point of view is determined by the **person, time,** and **tone** used in a composition. Person is indicated by personal pronouns. Time is determined by the words that indicate when the action discussed in the composition takes place (past, present, or future). Tone refers to the attitude that writers take toward their subjects. The tone may be serious, humorous, formal, informal, cynical, sarcastic, ironic, sympathetic, and so forth.

Prewriting Prewriting may involve **freewriting** and **brainstorming.** The purpose of prewriting is to get the writer started on defining the **main idea.** (See also **Brainstorming, Draft,** and **Freewriting.**)

Process Process is a **mode of development** used by writers to explain the method of performing a task, making or preparing something, or achieving a particular result. See chapter 7, "Process," for further discussion.

Purpose Purpose refers to a writer's reason for writing. Writers usually want to **inform** and to **instruct.**

Quotation Marks Quotation marks are a pair of punctuation marks (" ") used to indicate the beginning and end of **dialogue** or information cited verbatim from a source.

Revising The process of evaluating, reworking, and **rewriting a draft,** keeping **audience, purpose, thesis, development,** and, finally, mechanics (sentence structure, punctuation) in mind.

Rewriting Rewriting involves reworking and clarifying the **draft** of a piece of writing. (See also **Draft, Edit, Prewriting,** and **Revising.**)

Second Person See **Person.**

Sentence A sentence is a group of words that expresses a thought. A sentence usually contains a word or words that express who is doing an action or is being acted upon (the subject of the sentence) and a word or words that express the action that is taking place (the *verb* of the sentence). The first word of a sentence begins with a capital letter. The end of a sentence is marked by a period (.), a question mark (?), or an exclamation point (!).

Simile A simile is a **figure of speech** in which unlike items are compared. A simile is usually introduced by *like* or *as,* as in "He worked *like a horse* on the project" or "The chicken was as tasteless *as a piece of cardboard.*" (See also **Metaphor.**)

Spatial Order See **Order.**

Subjective Subjective writing is that in which the writer's own feelings about the topic are expressed. (By contrast, see **Objective.**)

Support Support refers to the information—specific details, **examples,** and so forth—used to develop or explain the **general idea** in a composition.

Symbol A symbol is a person, place, or object that represents something other than itself, usually something immaterial or abstract.

Synonym A synonym is a word or phrase that has the same meaning as another word or phrase. Writers sometimes use a synonym to clarify an unfamiliar word or phrase used in their compositions.

Thesis The thesis is the **main idea** of an essay. The thesis may be stated directly (see **Thesis Statement**) or only implied (see **Imply/Implied**).

Thesis Statement The thesis statement is the sentence or sentences in which the **main idea** of an **essay** is stated. The thesis statement is generally placed at or near the beginning of an essay.

Third Person See **Person.**

Time Time refers to the period (past, present, future) when the action discussed in the composition took place. Time is indicated by action words (verbs) and such words as *tomorrow, yesterday, next week,* and so on. (See also **Point of View.**)

Tone Tone refers to the attitude writers take toward their subjects. The attitude in a composition may be formal, informal, serious, humorous, and so forth. (See also **Point of View.**)

Topic The main idea of a **paragraph** is called its topic. The topic of a paragraph may be stated directly (see **Topic Sentence**) or only implied (see **Imply/Implied**).

Topic Sentence The topic sentence is the sentence (or sentences) in which the main **idea** of a **paragraph** is stated. The topic sentence is commonly placed at or near the beginning of a paragraph, but it may appear at any point in the paragraph.

Transitions Transitions are words and phrases such as *for example, on the other hand, first, second,* or *to illustrate* that help the reader identify the relationships among ideas in a composition.

Unified/Unity A **paragraph** or **essay** must be unified to be effective, which means each must deal with a single idea, and the information included in the paragraph or essay must be related to that idea. (See also **Main Idea** and **Coherence.**)

Acknowledgments

Carol Adams: "An Intruder in the House" by Carol Adams (student).

Kurt Anderson: Kurt Anderson, "Hush Timmy—This is Like a Church" Time, 4/15/85. © 1985 Time Inc. Reprinted by permission.

Magdoline Asfahani: "Time to Look and Listen" by Magdoline Asfahani. From NEWSWEEK, December 2, 1996. © 1996 Newsweek, Inc. All rights reserved. Reprinted by permission.

Isaac Asimov: From *Please Explain* by Isaac Asimov. Copyright © 1973 by Isaac Asimov. Reprinted by permission of Houghton Mifflin Company. All rights reserved.

James Baldwin: From NOTES OF NATIVE SON by James Baldwin. Copyright © 1955, renewed 1983, by James Baldwin. Reprinted by permission of Beacon Press, Boston.

Kirsten Bauman: Kirsten Bauman, "Poetry" (student).

Suzanne Britt: Suzanne Britt, "Neat People vs. Sloppy People" from SHOW AND TELL. Reprinted by permission of the author.

Leo Buscaglia: "The Wine Experience" by Leo Buscaglia from PAPA, MY FATHER, 1989, pp. 70-73. Reprinted by permission of the author.

Iu-Choi Chan: "Freedom" by Iu-Choi Chan (student).

Mary Boltz Chapman: Mary Boltz Chapman, "A Burning Issue," Copyright 2003 Reed Business Information, a division of Reed Elsevier Inc. Reprinted from CHAIN LEADER, Feb. 2003, with permission.

Jacques Cousteau: Selection from *The Bounty of the Sea*. Reprinted by permission of The Cousteau Society, Inc.

Gil Crandall: From "Letter to a Tobacco Company," by Gil Crandall in *READER'S DIGEST* Vol. 125, July 1984, pp. 64-65. Reprinted by permission of the author.

Diana Crane: Diana Crane, "The Social Meaning of T-shirts" from FASHION AND ITS SOCIAL AGENDAS, University of Chicago Press, 2000. Copyright © 2000 by the The University of Chicago Press. Reprinted by permission.

327

Michael Dobbs: "The ABCs of the U.S.A." by Michael Dobbs, The Washington Post, June 21, 1987. © 1987, The Washington Post, reprinted with permission.

Lt. Nicole A. Elwell: Lt. Nicole A. Elwell, "A Letter from the Desert," CLEVELAND PLAIN DEALER, 4/21/03, p. B7. Reprinted by permission of the author.

Ricardo Galvez: "My Suit" by Ricardo Galvez (student).
Julie Gifford: Julie Gifford, "The Art of Making Fimo Beads: A Step-by-Step Process" (student).
Ellen Gilchrist: Ellen Gilchrist, "Message in a Bottle" is reprinted by permission of Don Congdon Associates, Inc. First published in the February 2003 issue of REAL SIMPLE. Copyright © 2003 by Ellen Gilchrist.
Jeff Glasser: "Boomtown U.S.A.," U.S. NEWS & WORLD REPORT, 6/25/01, Vol. 130, Issue 25, p. 16. Copyright 2001 U.S. News & World Report, L.P. Reprinted with permission.
Bob Greene: "It Took This Night to Make Us Know," from *Johnny Deadline Reporter* by Bob Greene. Copyright © 1976 Nelson-Hall Inc. Reprinted by permission of the publisher.

S. I. Hayakawa and Alan R. Hayakawa: "How Dictionaries are Made" adapted from LANGUAGE IN THOUGHT AND ACTION, Fourth Edition by S. I. Hayakawa and Alan R. Hayakawa, copyright © 1978 by Harcourt, Inc., reprinted by permission of the publisher.
L. Rust Hills: "How to Eat An Ice-Cream Cone" from *How to do Things Right: The Revelations of a Fussy Man* (New York: Doubleday, 1972). Reprinted by permission of the author.
Roger Hoffmann: "There's Always the Dare" by Roger Hoffmann, THE NEW YORK TIMES, March 23, 1986. Copyright © 1986 by Roger Hoffmann. Reprinted by permission.
Mark Holston: Mark Holston, "Rhythm Four Strings," from AMERICAS, (English) Vol. 43, No. 1 (1991), p. 56(2). Reprinted from Americas, a bimonthly magazine published by The General Secretariat of The Organization of American States in English and Spanish.
Sue Hubbell: Excerpt from A BOOK OF BEES by Sue Hubbell. Copyright © 1988 by Sue Hubbell. Reprinted by permission of Houghton Mifflin Company. All rights reserved.
Bill Husted: Bill Husted, "Here's How to Revive a Computer after an Evil Wizard Kills the Beast." © 2004 The Atlanta Journal-Constitution. Reprinted with permission from the Atlanta Journal-Constitution.

Sara Askew Jones: Sara Askew Jones, "Starstruck" from SOUTHERN LIVING, December 2002, p. 30. © 2002 Southern Living. Reprinted with permission.

E. J. Kahn, Jr.: "The Discovery of Coca-Cola" from THE BIG DRINK: THE STORY OF COCA-COLA by E. J. Kahn, Jr. Copyright © 1950, 1959, 1960 by E. J. Kahn, Jr. Used by permission of Random House, Inc.
Tiffany Kay: Tiffany Kay, "Total Eclipse of the Son," PSYCHOLOGY TODAY, Jan/Feb 2003. Reprinted with permission from PSYCHOLOGY TODAY Magazine, Copyright © (2003) Sussex Publishers, Inc.

Coretta Scott King: Coretta Scott King, "The Death Penalty is a Step Back." Re-printed by arrangement with Coretta Scott King c/o Writers House as agent.

Stephen King: Stephen King, "Ever Et Raw Meat," THE NEW YORK TIMES BOOK REVIEW, December 6, 1987. Copyright © 1987 by the New York Times Co. Reprinted by permission.

Barbara Lewis: "The Cook" by Barbara Lewis (student).

Marc Levine: Marc Levine, "Super Bowl vs. The Oscars," from USA TODAY. Copyright March 14-16, 2003. Reprinted with permission.

Grace Lichtenstein: Excerpt from "Sold Only in the West, Coor's Beer is Smuggled to the East" by Grace Lichtenstein, NEW YORK TIMES, December 28, 1975. Copyright © 1975, The New York Times. Reprinted by permission.

Andy Lin: Andy Lin, "U.S. Parents Help Cause Teen Trouble," SANTA BARBARA NEWS PRESS, August 30, 1999, pp. B1-2. Reprinted by permission.

Rhonda S. Lucas: "Limbo," by Rhonda S. Lucas (student).

Carmen Machin: "The Deli," by Carmen Machin (student).

Robert MacKenzie: Robert MacKenzie, "The Pleasures of Age," NEW CHOICES, March 1993, p. 96. Reprinted by permission of the author.

Brian Manning: "The Thirsty Animal," by Brian Manning, THE NEW YORK TIMES, October 13, 1985. Copyright © 1985 by The New York Times Co.

David Mazie: Excerpted with permission from "Keep Your Teen-Age Driver Alive" by David Mazie, READER'S DIGEST June 1991. Copyright © 1991 by The Reader's Digest Assn., Inc.

Mary Mebane: From MARY by Mary Mebane, copyright © 1981 by Mary Elizabeth Mebane. Used by permission of Viking Penguin, a division of Penguin Group (USA) Inc.

Nancy Pritts Merrell: "Grandparents," by Nancy Pritts Merrell (student).

Cynthia Merriwether-deVries: Cynthia Merriwether-deVries, "Racial Stereotypes Go Underground," USA TODAY, 2/28/03. Reprinted by permission of the author.

Desmond Morris: "Secrets of Man's Unspoken Language" Extract from MAN-WATCHING: A FIELD GUIDE TO HUMAN BEHAVIOUR by Desmond Morris published by Jonathan Cape. Used by permission of The Random House Group Limited.

Alcestis "Cooky" Oberg: Alcestis "Cooky" Oberg, "The Internet Instills Family Values—Really," USA TODAY, 3/13/00 is reprinted by permission of the author. Alcestis Oberg © 2000. All rights reserved.

Marvin Olasky: "Aiming for Success?" by Marvin Olasky originally published in USA TODAY, August 14, 1997. Reprinted by permission of the author.

Jeanne Park: Jeanne Park, "Eggs, Twinkies and Ethnic Stereotypes," THE NEW YORK TIMES, April 20, 1990. Copyright © 1990 by the New York Times Co. Reprinted by permission.

John M. Parras: John M. Parras, "Cameras Give an Inside Look," Op-Ed, THE LOS ANGELES TIMES. Reprinted by permission of the author.

Ann Patchett: Ann Patchett, from "Southern Comforts," NEW YORK TIMES MAGAZINE (Dec. 30, 2001), p. 40. Copyright 2001, Ann Patchett. Reprinted by permission.

Holly Hubbard Preston: Holly Hubbard Preston, "Divorce is Hard for Adult Children Too" from NEWSWEEK, September 4, 2000, © 2000 Newsweek, Inc. All rights reserved. Reprinted by permission.

Carin C. Quinn: "The Jeaning of America – and the World," by Carin C. Quinn, American Heritage, Volume 30, number 3. Reprinted By Permission of AMERICAN HERITAGE Magazine, a division of Forbes Inc. © Forbes Inc., 1978.

Arturo E. Ramirez: "Back to Where the Seed was Planted" by Arturo E. Ramirez (student).

William Raspberry: William Raspberry, "The Handicap of Definition," from INSTILLING POSITIVE IMAGES. © **1982 Washington Post Writers Group. Reprinted with permission.**

Rick Reilly: Rick Reilly, "Earning Their Pinstripes," SPORTS ILLUSTRATED, Sept. 23, 2002, p. 92. Reprinted by permission of Sports Illustrated.

Peggy Robbins: "The Kickapoo Indian Medicine Company," by Peggy Robbins in AMERICAN HISTORY ILLUSTRATED, Vol. XV, #2, May 1980. Reprinted through the courtesy of Cowles Magazine, publishers of AMERICAN HISTORY ILLUSTRATED.

Andy Rooney: "Types" by Andy Rooney. Reprinted with the permission of Scribner, an imprint of Simon & Schuster Adult Publishing Group, from A FEW MINUTES WITH ANDY ROONEY by Andrew A. Rooney. Copyright © 1981, 1986 by Essay Productions, Inc.

Mike Royko: Mike Royko, "Death to the Killers," CHICAGO SUN TIMES. Reprinted with special permission from the Chicago Sun-Times, © 2001, 2004.

John Ruckdeschel: John Ruckdeschel, "Banning Smoking," CRAIN'S DETROIT BUSINESS, March 3, 2003, v. 19, issue 9, p. 9. Reprinted with permission from Crain's Detroit Business

Nancy Masterson Sakamoto: Conversational Ballgames from POLITE FICTIONS by NANCY MASTERSON SAKAMOTO. Reprinted by permission of the author.

Jonathan Schell: From THE FATE OF THE EARTH by Jonathan Schell. Copyright © 1982 by Jonathan Schell. Originally appeared in THE NEW YORKER. Reprinted by permission of Janklow and Nesbit.

Connie Schultz: Connie Schultz, "Daughter's Doll Teaches Mom Lesson on Race" © 2000 The Plain Dealer. All rights reserved. Reprinted with permission.

Nelliejean Smith: "On Being Unemployed," by Nelliejean Smith (student).

Bonnie Smith-Yackel: "My Mother Never Worked," by Bonnie Smith-Yackel. Reprinted with permission from WOMEN: A JOURNAL OF LIBERATION, Vol. 4, No. 2, Spring 1975.

Clifton L. Taulbert: Reprinted with permission of Council Oak Books from ONCE UPON A TIME WHEN WE WERE COLORED, by Clifton L. Taulbert; copyright © 1989 by Clifton L. Taulbert. (pp. 1-7).

Lester C. Thurow: Lester C. Thurow, "Brain Power" from "Brains Power Business Growth," USA TODAY, Monday, August 18, 1997, p. 13A. Reprinted by permission of the author.

James Tuite: "The Sounds of the City" by James Tuite. From THE NEW YORK TIMES, August 6, 1966. Copyright © 1966 by The New York Times Co. Reprinted by permission.

Eliot Wigginton: From THE FOXFIRE BOOK by Eliot Wigginton. Copyright © 1968, 1969, 1970, 1971, 1972 by The Foxfire Fund, Inc. Used by permission of Doubleday, a division of Random House, Inc.

George F. Will: George F. Will, "The Jury Room is No Place for TV," THE WASHINGTON POST, January 5, 2003. **© 2003, The Washington Post Writers Group. Reprinted with permission.**

Debra Aho Williamson: Williamson, Debra Aho, "Foreign Flavors, Mainstream Taste." Reprinted with permission from the July 8, 2002 issue of ADVERTISING AGE. Copyright, Crain Communications Inc. 2002.

Peter Wood: With permission of the publisher from DIVERSITY: THE INVENTION OF A CONCEPT by Peter Wood, Encounter Books, San Francisco, California (© 2002) **www.encounterbooks.com.**

Daniel Yergin and Robert Stabaugh: "Conservation" excerpted from ENERGY FUTURE by Daniel Yergin and Robert Stabaugh. Copyright 1979. Reprinted by permission of Daniel Yergin.

Index